MW01038860

Warfare On The Colonial American Frontier:

The Journals *of*

Major Robert Rogers

&

An Historical Account *of the* Expedition Against *the* Ohio Indians *in the* Year 1764, Under *the* Command *of*

Henry Bouquet, Esq.

DRESSLAR PUBLISHING

All Rights Reserved
Copyright © 1997 James Dresslar & Alan Gutchess
International Standard Book Number 0-89725-287-X
Library of Congress Catalog Card Number 96-72391

This is an enlarged facsimile reprint of a 1769 edition of *Rogers & Bouquet*. A certain amount of foxing or discoloration on the pages of the original will show through in such a reprint. We believe the saving of the period look and feel of the type warrants overlooking these small blemishes.

First Printing 1769
Second Printing January 1997

Additional copies of this book are available from:

Dresslar Publishing
Box 635
Bargersville, IN. 46106

Manufactured in the United States of America
Printed on 60# acid free paper

JOURNALS
OF
Major ROBERT ROGERS:

CONTAINING

An Account of the ſeveral Excurſions he made under the Generals who commanded upon the Continent of NORTH AMERICA, during the late War.

FROM WHICH MAY BE COLLECTED

The moſt material Circumſtances of every Campaign upon that Continent, from the Commencement to the Concluſion of the War.

TO WHICH IS ADDED

An Hiſtorical Account of the Expedition againſt the Ohio Indians in the Year 1764, under the command of Henry Bouquet, Eſq; Colonel of Foot, and now Brigadier General in America, including his Tranſactions with the Indians, relative to the Delivery of the Priſoners, and the Preliminaries of Peace. With an Introductory Account of the Proceeding Campaign, and Battle at Buſhy-Run.

DUBLIN:

Printed by R. ACHESON, at HORACES's-HEAD, William-ſtreet,

FOR

J. MILLIKEN, No. 10. in Skinner-row.

M,DCC,LX,IX.

INTRODUCTION.

IT would be offering an affront to the public, ſhould I pretend to have no private views in publiſhing the following JOURNALS; but they will excuſe me if I leave them to conjecture what my particular views are, and claim the merit of impartially relating matters of fact, without diſguiſe or equivocation. Moſt of thoſe which relate to myſelf can at preſent be atteſted by living witneſſes.

And ſhould the troubles in America be renewed, and the ſavages repeat thoſe ſcenes of barbarity they ſo often have acted on the Britiſh ſubjects, which there is great reaſon to believe will happen, I flatter myſelf, that ſuch as are immediately concerned may reap ſome advantage from theſe pages.

Should any one take offence at what they may here meet with, before they venture upon exhibiting a charge, they are deſired, in favour to themſelves, to conſider, that I am in a ſituation where they cannot attack me to their own advantage; that it is the ſoldier, not the ſcholar, that writes; and that many things here were wrote, not with ſilence and leiſure, but in deſarts and rocks and mountains, amidſt the hurries, diſorders, and noiſe of war, and under that depreſſion of ſpirits, which is the natural

tural consequence of exhausting fatigue. This was my situation when the following Journals or Accounts were transmitted to the generals and commanders I acted under, which I am not now at liberty to correct, except in some very gross and palpable errors.

It would perhaps gratify the curious to have a particular account of my life, preceding the war; but though I could easily indulge them herein, without any dishonour to myself, yet I beg they will be content with my relating only such circumstances and occurrences as led me to a knowledge of many parts of the country, and tended in some measure to quality me for the service I have since been employed in. Such, in particular, was the ſituation of the place in which I received my early education, a frontier town in the province of New Hampſhire, where I could hardly avoid obtaining ſome knowledge of the manners, cuſtoms, and language of the Indians, as many of them reſided in the neighbourhood, and daily converſed and dealt with the Engliſh.

Between the years 1743 and 1755 my manner of life was ſuch as led me to a general acquaintance both with the Britiſh and French ſettlements in North America, and eſpecially with the uncultivated deſart, the mountains, valleys, rivers, lakes, and ſeveral paſſes that lay between and contiguous to the ſaid ſettlements. Nor did I content myſelf with the ac-

counts

counts received from Indians, or the information of hunters, but travelled over large tracts of the country myſelf, which tended not more to gratify my curioſity, than to inure me to hardſhips, and, without vanity, I may ſay, to qualify me for the very ſervice I have ſince been employed in.

About this time the proceedings of the French in America, were ſuch as excited the jealouſy of the Engliſh, eſpecially in New-York and New-England; and as Crown-Point was the place from which, for many years, the Indians in the French intereſt had been fitted out againſt our ſettlements on the frontiers, a deſign was formed in the beginning of 1755 to diſpoſſeſs them of that poſt; purſuant to which, troops were levied in the ſeveral provinces of New England, New York, and New Jerſey. The general rendezvous was appointed at Albany in the province of New York, and the troops put under the command of Major General (ſince Sir William) Johnſon, I had the honour of commanding a company in the troops furniſhed by the province of New Hampſhire, with which I made ſeveral excurſions, purſuant to ſpecial orders from the governor of that province, on the northern and weſtern frontiers, with a view to deter the French and Indians from making inroads upon us that way. In this manner I was employed till the month of July, when I received orders to repair to Albany,

Albany, at which place I tarried till Auguſt 26th, and was then ordered with 100 men to eſcort the proviſion-waggons from thence to the Carrying-Place, then ſo called, ſince Fort-Edward. Here I waited upon the General, to whom I was recommended as a perſon well acquainted with the haunts and paſſes of the enemy, and the Indian method of fighting, and was by him diſpatched with ſmall parties on ſeveral tours towards the French poſts, and was on one of theſe up Hudſon's River on the 8th of September, when Baron Dieſkau was made priſoner, and the French and Indians, under his command defeated, at the ſouth-end of Lake George.

The 24th of September I received orders from the General to proceed with four men to Crown Point, and, if practicable, to bring a prisoner from thence; and with an account of the manner in which I executed these orders, I shall begin my JOURNALS.

A JOURNAL, &c.

September 24, 1755.

PURSUANT to orders of this date from Major-General Johnſon, Commander in chief of the Provincial Forces, raiſed for the reduction of Crown-Point, I embarked with four men upon Lake George, to reconnoitre the ſtrength of the enemy, and proceeding down the Lake twenty five miles, I landed on the weſt ſide, leaving two men in charge of the boat, while I marched with the

the other two 'till the 29th, when I had a fair view of the fort at Crown-Point, and discovered a large body of Indians round the Fort, and from their repeated irregular firing, supposed they were shooting at marks, (a diversion much in use among the savages). At night I crept through the enemy's guard into a small village lying south of the fort, and passing their centries to an eminence south-west of it, from whence I discovered they were building a battery, and had already thrown up an entrenchment on that side of the fort. The next day, from an eminence at a small distance from the former, I discovered an encampment, which extended from the fort south-east to a wind-mill, at about 30 yards distance; as near as I could judge, their number amounted to about 500 men: but finding no opportunity to procure a captive, and that our small party was discovered, I judged it proper to begin a retreat homeward the 1st of October. I took my route within two miles of Ticonderoga, from whence I observed a large smoak to arise, and heard the explosion of a number of small arms; but our provision being expended, we could not tarry to ascertain the number of the enemy there. On the 2d we arrived at the place where we left our boat in the charge of two men, but to our great mortification found they were gone, and no provisions left. This circumstance hastened us to the encampment with all possible speed, where we arrived the

4th,

4th, not a little fatigued and diſtreſſed with hunger and cold.

October 7, 1755, I received orders of this date from General Johnſon, to reconnoitre the French troops at Ticonderoga. Accordingly I proceeded at night to a point of land on the weſt ſide of the lake, where we landed, hid our canoe, and left two men in charge of it. The next day, with the other three, I marched to the point at Ticonderoga, where we arrived about noon. I here obſerved a body of men, which I judged to be about 200 in number, who had thrown up an entrenchment, and prepared large quantities of hewn timber in the adjacent woods. We remained here the ſecond night, and the next morning ſaw them lay the foundation of a fort, on the point which commands the paſs from Lake George, to Lake Champlain, and the entrance of South Bay, or Wood Creek. Having made what diſcoveries we could, we began our return, in which we found that the enemy had a large advanced guard at the north end of Lake George, where the river iſſues out of it into Lake Champlain. While we were viewing theſe, I perceived a bark-canoe, with nine Indians and a Frenchman in it, going up the Lake. We kept ſight of them 'till they paſſed the point of land, where our canoe and men were left, where, when we arrived, we had information from our people, that the above Indians and Frenchman had landed

landed on an iſland ſix miles to the ſouth of us, near the middle of the lake. In a ſhort time after, we ſaw them put off from the iſland, and ſteer directly towards us; upon which we put ourſelves in readineſs to receive them in the beſt manner we could, and gave them a ſalute at about 100 yards diſtance, which reduced their number to four. We then took boat and purſued them down the lake, till they were relieved by two canoes, which obliged us to retreat towards our encampment at Lake George, where we arrived the 10th of October.

October 15, 1755. Agreeable to orders of this date from General Johnſon, I embarked with forty men in five boats. Our deſign was to diſcover the ſtrength of the enemy's advanced guard, and, if poſſible, to decoy the whole, or part of them, into an ambuſh; but tho' we were indefatigable in our endeavours for ſeveral days, yet all our attempts of this kind proved abortive; and, as an account of our ſeveral movements during this ſcout would little gratify the reader, I ſhall omit giving a particular detail of them. We returned ſafe to our encampment at Lake George on the 19th.

October 21, 1755. I had orders from General Johnſon of this date, to embark for Crown Point, with a party of four men, in queſt of a priſoner. At night we landed on the weſt-ſide of Lake George,

twenty-

twenty-five miles from the Engliſh camp. The remainder of the way we marched by land, and the 26th came in ſight of the fort. In the evening we approached nearer, and next morning found ourſelves within about 300 yards of it. My men lay concealed in a thicket of willows, while I crept ſomething nearer, to a large pine-log, where I concealed myſelf, by holding buſhes in my hand. Soon after ſun-riſe the ſoldiers iſſued out in ſuch numbers, that my men and I could not poſſibly join each other without a diſcovery. About 10 o'clock a ſingle man marched out directly towards our ambuſh. When I perceived him within ten yards of me, I ſprung over the log, and met him, and offered him quarters, which he refuſed, and made a paſs at me with a dirk, which I avoided, and preſented my fuſee to his breaſt; but notwithſtanding, he ſtill puſhed on with reſolution, and obliged me to diſpatch him. This gave an alarm to the enemy, and made it neceſſary for us to haſten to the mountain. I arrived ſafe at our camp the 30th, with all my party.

November 4, 1755. Agreeable to orders from General Johnſon this day, I embarked for the enemy's advanced guard before mentioned, with a party of thirty men, in four battoes, mounted with two wall-pieces each. The next morning, a little before day-light, we arrived within half a mile of

them,

them, where we landed, and concealed our boats; I then sent out four men as spies, who returned the next evening, and informed me, that the enemy had no works round them, but lay entirely open to an assault; which advice I dispatched immediately to the General, desiring a sufficient force to attack them, which, notwithstanding the General's earnestness and activity in the affair, did not arrive till we were obliged to retreat. On our return, however, we were met by a reinforcement, sent by the General, whereupon I returned again towards the enemy, and the next evening sent two men to see if the enemy's centries were alert, who approached so near as to be discovered and fired at by them, and were so closely pursued in their retreat, that unhappily our whole party was discovered. The first notice I had of this being the case, was from two canoes with thirty men in them, which I concluded came out with another party by land, in order to force us between two fires; to prevent which, I with Lieutenant M'Curdy, and fourteen men, embarked in two boats, leaving the remainder of the party on shore, under the command of Captain Putnam—In order to decoy the enemy within the reach of our wall-pieces, we steered as if we intended to pass by them, which luckily answered our expectations; for they boldly headed us till within about an hundred yards, when we discharged the before mentioned pieces, which killed several of

them,

them, and put the reſt to flight, in which we drove them ſo near where our land-party lay, that they were again galled by them; ſeveral of the enemy were tumbled into the water, and their canoes rendered very leaky. At this time I diſcovered their party by land, and gave our people notice of it, who thereupon embarked likewiſe, without receiving any conſiderable injury from the enemy's fire, notwithſtanding it was for ſome time very briſk upon them. We warmly purſued the enemy, and again got an opportunity to diſcharge our wall-pieces upon them, which confuſed them much, and obliged them to diſperſe.—We purſued them down the lake to their landing, where they were received and covered by 100 men, upon whom we again diſcharged our wall-pieces, and obliged them to retire; but finding their number vaſtly ſuperior to ours, we judged it moſt prudent to return to our encampment at Lake George, where we ſafely arrived on the 8th of November.

Nov. 10, 1755. Purſuant to orders I received this day from Gen. Johnſon, in order to diſcover the enemy's ſtrength and ſituation at Ticonderago, I proceeded on the ſcout with a party of ten men on the 12th inſtant, and on the 14th arrived within view of the fort at that place, and found they had erected three new barracks and four ſtore-houſes in the fort, between which and the water they had eighty

eighty battoes hauled upon the beach, and about fifty tents near the fort; they appeared to be very busy at work. Having by these discoveries answered the design of our march, we returned, and arrived at our encampment the 19th of November.

December 19, 1755. Having had a month's repose, I proceeded, agreeable to orders from General Johnson, with two men, once more to reconnoitre the French at Ticonderoga. In our way we discovered a fire upon an island adjacent to the route we took, which, as we supposed, had been kindled by some of the enemy who were there. This obliged us to lie by and act like fishermen, the better to deceive them till night came on, when we proceeded and retired to the west-side of the lake 15 miles north of our fort. Here concealing our boat, the 20th we pursued our march by land, and on the 21st, at noon, were in sight of the French fort, where we found their people still deeply engaged at work, and discovered four pieces of cannon mounted on the south-east bastion, two at the north-east towards the woods, and two on the south. By what I judged, the number of their troops were about 500. I made several attempts to take a prisoner, by way-laying their paths; but they always passed in numbers vastly superior to mine, and thereby disappointed me. We approached very near their fort by night, and were driven by the cold (which now was very ſevere) to take ſhelter in one of their evacuated huts; before day, there was a fall of ſnow, which obliged us with all poſſible ſpeed to march homeward, leſt the enemy ſhould perceive our tracks, and purſue us.

We found our boat in ſafety, and had the good fortune (after being almoſt exhauſted with hunger, cold, and fatigue) to kill two deer, with which being refreſhed, on the 24th we returned to Fort William Henry (a fortreſs erected in this year's campaign) at the ſouth end of Lake George. About this time General Johnſon retired to Albany, to which place commiſſioners were ſent from the ſeveral governments whoſe troops had been under his command (New Hampſhire only excepted) Theſe commiſſioners were empowered by their reſpective conſtituents with the aſſent of a council of war, to garriſon Fort William Henry and Fort Edward, for the winter, with part of the troops that had ſerved the preceding year. Accordingly a regiment was formed, to which Boſton government furniſhed a Colonel—Connecticut a Lieutenant-Colonel—and New York a Major: after which it was adjudged, both by Gen. Johnſon and theſe Commiſſioners, that it would be of great uſe to leave one company of woodſmen or rangers under my command, to make excurſions towards the enemy's forts during the winter; I accordingly remained, and did duty

the

the whole winter, until called upon by General Shirley.

January 14, 1756. I this day marched with a party of ſeventeen men, to reconnoitre the French forts; we proceeded down the lake, on the ice, upon ſkaits, and halted for refreſhment near the fall out of Lake George into Lake Champlain.—At night we renewed our march, and, by day-break on the 16th, formed an ambuſh on a point of land on the eaſt ſhore of Lake Champlain, within gun-ſhot of the path in which the enemy paſſed from one fort to the other. About ſun-riſe, two ſledges laden with freſh beef were preſented to our view, we intercepted the drivers, deſtroying their loading, and afterwards returned to Fort William Henry, where I arrived with my priſoners and party in good health the 17th.

January 26, 1756. Purſuant to orders of this date, from Colonel Glaſier, I marched from Lake George with a party of fifty men, with a deſign to diſcover the ſtrength and works of the enemy at Crown Point.

On the 2d of February, we arrived within a mile of that fortreſs, where we climbed a very ſteep mountain, from which we had a clear and full proſpect of the fort, and an opportunity of taking a plan a plan of the enemy's works there. In the evening we retired to a ſmall village, half a mile from the fort, and formed an ambuſcade on each ſide of the road leading from the fort to the village. Next morning a Frenchman fell into onr hands; ſoon after we diſcovered two more, but they unluckily got ſight of us before they were in our power, and haſtily retired to the fort. Finding ourſelves diſcovered by the enemy by this accident, we employed ourſelves while we dared ſtay in ſetting fire to the houſes and barns of the village, with which were conſumed large quantities of wheat, and other grain; we alſo killed about fifty cattle, and then retired, leaving the whole village in flames, and arrived ſafe at our fort, with our priſoner, the 6th of February.

February 29, 1756. Agreeable to orders from Colonel Glaſier, I this day marched with a party of fifty-ſix men down the weſt-ſide of Lake George. We continued our route north-ward till the 5th of March, and then ſteered eaſt to Lake Champlain, about ſix miles north of Crown Point, where, by the intelligence we had from the Indians, we expected to find ſome inhabited villages.—We then attempted to croſs the lake, but found the ice too weak. The 17th we returned and marched round the bay to the weſt of Crown Point, and at night got into the cleared land among their houſes and barns;

barns; here we formed an ambufh, expecting their labourers out to tend their cattle, and clean their grain, of which there were feveral barns full; we continued there that and the next day till dark, when difcovering none of the enemy, we fet fire to the houfes and barns, and marched off. In our return I took a frefh view of Ticonderoga, and reconnoitred the ground between that fort and the advanced guard on Lake George, approaching fo near as to fee their centries on the ramparts, and obtained all the knowledge of their works, ftrength, and fituation, that I defired.

The 14th of March, we returned fafe to Fort William-Henry.

The next day, after my return from this fcout, I received a letter, dated February 24, 1756, from Mr. William Alexander of New-York, who was fecretary to Mr. Shirley, Commander in chief of the troops at Ofwego the preceding year, and who now, upon the deceafe of General Braddock, fucceeded to the chief command of all his Majefty's forces in North-America, and was now at Bofton, preparing for the enfuing campaign, being previoufly recommended to this gentleman by General Johnfon. I was defired by the above-mentioned letter to wait on him at Bofton; of which I informed the commanding officer at the fort, and, with his

his approbation, I ſet out on the 17th of March, leaving the command of my company to Mr. Noah Johnſon, my Enſign; my brother Richard Rogers, who was my Lieutenant, being ſent to Boſton by the commanding officer on ſome diſpatches previous to this.

On the 23d, I waited on the General, and met with a very friendly reception; he ſoon intimated his deſign of giving me the command of an independent company of rangers, and the very next morning I received the commiſſion, with a ſet of inſtructions.

According to the General's orders, my company was to conſiſt of ſixty privates, at 3s. New York currency per day, three ſearjents at 4s. an Enſign at 5s. a Lieutenant at 7s. and my own pay was fixed at 10s. per day. Ten Spaniſh dollars were allowed to each man towards providing cloaths, arms, and blankets. My orders were to raiſe this company as ſoon as poſſible, to inliſt none but ſuch as were uſed to travelling and hunting, and in whoſe courage and fidelity I could confide; they were, moreover to be ſubject to military diſcipline, and the articles of war.

Our rendezvous was appointed at Albany, from thence to proceed in four whale-boats to lake George,

George, and, " from time to time, to uſe my beſt " endeavours to diſtreſs the French and their allies, by ſacking, burning, and deſtroying their houſes, " barns, barracks, canoes, battoes, &c. and by kill- " ing their cattle of every kind; and at all times to endeavour to way-lay, attack and deſtroy their convoys of proviſions by land and water, in any " part of the country where I could find them."

With theſe inſtructions, I received letters to the commanding officers at Fort William-Henry and Fort Edward directing them to forward the ſervice, with which I was now particularly charged.

When my company was completed, a part marched under the command of Lieutenant Rogers to Albany; with the remainder, I was ordered to march through the woods to No. 4, then a frontier town greatly expoſed to the enemy; where,

April 28, 1756, I received orders to march from thence to Crown Point, in purſuance of which we travelled through deſarts and mountains. The ſecond day of our march, my ſecond Lieutenant, Mr. John Stark was taken ſick, and obliged to return, with whom I ſent ſix men to guard him to Fort Edward.

We

We continued our march till the 5th of May, when I arrived with nine men at Lake Champlain, four miles ſouth of Crown Point. Here we concealed our packs, and marched up to a village on the eaſt-ſide, about two miles diſtant from Crown Point, but found no inhabitant there. We lay in wait the whole day following, oppoſite to Crown Point, expecting ſome party to croſs the lake; but nothing appeared except about four or five hundred men in canoes and battoes, coming up the lake from St. John's to Crown Point. We kept our ſtations till next day, ten o'clock A. M. to obſerve the motions of the enemy, but finding no opportunity to trapan any of them, we killed twenty-three head of cattle, the tongues of which were a very great refreſhment to us on our journey. We at this time diſcovered eleven canoes manned with a conſiderable number of French and Indians croſſing the lake directly towards us, upon which we retired; and the better to eſcape our purſuers we diſperſed, each man taking a different route. We afterwards aſſembled at the place where we concealed our packs, and on a raft croſſed over to the weſt-ſide of the lake. In our way we had a view of the French and Indians, encamped at the old Indian carrying-place, near Ticonderoga, and the 11th of May arrived ſafe at Fort William-Henry. Mr. Stark, with his party, arrived at Fort-Edward three days before. In their way they diſcovered a ſcouting

ing party of three or four hundred Indians. Lieutenant Rogers with his party had arrived ſome days before this, and was at this time out upon a ſcout.

May 20, 1756. Agreeable to orders from the General, I ſet out with a party of eleven men to reconnoitre the French advanced guards. The next day, from the top of a mountain, we had a view of them, and judged their number to be about 300; they were buſy in fortifying themſelves with paliſadoes. From the other ſide of the mountain we had a proſpect of Ticonderoga fort, and from the groundtheir encampment took up, I judged it to conſiſt of 1000 men. This night we lodged on the mountain, and next morning marched to the Indian carrying-path, that leads from lake George to Lake Champlain, and formed an ambuſcade between the French guard and Ticonderoga fort. About ſix o'clock 118 Frenchmen paſſed by without diſcovering us; in a few minutes after, twenty-two more came the ſame road, upon whom we fired, killed ſix, and took one a priſoner; but the large party returning, obliged us to retire in haſte, and we arrived ſafe with our priſoner, at Fort William-Henry the 23d.

The

The prisoner we had taken reported, " that a party of 220 French and Indians were preparing to invest the out-parties at Fort Edward," which occasioned my marching the next morning with a party of 78 men, to join a detachment of Col. Bayley's regiment, to scour the woods as far as South Bay, if possible to intercept the enemy; but we could not discover them.

June 13, 1756. Agreeable to orders this evening, I embarked with a party of 26 men in battoes upon Lake George, to revisit the French advanced guard; excessive thunder and lightning obliged us to land at about ten miles distance from our fort, where we spent the night. The next morning about sun-rise, we heard the explosion of upwards of twenty small arms, on the opposite side of the lake, which we supposed to be a party of French and Indians, cleaning their guns after the rain. In the evening we embarked again, and early in the morning of the 16th drew up our battoes about four miles distant from the advanced guard, and afterwards lay in ambush by a path leading from thence to a mountain, in order to surprize the enemy, who went there daily in parties, to take a view of the lake; but finding they were not at that place, we marched to the spot where the enemy had posted their advanced guard, but they had retired and demolished all their works there;

we

we then continued our march towards Ticonderoga, near which place we aſcended an eminence, and had a clear view of their works. I judged that their garriſon and encampment conſiſted of about 3000 men: We then ſet out on our return, and arrived at Fort William-Henry the 18th inſtant, except one man, who ſtrayed from us, and who did not get in till the 23d, then almoſt famiſhed for want of ſuſtenance.

About this time the General augmented my company to ſeventy men, and ſent me ſix light whale-boats from Albany, with order to proceed immediately to Lake Champlain, to cut off, if poſſible, the proviſions and flying parties of the enemy. Accordingly,

June 28, 1756. I embarked with fifty men in five whale-boats, and proceeded to an iſland in Lake George. The next day, at about five miles diſtance from this iſland we landed our boats, and carried them about ſix miles over a mountain to South Bay, where we arrived the 3d of July. The following evening we embarked again, and went down the bay to within ſix miles of the French fort, where we concealed our boats till the evening. We then embarked again, and paſſed by Ticonderoga undiſcovered, tho' we were ſo near the enemy as to hear their centry's watch-word. We judged from the

the number of their fires, that they had a body of about 2000 men, and the lake in this place to be near 400 yards wide. About five miles further down, we again concealed our boats, and lay by all day. We saw several battoes going and coming upon the lake. At night we put off again, with a design to pass by Crown Point, but afterwards judged it imprudent by reason of the clearness of the night, so lay concealed again the next day, when near a hundred boats passed by us, seven of which came very near the point where we were, and would have landed there; but the officer insisted, in our hearing, upon going about 150 yards further, where they landed, and dined in our view. About nine o'clock we re-imbarked, and passed the fort at Crown Point, and again concealed our boats at about 10 miles distance from it. This day, being July 7th, 30 boats, and a schooner of about 30 or 40 tons, passed by us towards Canada. We set out again in the evening, and landed about fifteen miles further down; from which place I sent a party for further discovery, who brought intelligence of a schooner at anchor, about a mile from us; we immediately lightened our boats, and prepared to board her; but were prevented by two lighters coming up the lake, who, we found intended to land where we were posted; these we fired upon, then hailed them, and offered them quarters, if they would come ashore; but they hastily pushed towards the

 opposite

opposite shore, where we pursued and intercepted them: we found their number to be twelve, three of which were killed by our fire, and two wounded, one of them in such a manner that he soon died. We sunk and destroyed their vessels and cargoes, which consisted chiefly of wheat and flour, wine and brandy; some few casks of the latter we carefully concealed. The prisoners informed us, that they were a part of 500 men, the remainder of which were not far behind on their passage, which induced us to hasten our return to our garrison, where, with our prisoners, we safely arrived the 15th of July. These prisoners, upon examination, reported, "That a great number of regular troops and militia were assembling at Chamblee, and destined for Carillon, or Ticonderoga *: that great quantities of provisions were transporting there, and a new General † with two regiments lately arrived from France: that there was no talk of any design upon our Forts on this side; but that a party of 300 French, and 20 Indians, had already set out to intercept our convoys of provisions between Albany and Lake George: that 60 livres was the reward for an

* The former is the French, the latter the Indian name, signifying the meeting or confluence of three waters.

† The Marquis de Montcalm, who commanded in the reduction of Oswego this year, and of Fort William-Henry, the year following.

an Engliſh ſcalp, and that the priſoners were ſold in Canada for 50 crowns each: that their proſpect of an harveſt was very encouraging, but that the ſmall-pox made great havock amongſt the inhabitants." About the time of my ſetting out upon this ſcout, Major General Shirley was ſuperſeded in his command by Major General Abercrombie, who arrived at the head-quarters in Albany on the 25th of June, and brought with him two regiments of regular troops from England. I therefore, upon my return, wrote to his Excellency, deſiring leave to lay before him the minutes of my laſt ſcout, and to recommend to his conſideration an augmentation of the rangers. The General permitted me, with my brother Richard Rogers, to wait upon him at Albany. In this interview we diſcourſed on the ſubject of my letter, in conſequence of which he immediately ordered a new company of rangers to be raiſed, and gave the command of it to my brother *, appointed Noah Johnſon, my former Enſign, his Firſt Lieutenant, Nathaniel Abbot his Second Lieutenant, and Caleb Page his Enſign. John Stark, formerly my Second Lieutenant, was appointed my Firſt, John M'Curdy ſucceeded to his place, and Jonathan Burbank was appointed my Enſign. August

* He compleated his company in 28 days, and by the General's orders, went up Mohawke river, to ſerve as a ſcouting party for the troops that way.

Auguſt 2, 1756. Agreeable to orders received of General Abercrombie at Albany, the 23d of July, I embarked this day at Fort William-Henry, on board one of the lighters built there this ſummer, with twenty-five of my company, in order to reconnoitre the enemy at Ticonderoga and Crown Point, and ſixty men under Capt. Larnard of the provincials, who had General Winſlow's || orders to proceed with his men to the French advanced guard; but he not being acquainted with the way thither, put himſelf under my command. We landed this morning about fifteen miles down Lake George, and proceeded with the party till the 4th in the evening, and encamped about a mile from the advanced guard. The 5th in the morning we muſtered the whole party, and got to the ſummit of a hill, weſt of the advanced guard, where we diſcovered two advanced poſts, which I then imagined was the whole of the guard, one of them on the weſt-ſide, half a mile ſouthward of Lake Champlain, the other on the eaſt-ſide of the Lake, oppoſite the former, at the old Indian carrying-place. We judged there were about 400 men on the eaſt, and 200 on the weſt. After deliberating with Capt. Larnard upon the ſtrength and diſpoſition of the enemy,

|| General Winſlow commanded the provincial troops this year by virtue of a commiſſion from the ſeveral provinces, who were concerned in 1755, in the ſame expedition, and was now with the greateſt part of the provincial troops at Lake George.

enemy, and the report of our advanced party we, concluded it unadviſeable to continue there any longer. He returned towards Fort William-Henry, and I went on with my own party till we came within view of Ticonderoga Fort, where, from an eminence, I diſcovered the ſituation, but could not aſcertain the ſtrength of it to my ſatisfaction.

Auguſt 6, I went down towards Crown Point, by the weſt-ſide of Lake Champlain, and diſcovered ſeveral battoes paſſing from that place to Ticonderoga with troops on board. We then proceeded to the place where we burnt the village, as mentioned before, and there encamped, and perceived a party ſallying out, driving a number of horſes to feed.

The 7th we lay in ambuſh by the road, with a deſign to intercept ſuch as might come out to drive in the cattle; but no one appearing for that purpoſe, we approached nearer, to within half a mile of the fort, where we were diſcovered by two Frenchmen, before they were in our power. This accident obliged us to make a retreat, in which we killed upwards of forty cattle. We arrived at Fort William-Henry, Auguſt 10.

A company of Stockbridge Indians was this year employed in his Majeſty's ſervice, commanded by

Indian officers, properly commiſſioned by General Shirley, before he was ſuperſeded in his command. General Abercrombie was ſomewhat at a loſs how to diſpoſe of this company, and applied to Sir William Johnſon, who adviſed, that a part *, viz. thirty privates and a Lieutenant, ſhould ſcout and ſcour the woods under my direction, which party had arrived while I was out upon my laſt ſcout, and Lieutenant Stark had ſtrengthened their party with ſome of our people, and ſent them out with particular directions what route to take, the day before I arrived.

About this time his Excellency the Earl of Loudoun arrived at Albany, and had taken upon him the command of the army, to whom I applied as I had done before to Gen. Abercrombie, tranſmitting to him an account of the Indian ſcout abovementioned (who returned the 13th with two French ſcalps, agreeable to their barbarous cuſtom) and deſiring that with them I might attempt to penetrate into Canada, and diſtreſs the inhabitants, by burning their harveſt (now nearly ripe) and deſtroying their cattle.

Accordingly, Auguſt 16, we embarked in whaleboats in two departments, the one commanded by Lieutenant

* The remainder of this Indian company, with their Captain, were ſent to Saratoga, to be under the direction of Colonel Burton.

Lieutenant Stark, the other by myſelf.—The next morning we joined each other, at which time alſo fell in with us a party of eight Mohocks, who had marched out from Fort William-Henry the day before. We then marched directly to the place where we left our whale-boats the 7th of July, proceeding about twenty-five miles northward of Crown Point fort, on the weſt-ſide of Lake Champlain, where we all (excepting one man who ſtrayed from us and returned) arrived ſafe the 24th. We embarked again in our boats, and ſteered down the lake toward St. John's. The 25th we proceeded twenty miles further, and about midnight diſcovered a ſchooner ſtanding up the lake with a fair wind towards Crown Point; they paſſed us ſo ſwiftly that we could not poſſibly board her, as we intended.

The 26th we landed, and the Mohocks left us to join another party of theirs then out on a ſcout.

The 27th we got on a point, with a deſign to intercept the enemy's battoes, that might paſs up and down the lake; but not diſcovering any, and our proviſions growing ſhort, we returned up the lake, and landed eight miles north of the fort at Crown Point, on the eaſt-ſide of the lake.

The 29th in the morning we marched to a village lying eaſt of the fort, and in our way took priſoners,

ſoners, a man, his wife, and daughter, (a girl about fourteen years of age); with theſe priſoners we returned, and arrived ſafe at Fort William-Henry, Sept. 22, 1756.

The man-priſoner, above-mentioned, upon examination, reported, "That he was born at Vaiſac, "in the province of Guienne in France: that he "had been in Canada about fifteen years, and in "the colonies ſervice about ſix, and two years at "Crown Point: that there were only 300 men at "Crown Point, and thoſe chiefly inhabitants of "the adjacent villages; that there were 4000 men "at Ticonderoga or Carillon, 1500 of which were "regular troops, who had a ſufficiency of all kinds "of proviſions: that he never was at Ticonderoga "or at the advance guard, but heard there were "only fifteen men at the latter: that the French "had 600 Indians at Ticonderoga, and expected "600 more: that 1200 were arrived at Quebec "for Carillon, which laſt 1800 were under the "command of Monſ. Scipio de la Maſure: that "they had a great quantity of cannon, mortars, "ſhells, &c. at Ticonderoga, but he did not know "the number or quantity: that they expected the "above re-inforcement in two or three days at "Ticonderoga, having ſent boats to Montreal to "fetch them: that they underſtood by a letter that "Oſwego had fallen into their hands, but the news

"was

"was not confirmed: that they had heard we intended to invest Carillon, but did not know what movements were intended on their side should we neglect it: that they had 150 battoes on Lake Champlain, which were kept at Carillon, thirty-five of which constantly plied between Montreal and that fortress: that Monf. Montcalm commanded at Frontiniac with 5000 men, but did not know whether these troops were regulars or provincials: that a great number of vessels had arrived at Canada with provisions and military stores: that they heard we had several ships in the river St. Lawrence: that Monf. le Conte de Levi commanded at Carillon, and came last May from France; and that, since the two last shallops or lighters (before-mentioned) were taken, they had augmented the number of men on board the large schooner in Lake Champlain from twelve to thirty."

Upon my return to the fort, I received orders from my Lord Loudoun to wait upon Col. Burton, of the 48th regiment, for instructions, he being then posted at Saratoga. By him I was ordered to return to my company at Fort William-Henry, and march them to the South Bay, thence east to the Wood Creek, then to cross it southerly, opposite to Saratoga, and return and make my report to him.

In

In this tour we apprehended four deserters from Otway's regiment, who were going to the enemy, and whom I sent back to Fort Edward, with a part of my detachment, under the command of Lieutenant Stark, and proceeded with the remainder to compleat my orders, after which I returned to Saratoga to make my report.

There I met my brother Capt. Richard Rogers with his company, he being ordered back from Mohock river, to join me with the remainder of the Stockbridge Indians; and I marched both companies to Fort Edward, where I was ordered to form an encampment. A part of the Indian company were sent out to the east-side of Lake Champlain to alarm the enemy at Ticonderoga, whilst I, with a detachment of my own, and Capt. Richard Rogers's company, was ordered on another party down Lake George, in whale-boats, and the remainder of the companies were employed in reconnoitering round the encampment, and also served as flankers to the parties that guarded provisions to Lake George. Capt. Jacob, who commanded the Indian party before-mentioned, returned two days before me with four French scalps, which they took opposite to Ticonderoga on the east-side.

Sept. 7, 1756. Agreeable to orders, I this day embarked on Lake George, with a party of fourteen

teen men in a whale-boat, which we landed, and concealed the evening following, on the eaft fhore, about four miles fouth of the French advance guard. Here I divided my party, taking feven men with me leaving the remainder in charge of Mr. Chalmer (a volunteer fent me by Sir John Sinclair) with orders, upon his difcovering the enemy's boats going up the lake, &c. to make the beft of his way with the intelligence to Fort William-Henry.

I was the 9th current within half a mile of Ticonderoga fort, where I endeavoured to reconnoitre the enemy's works and ftrength. They were engaged in raifing the walls of the fort, and had erected a large block-houfe near the fouth-eaft corner of the fort, with ports in it for cannon. Eaft from the block-houfe was a battery, which I imagined commanded the lake. I difcovered five houfes fouth of the fort clofe to the water-fide, and 160 tents fouth-weft of the fort, and twenty-feven battoes hauled upon the beach.

Next morning, with one private, I went to view the falls betwixt Lake Champlain and Lake George (where I had heard the explofion of feveral guns the evening before and had at that time fent Serjeant Henry to difcover the reafon of it) leaving the remainder of my party in charge of Mr. Gibbs, another volunteer, to wait our return. Serjeant Henry followed

followed ſoon after me, and reported, "that the "French were building a ſmall fort at the head of "the falls on the eaſt-ſide of the lake; that he alſo "diſcovered their guard to the weſtward, and ima-"gined both conſiſted of 500 men." I returned, after finding the French were engaged in building a ſaw-mill at the lower end of the falls, and found my boats with proviſions left, as I ſuppoſe, by Mr. Chalmer and his party, whom I waited for till ſeven o'clock next day; but he not returning, and I judging from their tracks that they were returned to Fort William-Henry, we likewiſe began our return, and arrived ſafe the 11th of September, where I found Mr. Chalmer and the party left with him, he having punctually obeyed the orders given him above. Upon my return, I communicated my obſervations upon the Lakes George and Champlain to my Lord Loudoun, giving him as juſt a deſcription as I could of their ſituation.

September 24, General Abercrombie iſſued out orders, that three commiſſioned officers of the rangers, with 20 privates each, ſhould reconnoitre the Wood Creek, South Bay and Ticonderoga; and theſe were alternately ſent out, ſo that a continual ſcout was kept up for a conſiderable time.

October 22, 1756. The greateſt part of the army was now at Fort-Edward, under the command

mand of General Abercrombie, and Lord Loudoun arriving about this time with the remainder, it was generally expected that the army would croſs the lake, and endeavour to reduce the French forts, notwithſtanding the ſeaſon was ſo far advanced; but his Lordſhip taking into conſideration the probability that thoſe lakes would freeze (which they generally do in the month of December) in which caſe no ſupplies could be had from, nor any communication kept up with Fort William-Henry; he determined to deſiſt from this deſign, and contented himſelf with keeping the field till Monſ. Montcalm retired to winter-quarters, and accordingly ſought all opportunities to learn his ſituation and movements.

Agreeable to orders from his Lordſhip, I this day embarked in two whale-boats, with a party of twenty men, upon Lake George, with an intent to bring a priſoner from Ticonderoga. We paſſed the Narrows twenty miles from our embarkation, when Capt. Shephard (who was made a captive in Auguſt laſt and carried to Canada) hailed our boat; I knew his voice, and took him on board with three other men, one of whom was taken with him. He reported, that he left Canada fifteen days before. I went on my courſe till the 27th, towards Carillon, and landed that night on the weſt-ſide of the lake, concealed our boats, and travelled by land to within

within a mile of the fort. I kept ſpies out the day after to improve any opportunity that might offer, and the next day ſent them ſtill nearer, but to no good purpoſe: I at length diſcovered two men centries to the piquet guard of theFrench army, one of which was poſted on the road that leads from the fort to the woods: I took five of my party, and marched directly down the road in the middle of the day, till we were challenged by the centry. I anſwered in French, ſignifying that we were friends; the centinel was thereby deceived, till I came cloſe to him, when perceiving his miſtake, in great ſurprize he called, Qui etes vous? I anſwered Rogers, and led him from his poſt in great haſte, cutting his breeches and coat from him, that he might march with the greater eaſe and expedition. With this priſoner we arrived at Fort William-Henry, Oct. 31, 1756.Upon examination, he reported, "That he belonged to the regi-
" ment of Languedoc: that he left Breſt laſt A-
" pril was a twelve-month, and had ſerved ſince
" at Lake Champlain, Crown Point, and Carillon,
" was laſt year with General Dieſkaw in the battle
" at Fort William-Henry: that they loſt in that en-
" gagement of regulars, Canadians, and Indians, a
" great number: that at Carillon were at this time
" mounted thirty-ſix pieces of cannon, viz. twelve
" eighteen pounders, fifteen twelve pounders, and
" nine eight pounders, that at Crown Point were

" eighteen

" eighteen pieces, the largeſt of which were eigh-
" teen pounders : that Monſ. Montcalm's forces
" this year at Carillon were 3000 regulars, and 2000
" Canadians and Indians : that Montcalm himſelf
" was drawn off with one batallion, and that the for-
" ces then in that neighbourhood conſiſted of five ba-
" tallions and about 800 Canadians : that the Indi-
" ans were all gone off, 200 of whom talked
" of returning to ſpend the winter at Carillon: that
" the advanced guard on the weſt-ſide above the
" falls were all drawn in, and that on the eaſt con-
" ſiſted of 600 men, who were to decamp the 1ſt
" of November : that they had a camp of five bat-
" allions and ſixty Canadians, about half a league
" from Carillon, and that the reſt of the army
" were under the fort : that they had barracks ſuffi-
" cient for 500 men, which he underſtood were
" to quarter there: that they had one ſchooner and
" 200 battoes on on Lake Champlain, and but five
" or ſix on Lake George : that Monſ. the Chevalier
" de Levi commanded in Monſ Montcalm's ab-
" ſence, and that the Canadians were commanded
" by Meſſieurs Le Corn and Columbie : that when
" Monſ. Montcalm went off, he ſaid he had done
" enough for this year, and would take Fort Will-
" liam Henry early in the ſpring ; that the French
" had taken four of Captain Rogers's whale-boats
" in lake Champlain: that when he was taken pri-
" ſoner, he imagined himſelf to be about a gun-ſhot
" and

" and half from the fort, and that the French camp " was pretty healthy."

From this time we were conſtantly employed in patrolling the woods about Fort Edward till the 19th of November 1756, when I had his Lordſhip's orders to take another excurſion down the Lake. Captain Abercrombie, Aid-de-camp and nephew to General Abercrombie, did me the honour to accompany me; but nothing material being in our power to effect, except taking a view of the fort and works of the enemy at Ticonderoga, we returned ſafe to Fort Edward the 25th in the evening.

About this time his Lordſhip drew off the main body of the troops from Fort Edward to be quartered at Albany and New York.

Both armies being now retired to winter-quarters, nothing material happened to the end of this year. The rangers were ſtationed at the Forts William-Henry and Edward, to which alſo two new companies of rangers were ſent this fall, commanded by Captain Spikeman and Captain Hobbs, in one of which my brother James Rogers was appointed an Enſign.

Theſe

Theſe two companies were ſttationed at Fort William-Henry, mine and my brother Richard's at Fort Edward.

Captain Richard Rogers had leave go into New England for recruits to complete our two companies. He this winter waited upon the government of Boſton, to obtain pay for our ſervices in the winter 1755 before-mentioned, but could obtain none, notwithſtanding Lord Loudoun, who was then at Boſton, generouſly ſupported and enforced our ſolicitations with his intereſt.

January 15, 1757. Agreeable to orders from the commanding officer at Fort Edward, I this day marched with my own Lieutenant Mr. Stark, Enſign Page of Captain Richard Rogers's company, and fifty privates of ſaid companies, to Fort William-Henry, where we were employed in providing proviſions, ſnow-ſhoes, &c. till the 17th, when being joined by Captain Spikeman, Lieutenant Kennedy and Enſign Brewer of his company, and fourteen of their men, together with Enſign James Rogers, and fourteen men of Captain Hobbs's company, and Mr. Baker, a volunteer of the 44th regiment of foot, we began our march on the ice down Lake George, and at night encamped on the eaſt-ſide of the Firſt Narrows. The next morning, finding that ſome of the detachment had hurt themſelves

themſelves in the march the day before, as many were diſmiſſed to return to the fort, as reduced our party to ſeventy-four men, officers included.

The 18th we marched twelve miles down the lake, and encamped on the weſt-ſide of it.

The 19th we marched three miles from our encampment further down the lake, and then took the land, and, upon ſnow-ſhoes, travelled north-weſt about eight miles from our landing, and three from the lake, where we encamped.

The 20th we marched north-by-eaſt the whole day, and at night encamped on the weſtern ſide, oppoſite to, and about three miles diſtant from lake Champlain.

The 21ſt we marched eaſt, till we came to the lake, about mid-way between Crown Point and Ticonderoga, and immediately diſcovered a ſled going from the latter to the former. I ordered Lieutenant Stark, with twenty men to head the ſled, while I, with a party, marched the other way to prevent its retreating back again, leaving Captain Spikeman in the center with the remainder. I ſoon diſcovered eight or ten ſleds more following down the lake, and endeavoured to give Mr. Stark intelligence of it before he ſallied on the lake and

and diſcovered himſelf to them, but could not. They all haſtily returned towards Ticonderoga. We purſued them, and took ſeven priſoners, three ſleds, and ſix horſes; the remainder made their eſcape. We examined the captives ſeparately, who reported, " That 200 Canadians and 45 Indians " were juſt arrived at Ticonderoga, and were to " be reinforced that evening, or next morning, " by fifty Indians more from Crown Point: that " there were 600 regular troops at that fortreſs, " and 350 at Ticonderoga, where they ſoon " expected a large number of troops, who in the " ſpring were to beſiege our forts: that they had " large magazines of proviſions in their forts, " and that the above-mentioned party were well " equipped, and in a condition to march upon a-" ny emergency at the leaſt notice, and were de-" ſigned ſoon to way-lay and diſtreſs our convoys " between the forts."

From this account of things, and knowing that thoſe who eſcaped would give early notice of us at Ticonderoga, I concluded it beſt to return; and ordered the party, with the utmoſt expedition, to march to the fires we had kindled the night before, and prepare for a battle, if it ſhould be offered, by drying our guns, it being a rainy day, which we effected; and then marched in a ſingle file, myſelf and Lieutenant Kennedy in the front, Lieutenant Stark

Stark in the rear, and Captain Spikeman in the center, Enſigns Page and Rogers were between the front and center, and Enſign Brewer between the center and rear, Serjeant Walker having the command of a rear-guard. In this manner we advanced half a mile, or thereabouts, over broken ground, when paſſing a valley of about fifteen rods breadth, the front having reached the ſummit of a hill on the weſt-ſide of it; the enemy, who had here drawn up in the form of a half-moon, with a deſign, as we ſuppoſed, to ſurround us, ſaluted us with a volley of about 200 ſhot, at the diſtance of about five yards from the neareſt or front, and thirty from the rear of their party. This fire was about two o'clock in the afternoon, and proved fatal to Lieutenant Kennedy, and Mr Gardner, a volunteer in my company, and wounded me and ſeveral others; myſelf, however, but ſlightly in the head. We immediately returned their fire. I then ordered my men to the oppoſite hill, where I ſuppoſed Lieutenant Stark and Enſign Brewer had made a ſtand with forty men to cover us, in caſe we were obliged to retreat. We were cloſely purſued, and Capt. Spikeman, with ſeveral of the party, were killed, and others made priſoners. My people, however, beat them back by a briſk fire from the hill, which gave us an opportunity to aſcend, and poſt ourſelves to advantage. After which I ordered Lieutenant Stark and

and Mr. Baker in the center, with Enſign Rogers; Serjeants Walter and Phillips, with a party, being a reſerve, to prevent our being flanked, and watch the motions of the enemy. Soon after we had thus formed ourſelves for battle, the enemy attempted to flank us on the right, but the above reſerve bravely attacked them, and giving them the firſt fire very briſkly, it ſtopped ſeveral from retreating to the main body. The enemy then puſhed us cloſely in the front ; but having the advantage of the ground, and being ſheltered by large trees, we maintained a continual fire upon them, which killed ſeveral, and obliged the reſt to retire to their main body. They then attempted to flank us again, but were again met by our reſerved party, and repulſed. Mr. Baker about this time was killed. We maintained a pretty conſtant fire on both ſides, till the darkneſs prevented our ſeeing each other, and about ſun-ſet I received a ball thro' my hand and wriſt, which diſabled me from loading my gun. I however found means to keep my people from being intimidated by this accident ; they gallantly kept their advantageous ſituation, till the fire ceaſed on both ſides. The enemy, during the action, uſed many arts and ſtratagems to induce us to ſubmit, ſometimes threatening us with ſeverity if we refuſed, aſſuring us that they every moment expected a large reinforcement, which ſhould cut us to pieces without mercy: at other times flattering and cajoling us, declaring it was a pity ſo many brave men ſhould be loſt; that we ſhould, upon our ſurrender, be treated with the greateſt compaſſion and kindneſs; calling me by name, they gave me the ſtrongeſt aſſurances of their eſteem and friendſhip that words could do; but no one being diſmayed by their menaces, or flattered by fair promiſes, we told them our numbers were ſufficient, and that we were determined to keep our ground as long as there were two left to ſtand by each other.

After the action, in which we had a great number ſo ſeverely wounded that they could not travel without aſſiſtance, and our ammunition being nearly expended, and conſidering that we were near to Ticonderoga, from whence the enemy might eaſily make a deſcent, and overpower us by numbers, I thought it expedient to take the advantage of the night to retreat, and gave orders accordingly; and the next morning arrived at Lake George, about ſix miles ſouth of the French advanced guard, from whence I diſpatched Lieutenant Stark with two men to Fort William Henry, to procure conveyances for our wounded men thither; and the next morning we were met by a party of fifteen men and a ſled, under the command of Lieutenant Buckley, of Hobbs's company of Rangers, at the firſt narrows at Lake George.

Our

Our whole party, which now conſiſted of only forty-eight effective, and ſix wounded men, arrived at Fort William Henry the ſame evening, being the 23d of January 1757.

The neareſt computation we could make of the number which attacked us, was, that it conſiſted of about 250 French and Indians; and we afterwards had an account from the enemy, that their loſs in this action, of thoſe killed, and who afterwards died of their wounds, amounted to 116 men.

Both the officers and ſoldiers I had the honour to command, who ſurvivedthe firſt onſet, behaved with the moſt undaunted bravery and reſolution, and ſeemed to vie with each other in their reſpective ſtations who ſhould excel.

The following is the RETURN which was made of the Killed, Wounded, and Miffing, in the above action.

Captain Rogers's Company.	Captain Robert Rogers	——	——	wound
	Mr. Baker, Volunteer	Killed	——	——
	Mr. Gardner, ditto	ditto	——	——
	Thomas Henfon	ditto	——	——
	Serjeant Martin	——	——	tto
	Thomas Burnfide	——	——	ditto
	Serjeant Henry	——	miffing	——
	William Morris	——	ditto	——
	John Morrifon	——	ditto	——
C Rd Rogers's do	Jofeph Stephens	ditto	——	——
	Benjamin Woodall	——	ditto	——
	David Kemble	——	ditto	——
	Enfign Caleb Page	ditto	——	——
	David Page	——	——	ditto
Cap. Hobbs's dit.	Serjeant Jon. Howard	ditto	——	——
	Phineas Kemp	ditto	——	——
	John Edmonds	ditto	——	——
	Thomas Farmer	ditto	——	——
	Emanuel Lapartaquer	ditto	——	——
Capt. Spikeman's dit.	Capt. Spikeman	ditto	——	——
	Lieut. Kennedy	ditto	——	——
	Robert Avery	ditto	——	——
	Thomas Brown	——	ditto	——
	Samuel Fifk	ditto	——	——
	Serjeant Moore	——	——	ditto
	John Cahall	——	——	ditto
	Total,	14	6	6

N. B. Thofe returned as miffing, we afterwards found had been taken prifoners by the enemy.

Having

Having laid this return before Major Sparks, commanding officer at Fort Edward, he tranſmitted the ſame to the General; and the 30th of January following, I wrote to Capt. James Abercrombie, then at Albany, recommending ſuch officers as I thought moſt deſerving, to fill up the vacancies occaſioned by our late action, among whom were Lieutenant Stark to be Captain of Spikeman's company, and Serjeant Joſhua Martin to be Enſign in Captain Richard Rogers's company; and I alſo mentioned ſeveral things in favour of the Rangers. In conſequence of which I received the following anſwer.

Dear Sir, *Albany, Feb.* 6, 1757.

"The General received your letter that was ſent by Major Sparks, and returns you and your men thanks for their behaviour, and has recommended both you and them ſtrongly to my Lord Loudoun, as alſo that they have payment for the priſoners they took. Upon receiving an account of your ſkirmiſh we ſent an expreſs to Boſton, and, by the ſaid opportunity, recommended, for Spikeman's company, your brother * for a Lieutenant. We expect the expreſs back in a day or two, by whom I dare ſay, we ſhall have my Lord's approbation of the Rangers. Pleaſe to ſend me the names of the officers you would recommend for your own com-

* James Rogers.

company, and alſo to fill up the vacancies in the others; as I am certain you have the good of the ſervice at heart, your recommendation will be paid great regard to. I yeſterday received your's of the 30th of January. You cannot imagine how all ranks of people here are pleaſed with your conduct, and your mens behaviour; for my part, it is no more than I expected: I was ſo pleaſed with their appearance when I was out with them, that I took it for granted they would behave well whenever they met the enemy. When I returned I reported them as ſuch, and am glad they have anſwered my expectation.

"I am heartily ſorry for Spikeman and Kennedy, who I imagined would have turned out well, as likewiſe for the men you have loſt; but it is impoſſible to play at bowls without meeting with rubs. We muſt try to revenge the loſs of them. There is few people that will believe it; but upon honour, I could be glad to have been with you, that I might have learned the manner of fighting in this country. The chance of being ſhot is all ſtuff, and King William's opinion and principle is much the beſt for a ſoldier, viz. "that every bullet has its billet," and that "it is allotted how every man ſhall die;" ſo that I am certain that every one will agree, that it is better to die with the reputation of a brave man, fighting for his country in a good cauſe, than either ſhamefully running away to preſerve one's one's liſe, or lingering out an old age, and dying in one's bed, without having done his country or his King any ſervice.

" The hiſtories of this country, particularly, are full of the unheard-of cruelties committed by the French, and the Indians, by their inſtigation, which I think every brave man ought to do his utmoſt to humble that haughty nation, or reduce their bounds of conqueſt in this country to a narrow limit. As ſoon as General Abercrombie receives my Lord's inſtructions in regard to the Rangers, I ſhall ſend you notice of it; in the interim, I hope you'll get the better of your wound. If I can be of any ſervice to you or your men as long as they continue to behave ſo well, you may command

Your moſt humble ſervant,

To Capt. Robert Rogers.

James Abercrombie,
Aid de Camp."

My wound growing worſe, I was obliged to repair to Albany for better aſſiſtance, and there received the following inſtructions from General Abercrombie, viz.

Inſtructions for Capt. ROBERT ROGERS.

" His Excellency the Earl of Loudoun having given authority to me to augment the company of Rangers under your command, to 100 men each, viz.

One

One Captain,
Two Lieutenants, } upon an Engliſh pay;
One Enſign,

Four Serjeants at 4s. each, New York currency; 100 private men, at 2s. and 6d. each ditto per day; "And whereas there are ſome private men of your company ſerving at preſent upon higher pay than the above eſtabliſhment, you are at liberty to diſcharge them, in caſe they refuſe to ſerve at the ſaid eſtabliſhment, as ſoon as you have other men to replace them. If your men agree to remain with you and ſerve upon the above eſtabliſhment, you may aſſure them they will be taken notice of, and be firſt provided for; each man to be allowed ten dollars bounty-money, and to find their own cloaths, arms, and blankets, and to ſign a paper ſubjecting themſelves to the rules and articles of war, and to ſerve during the war. You are to inliſt no vagrants, but ſuch as you and your officers are acquainted with, and who are every way qualified for the duty of Rangers; and you and your officers are to uſe your beſt endeavours to complete your companies as ſoon as poſſible, and bring them to Fort Edward.

James Abercrombie,
Major General."

About this time I again wrote to his Lordſhip, earneſtly ſoliciting his friendly interpoſition and aſſiſtance,

ſiſtance, to obtain from the government here, an order for payment of what was due to me and my men, for our reſpective ſervices during the winter 1755; but if that could not be obtained, that he would be pleaſed to direct me what method to take for the recovery thereof. Whereto his Lordſhip replied, that as theſe ſervices were antecedent to his command here, it was not in his power to reward them. General Amherſt, afterwards, on a like application, gave me much the ſame anſwer.

Theſe applications not being attended with any ſucceſs, and ſuits of law being afterwards commenced againſt me, by, and on the behalf of thoſe who ſerved under me in that campaign, and verdicts obtained in their favour, I was not only obliged to anſwer their ſeveral demands, to the amount of £. 828 : 3 : 3 ſterling, which I paid out of my private fortune, but alſo a conſiderable ſum for law-charges, excluſive of what I ought to have received for my own ſervices during that ſevere ſeaſon. But for all which I have not at any time ſince received one ſhilling conſideration.

In the ſame letter I likewiſe informed his Lordſhip of the death of Capt. Hobbs of the Rangers who died a few days before, and recommended Lieutenant Bulkley of the ſame company, as a proper perſon to ſucceed him in that command.

March 5, I was taken ill with the ſmall-pox, and not able to leave my room till the 15th of April following, during which time my officers were recruiting, agreeable to his Lordſhip's inſtructions. Not long after I received the following letter from Capt. Abercrombie.

Sir, *New York, April* 22, 1757.

" As there is another ranging company ſent up to Albany, with orders to proceed to the forts, you will acquaint Colonel Gage, that it is my Lord Loudoun's orders, that the two companies at Fort William-Henry, and your own from Fort Edward, come down immediately to Albany, to be ready to embark for this place. Shew this letter to Colonel Gage, that he may acquaint Colonel Monro of his Lordſhip's orders, and that quarters may be provided for your companies in the houſes about Albany. You will take particular care that the companies have provided themſelves with all neceſſaries, and ſee that they are complete and good men. Since his Lordſhip has put it in your charge, I hope you will be very diligent in executing the truſt, for, upon a review of the men, if any are found inſufficient for the ſervice, the blame will be laid upon you. If the officers of this ranging company that is gone up, are not acquainted with the woods about Fort William-Henry, your brother muſt ſend ſome

ſome officers and men of his company along with them, to let them know the different ſcouts.

I am, Sir,

Your moſt humble ſervant,

To Capt.
Robert Rogers,
at Albany.

James Abercrombie,
Aid de Camp."

Capt. Richard Rogers, with his own, and the new company of Rangers before-mentioned, which was raiſed in the Jerſies, and commanded by Capt. Burgin, being left at Fort William-Henry, my own company from Fort-Edward, and Capt. Stark's and Capt. Bulkeley's from Fort William-Henry, agreeable to the above inſtructions, marched down to Albany, and from thence embarked for New York, where we were joined by another new-raiſed company of Rangers, under the command of Capt. Shephard from New Hampſhire, and after ſome ſmall ſtay there, re-embarked on board a tranſport, and left Sandy Hook on the 20th of June, with a fleet of near an hundred ſail, bound to Halifax, where we ſoon arrived, and, according to orders, I encamped on the Dartmouth ſide of the harbour, while the army lay encamped on the Halifax-ſide. The Rangers were here employed in various ſervices.

On

On July 3d, by orders, I commanded a party to Lawrence Town, and from thence to Schitzcook; ſome were left there to cut and make up hay in the meadows, for the horſes intended to be uſed in an expedition to Louiſburg; others covered the hay-makers, and others were diſpatched on ſcouts, to make diſcoveries; in one of which two deſerters from the 45th regiment were ſeized and brought in.

About the latter end of this month forty Rangers were ſent acroſs the iſthmus of Nova Scotia, to the ſettlements on the Bay of Fundy, and a party down to the north-weſt arm, to ſcour the woods for deſerters, &c. and brought in ſeveral, both from the army and navy.

About this time Admiral Holbourn arrived with a fleet from England, with ſeveral regiments of regular troops on board, which were landed, and likewiſe encamped at Halifax, upon which all ſcouting parties were called in; but certain intelligence being received that a French fleet of ſuperior force had actually arrived at Louiſburg, the intended expedition againſt that place was laid aſide, and thereupon the Rangers were remanded back to the weſtern frontiers.

Great numbers of the Rangers having been carried off this ſummer by the ſmall-pox, I ſent ſeveral of of my officers by his Lordſhip's command, to recruit in New Hampſhire, and the Maſſachuſet's provinces, with orders to join me at Albany. I afterwards embarked with the Rangers under my command, on board the fleet which carried the regular troops to New York, and from thence proceeded in ſmall veſſels up Hudſon's River to Albany, where I was ſoon after joined by the new-raiſed recruits.

I then proceeded to Fort Edward, which was the only remaining cover to the northern frontiers of New York, and the more eaſtern provinces, Fort William-Henry * having been taken by the French, under the command of Monſ. Montcalm, the Auguſt before. General Webb was then commanding officer at Fort Edward, and by his orders we were continually employed in patrolling the woods between this fort and Ticonderoga. In one of theſe parties, my Lord Howe did us the honour to accompany us, being fond, as he expreſſed himſelf, to learn our method of marching, ambuſhing, retreating,

* My brother Captain Richard Rogers died with the Small-pox a few days before this fort was beſieged; but ſuch was the cruelty and rage of the enemy after their conqueſt, that they dug him up out of his grave, and ſcalped him. In conſequence of the articles of capitulation at the ſurrender of this fort, the two companies of Rangers there were diſbanded, and diſmiſſed the ſervice.

ing, &c. and, upon our return, expreſſed his good opinion of us very generouſly.

About this time Lord Loudoun ſent the following volunteers in the regular troops, to be trained to the ranging, or wood-ſervice, under my command and inſpection; with particular orders to me to inſtruct them to the utmoſt of my power in the ranging-diſcipline, our methods of marching, retreating, ambuſhing, fighting, &c. that they might be the better qualified for any future ſervices againſt the enemy we had to contend with, deſiring me to take particular notice of each one's behaviour, and to recommend them according to their deſerts, *viz.*

Walter Crofton Mr. Lyſhat Mr. Roberts	of the 4th regiment of foot.
Charles Humbles Richard Edlington Andrew Crawley Thomas Millet	of the 22d ditto
John Wilcox John Wrightſon Michael Kent Mr. Monſel Francis Creed	of the 27th ditto.

Alexander

Alexander Robertſon William Frazier John Graham Andrew Roſs William Frazier, jun. Archibald Campbell Arch. Campbell, jun. Auguſ. Campbell Charles Menzies John Robertſon	of the 42d ditto.
Will. Ervin, or Irwin Thomas Drought William Drought Francis Carruthers John Clarke	of the 44th ditto.
Walter Paterſon Mr. Nicholſon Richard Boyce Charles Perry	of the 48th ditto.
Mr. Chriſtopher Mr. Still Mr. Hamilton Mr. Young	of the 55th ditto.

Allen

Allen Grant Jonathan M'Dougal Mr. Friſborough	of the ſecond battalion of Royal Americans.
Nicholas Ward James Hill	of the 3d ditto.
John Schloſer George Wardoman Francis Barnard Engelbertus Horſt Ericke Reinhault Andrew Wackerberg Luhainſans Dekeſar Donald M'Bean Henry Ven Bebber John Boujour	of the 4th ditto.
Edward Crafton James Pottinger Simon Stephens Archibald M'Donald Hugh Sterling Mr. Bridge	Rangers.

Theſe volunteers I formed into a company by themſelves, and took the more immediate command and management of them to myſelf; and for their benefit and inſtruction reduced into writing

ting the following rules or plan of difcipline, which, on various occafions, I had found by experience to be neceffary and advantageous, viz.

I. All Rangers are to be fubject to the rules and articles of war; to appear at roll-call every evening on their own parade, equipped, each with a firelock, fixty rounds of powder and ball, and a hatchet, at which time an officer from each company is to infpect the fame, to fee they are in order, fo as to be ready on any emergency to march at a minute's warning; and before they are difmiffed, the neceffary guards are to be draughted, and fcouts for the next day appointed.

II. Whenever you are ordered out to the enemies forts or frontiers for difcoveries, if your number be fmall, march in a fingle file, keeping at fuch a diftance from each other as to prevent one fhot from killing two men, fending one man, or more, forward, and the like on each fide, at the diftance of twenty yards from the main body, if the ground you march over will admit of it, to give the fignal to the officer of the approach of an enemy, and of their number, &c

III. If you march over marfhes or foft ground, change your pofition, and march abreaft of each other to prevent the enemy from tracking you

you (as they would do if you marched in a ſingle file) till you get over ſuch ground, and then reſume your former order, and march till it is quite dark before you encamp, which do, if poſſible, on a piece of ground that may afford your centries the advantage of ſeeing or hearing the enemy ſome conſiderable diſtance, keeping one half of your whole party awake alternately through the night.

IV. Some time before you come to the place you would reconnoitre, make a ſtand, and ſend one or two men in whom you can confide, to look out the beſt ground for making your obſervations.

V. If you have the good fortune to take any priſoners, keep them ſeparate, till they are examined, and in your return take a different route from that in which you went out, that you may the better diſcover any party in your rear, and have an opportunity, if their ſtrength be ſuperior to yours, to alter your courſe, or diſperſe, as circumſtances may require.

VI. If you march in a large body of three or four hundred, with a deſign to attack the enemy, divide your party into three columns, each headed by a proper officer, and let thoſe columns march in ſingle files, the columns to the right and left keeping at twenty yards diſtance or more from that

that of the center, if the ground will admit, and let proper guards be kept in the front and rear, and ſuitable flanking parties at a due diſtance as before directed, with orders to halt on all eminences, to take a view of the ſurrounding ground, to prevent your being ambuſcaded, and to notify the approach or retreat of the enemy, that proper diſpoſitions may be made for attacking, defending, &c. And if the enemy approach in your front on level ground, form a front of your three columns or main body with the advanced guard, keeping out your flanking parties, as if you were marching under the command of truſty officers, to prevent the enemy from preſſing hard on either of your wings, or ſurrounding you, which is the uſual method of the ſavages, if their number will admit of it, and be careful likewiſe to ſupport and ſtrengthen your rear-guard.

VII. If you are obliged to receive the enemy's fire, fall, or ſquat down, till it is over, then riſe and diſchargeat them. If their main body is equal to yours, extend yourſelves occaſionally; but if ſuperior, be careful to ſupport and ſtrengthen your flanking parties, to make them equal to theirs, that if poſſible you may repulſe them to their main body, in which caſe puſh upon them with the greateſt reſolution with equal force in each flank and in the center, obſerving to keep at a due diſt-

ance

ance from each other, and advance from tree to tree, with one half of the party before the other ten or twelve yards. If the enemy puſh upon you, let your front fire and fall down, and then let your rear advance thro' them and do the like, by which time thoſe who before were in front will be ready to diſcharge again, and repeat the ſame alternately, as occaſion ſhall require; by this means you will keep up ſuch a conſtant fire, that the enemy will not be able eaſily to break your order, or gain your ground.

VIII. If you oblige the enemy to retreat, be careful, in your purſuit of them, to keep out your flanking parties, and prevent them from gaining eminences, or riſing grounds, in which caſe they would perhaps be able to rally and repulſe you in their turn.

IX. If you are obliged to retreat, let the front of your whole party fire and fall back, till the rear hath done the ſame, making for the beſt ground you can; by this means you will oblige the enemy to purſue you, if they do it at all, in the face of a conſtant fire.

X. If the enemy is ſo ſuperior that you are in danger of being ſurrounded by them, let the whole body diſperſe, and every one take a different road

to

to the place of rendezvous appointed for that evening, which muſt every morning be altered and fixed for the evening enſuing, in order to bring the whole party, or as many of them as poſſible, together, after any ſeparation that may happen in the day; but if you ſhould happen to be actually ſurrounded, form yourſelves into a ſquare, or if in the woods, a circle is beſt, and, if poſſible, make a ſtand till the darkneſs of the night favours your eſcape.

XI. If your rear is attacked, the main body and flankers muſt face about to the right and left, as occaſion ſhall require, and form themſelves to oppoſe the enemy, as before directed; and the ſame method muſt be obſerved, if attacked in either of your flanks, by which means you will always make a rear of one of your flank-guards.

XII. If you determine to rally after a retreat, in order to make a freſh ſtand againſt the enemy, by all means endeavour to do it on the moſt riſing ground you come at, which will give you greatly the advantage in point of ſituation, and enable you to repulſe ſuperior numbers.

XIII. In general, when puſhed upon by the enemy, reſerve your fire till they approach very near, which will then put them into the greateſt ſurprize and conſternation, and give you an op-pportunity of ruſhing upon them with your hatch-ets and cutlaſſes to the better advantage.

XIV. When you encamp at night, fix your cen-tries in ſuch a manner as not to be relieved from the main body till morning, profound ſecrecy and ſilence being often of the laſt importance in theſe caſes. Each centry therefore ſhould conſiſt of ſix men, two of whom muſt be conſtantly alert, and when relieved by their fellows, it ſhould be done without noiſe; and in caſe thoſe on duty ſee or hear any thing, which alarms them, they are not to ſpeak, but one of them is ſilently to retreat, and acquaint the commanding officer thereof, that pro-per diſpoſitions may be made; and all occaſional centries ſhould be fixed in like manner.

XV. At the firſt dawn of day, awake your whole detachment; that being the time when the ſavages chuſe to fall upon their enemies, you ſhould by all means be in readineſs to receive them.

XVI. If the enemy ſhould be diſcovered by your detachments in the morning, and their num-bers are ſuperior to yours, and a victory doubtful, you ſhould not attack them till the evening, as then they will not know your numbers, and if you are

are repulſed, your retreat will be favoured by the darkneſs of the night.

XVII. Before you leave your encampment, ſend out ſmall parties to ſcout round it, to ſee if there be any appearance or track of an enemy that might have been near you during the night.

XVIII. When you ſtop for refreſhment, chuſe ſome ſpring or rivulet if you can, and diſpoſe your party ſo as not to be ſurpriſed, poſting proper guards and centries at a due diſtance, and let a ſmall party waylay the path you came in, leſt the enemy ſhould be purſuing.

XIX. If, in your return, you have to croſs rivers, avoid the uſual fords as much as poſſible, leſt the enemy ſhould have diſcovered, and be there expecting you.

XX. If you have to paſs by lakes, keep at ſome diſtance from the edge of the water, leſt, in caſe of an ambuſcade or an attack from the enemy, when in that ſituation, your retreat ſhould be cut off.

XXI. If the enemy purſue your rear, take a circle till you come to your own tracks, and there form an ambuſh to receive them, and give them the firſt fire.

XXII.

XXII. When you return from a ſcout, and come near our forts, avoid the uſual roads, and avenues thereto, leſt the enemy ſhould have headed you, and lay in ambuſh to receive you, when almoſt exhauſted with fatigues.

XXIII. When you purſue any party that has been near our forts or encampments, follow not directly in their tracks, leſt they ſhould be diſcovered by their rear-guards, who, at ſuch a time, would be moſt alert; but endeavour, by a different route, to head and meet them in ſome narrow paſs, or lay in ambuſh to receive them when and where they leaſt expect it.

XXIV. If you are to embark in canoes, battoes, or otherwiſe, by water, chuſe the evening for the time of your embarkation, as you will then have the whole night before you, to paſs undiſcovered by any parties of the enemy, on hills, or other places, which command a proſpect of the lake or river you are upon.

XXV. In padling or rowing, give orders that the boat or canoe next the ſternmoſt, wait for her, and the third for the ſecond, and the fourth for the third, and ſo on, to prevent ſeparation, and that you may be ready to aſſiſt each other on any emergency.

XXVI. Appoint one man in each boat to look out for fires, on the adjacent ſhores, from the numbers and ſize of which you may form ſome judgment of the number that kindled them, and whether you are able to attack them or not.

XXVII. If you find the enemy encamped near the banks of a river or lake, which you imagine they will attempt to croſs for their ſecurity upon being attacked, leave a detachment of your party on the oppoſite ſhore to receive them, while, with the remainder, you ſurprize them, having them between you and the lake or river.

XXVIII. If you cannot ſatisfy yourſelf as to the enemy's number and ſtrength, from their fire, &c. conceal your boats at ſome diſtance, and aſcertain their number by a reconnoitring party, when they embark, or march, in the morning, marking the courſe they ſteer, &c. when you may purſue, ambuſh, and attack them, or let them paſs, as prudence ſhall direct you. In general, however, that you may not be diſcovered by the enemy on the lakes and rivers at a great diſtance, it is ſafeſt to lay by, with your boats and party concealed all day, without noiſe or ſhew, and to purſue your intended route by night; and whether you go by land or water, give out parole and counterſigns, in order to know one another in the dark, and likewiſe appoint a ſtation for every man to repair to, in caſe of any accident that may ſeparate you."

Such in general are the rules to be obſerved in the Ranging ſervice; there are, however, a thouſand occurrences and circumſtances which may happen, that will make it neceſſary, in ſome meaſure, to depart from them, and to put other arts and ſtratagems in practice; in which caſes every man's reaſon and judgment muſt be his guide, according to the particular ſituation and nature of things; and that he may do this to advantage, he ſhould keep in mind a maxim never to be departed from by a commander, viz. to preſerve a firmneſs and preſence of mind on every occaſion.

My Lord Loudoun about this time made a viſit to Fort Edward, and after giving directions for quartering the army the approaching winter, left a ſtrong garriſon there under the command of Colonel Haviland, and returned to Albany. The Rangers * with the before-mentioned volunteers, were

* Several of them were diſmiſſed with an allowance of thirteen days pay to carry them home, being rendered unfit for immediate ſervice by their paſt fatigues, and ſeveral officers were ſent recruiting in order to have the companies complete by the opening of the ſpring.

were encamped and quartered in huts on an adjacent iſland in Hudſon's River, and were ſent out on various ſcouts, in which my ill ſtate of health at this time would not permit me to accompany them, till December 17, 1757, when, purſuant to orders from Lieutenant Colonel Haviland, commanding officer at Fort Edward, I marched from thence with a party of 150 men to reconnoitre Carillon, alias Ticonderoga, and if poſſible to take a priſoner. We marched ſix miles and encamped, the ſnow being then about three inches deep; and before morning it was fifteen: we however purſued our route.

On the 18th in the morning, eight of my party being tired, returned to the fort; with the remainder I marched nine miles further, and encamped on the eaſt-ſide of Lake-George, near the place where Monſ. Montcalm landed his troops when he beſieged and took Fort William-Henry, where I found ſome cannon-ball and ſhells, which had been hid by the French, and made a mark by which I might find them again.

The 19th we continued our march on the weſt-ſide of the lake nine miles further, near the head of the north-weſt bay.

The 21ſt, ſo many of my party tired and returned as reduced our number to 123 officers included, with whom I proceeded ten miles further, and encamped at night, ordering each man to leave a day's provisions there till our return.

The next day we marched ten miles further, and encamped near the great brook that runs into Lake George, eight miles from the French advanced guard.

The 23d we marched eight miles, and the 24th six more, and then halted within 600 yards of Carillon fort. Near the mills we discovered five Indian's tracks, that had marched that way the day before as we supposed, on a hunting party. On my march this day between the advanced guard and the fort, I appointed three places of rendezvous to repair to, in case of being broke in an action, and acquainted every officer and soldier that I should rally the party at the nearest post to the fort, and if broke there to retreat to the second, and at the third to make a stand till the darkness of the night would give us an opportunity to get off. Soon after I halted I formed an ambush on a road leading from the fort to the woods, with an advanced party of twenty men, and a rear-guard of fifteen. About eleven o'clock a serjeant of marines came from the fort up the road to my advanced party, who let him pass to the main body, where I made him prisoner.
Upon

Upon examination, he reported, "that there were "in the garrison 350 regulars, about fifty work- "men, and but five Indians: that they had plen- "ty of provisions, &c. and that twelve masons were "constantly employed in blowing up rocks in the "entrenchment, and a number of soldiers to assist "them: that at Crown Point there were 150 sol- "diers and fourteen Indians: that Monf. Mont- "calm was at Montreal: that 500 Ottawawas In- "dians wintered in Canada, and that 500 Rangers "were lately raised in Canada, each man having a "double-barrelled fuzee, and put under an expe- "rienced officer, well acquainted with the coun- "try: that he did not know whether the French "intended to attack any of the English forts this "winter or not; but that they expected a great "number of Indians as soon as the ice would bear "them, in order to go down to the English forts; "and that all the bakers in Carillon were employ- "ed in baking biscuit for the scouts above-menti- "oned."

About noon, a Frenchman, who had been hunting, came near my party in his return, when I ordered a party to pursue him to the edge of the cleared ground, and take him prisoner, with this caution, to shoot off a gun or two, and then retreat to the main body, in order to intice the enemy from their fort; which orders were punctually obeyed, but not one of them ventured out.

The last prisoner, on examination, gave much the same account as the other, but with this addition, "that he had heard the English intended to at-" "tack Ticonderoga, as soon as the lake was froze" "so as to bear them."

When I found the French would not come out of the fort, we went about killing their cattle, and destroyed seventeen head, and set fire to the wood, which they had collected for the use of the garrison, and consumed five large piles; the French shot off some cannon at the fires, but did us no harm. At eight o'clock at night I began my march homewards, and arrived at Fort Edward with my prisoners the 27th. In my return, I found at the north-end of Lake George, where the French had hid the boats they had taken at Fort William Henry, with a great number of cannon-balls; but as the boats were under water we could not destroy them. Upon my return to Fort Edward, I received a letter from Captain Abercrombie, informing me that the Earl of Loudoun, who was then at New York, had thoughts of augmenting the Rangers, and had desired General Abercrombie to command me down to receive his directions. I accordingly prepared for my journey, and upon my arrival was received by by his Lordſhip in a very friendly manner; and, after much converſation upon the ſubject, he was pleaſed to inform me of his intentions of levying five additional companies of Rangers, deſiring me to name the perſons whom I thought fit for officers, and ſuch as might be depended upon, to levy the men his Lordſhip deſired; which I accordingly did, and then received from him the following inſtructions.

"By his Excellency John Earl of Loudoun, Lord Machline and Tairenſeen &c. &c. &c. one of the ſixteen peers of Scotland, Governor and Captain General of Virginia, and Vice Admiral of the ſame, Colonel of the 13th Regiment of foot, Colonel in chief of the Royal American regiment, Major General and Commander in Chief of all his Majeſty's forces, raiſed or to be raiſed in North-America:

"Whereas I have this day thought proper to augment the Rangers with five additional companies, that is, four New England and one Indian company, to be forthwith raiſed and employed in his Majeſty's ſervice; and whereas I have an entire confidence in your ſkill and knowledge, of the men moſt fit for that ſervice; I do therefore by theſe preſents appoint you to raiſe ſuch a number of non-commiſſion officers and private men as will be neceſſary to compleat the ſaid five companies, upon the following eſtabliſhment, viz. each company to conſiſt of one Captain, two Lieutenants, one Enſign, four Serjeants and 100 privates. The officers to have Britiſh pay, that is, the ſame as an officer of the like rank in his Majeſty's regular forces; the Serjeants 4s. New York currency per day, and the private men 2s. 6d currency per day. And the better to enable you to make this levy of men, you ſhall have one month's pay for each of the ſaid five companies advanced to you; upon theſe conditions, that, out of the firſt warrants that ſhall hereafter be granted for the ſubſiſtence of theſe companies, ſhall be deducted the ſaid month's pay now advanced. Your men to find their own arms, which muſt be ſuch as upon examination, ſhall be found fit, and be approved of. They are likewiſe to provide themſelves with good warm cloathing, which muſt be uniform in every company, and likewiſe with good warm blankets. And the company of Indians to be dreſſed in all reſpects in the true Indian faſhion, and they are all to be ſubject to the rules and articles of war. You will forthwith acquaint the officers appointed to theſe companies, that they are immediately to ſet out on the recruiting ſervice, and you will not fail to inſtruct them that they are not to inliſt any man for a leſs term than one year, nor any but what are able-bodied, well acquainted with the woods, uſed to hunting,

and

and every way qualified for the Ranging ſervice. You are alſo to obſerve that the number of men requiſite to compleat the ſaid five companies, are all to be at Fort Edward on or before the 15th day of March next enſuing, and thoſe that ſhall come by the way of Albany are to be muſtered there by the officer commanding, as ſhall thoſe who go ſtrait to Fort Edward by the officer commanding there. Given under my hand, at New York, the 11th day of January 1758.

LOUDOUN.

By his Excellency's command,
To Capt. J. APPY."
Robert Rogers.

In purſuance of the above inſtructions I immediately ſent officers into the New England provinces, where, by the aſſiſtance of my friends, the requeſted augmentation of Rangers was quickly compleated, the whole five companies being ready for ſervice by the 4th of March.

Four of theſe companies were ſent to Louiſburg to join General Amherſt, and one joined the corps under my command; and tho' I was at the whole expence of raiſing the five companies, I never got the leaſt allowance for it, and one of the captains dying, to whom I had delivered a thouſand dollars as advance pay for his company, which, agreeable to the inſtructions I received, had a right to do; yet was I obliged to account with the government for this money, and entirely loſt every penny of it. It has already been mentioned, that the garriſon at Fort Edward, was this winter under the command of Lieut. Col. Haviland. This gentleman, about the 28th of February, ordered out a ſcout under the direction of one Putnam, Captain of a company of one of the Connecticut provincial regiments, with ſome of my men, given out publickly at the ſame time, that, upon Putnam's return, I ſhould be ſent to the French forts with a ſtrong party of 400 Rangers.

This was known not only to all the officers, but ſoldiers alſo, at Fort Edward before Putnam's departure.

While this party was out, a ſervant of Mr. Beſt, a ſutler to the Rangers, was captivated by a flying party of the enemy from Ticonderoga; unfortunately too, one of Putnam's men had left him at Lake George, and deſerted to the enemy. Upon Captain Putnam's return, we were informed he had ventured within eight miles of the French fort at Ticonderoga, and that a party he had ſent to make diſcoveries had reported to him, that there were near 600 Indians not far from the enemy's quarters.

March 10, 1758. Soon after the ſaid Captain Putnam's return, in conſequence of poſitive orders from Col. Haviland, I this day began a march from

Fort

Fort Edward for the neighbourhood of Carillon, not with a party of 400 men, as at firſt given out, but of 180 men only, officers included, one Captain, one Lieutenant, and one Enſign, and three volunteers, viz. Meſſ. Creed, Kent and Wrightſon, one ſerjeant, and one private, all of the 27th regiment; and a detachment from the four companies of Rangers, quartered on the iſland near Fort Edward, viz. Capt Buckley, Lieutenants Philips, Moore, Crafton, Campbell, and Pottinger; Enſigns Roſs, Wait, M'Donald, and White, and 162 private men. I acknowledge I entered upon this ſervice, and viewed this ſmall detachment of brave men march out, with no little concern and uneaſineſs of mind; for as there was the greateſt reaſon to ſuſpect, that the French were, by the priſoner and deſerter above mentioned, fully informed of the deſign of ſending me out upon Putnam's return: what could I think to ſee my party, inſtead of being ſtrengthend and augmented, reduced to leſs than one half the number at firſt propoſed. I muſt confeſs it appeared to me (ignorant and unſkilled as I then was in politicks and the art of war) incomprehenſible; *but my commander doubtleſs had his reaſons, and is able to vindicate his own conduct.* We marched to the half-way brook, in the road leading to Lake George, and there encamped the firſt night.

The 11th we proceeded as far as the firſt Narrows on Lake George, and encamped that even-

in

ing on the eaſt-ſide of the lake; and after dark, I ſent a party three miles further down, to ſee if the enemy might be coming towards our forts, but they returned without diſcovering any. We were however on our guard, and kept parties walking on the lake all night, beſides centries at all neceſſary places on the land.

The 12th we marched from our encampment at ſun-riſe, and having diſtanced it about three miles, I ſaw a dog running acroſs the lake, whereupon I ſent a detachment to reconnoitre the iſland, thinking the Indians might have laid in ambuſh there for us; but no ſuch could be diſcovered; upon which I thought it expedient to put to ſhore and lay by till night, to prevent any party from deſcrying us on the lake, from hills, or otherwiſe. We halted at a place called Sabbath-day Point, on the weſt-ſide of the lake, and ſent our parties to look down the lake with perſpective glaſſes, which we had for that purpoſe. As ſoon as it was dark we proceeded down the lake. I ſent Lieutenant Phillips with fifteen men, as an advanced guard, ſome of whom went before him on ſcates, while Enſign Roſs flanked us on the left under the weſt-ſhore, near which we kept the main body, marching as cloſe as poſſible, to prevent ſeparation, it being a very dark night. In this manner we continued our march till within eight miles of the

ſhore,

French advanced guards, when Lieutenant Phillips ſent a man on ſcates back to me, to deſire me to halt; upon which I ordered my men to ſquat down upon the ice. Mr. Phillips ſoon came to me himſelf, leaving his party to look out, and ſaid, he imagined he had diſcovered a fire * on the eaſt-ſhore, but was not certain; upon which I ſent with him Enſign White, to make further diſcovery. In about an hour they returned, fully perſuaded that a party of the enemy was encamped there. I then called in the advanced guard, and flanking party, and marched on to the weſt-ſhore, where, in a thicket, we hid our ſleys and packs, leaving a ſmall guard with them, and with the remainder I marched to attack the enemy's encampment, if there was any; but when we came near the place, no fires were to be ſeen, which made us conclude that we had miſtaken ſome bleach patches of ſnow, or pieces of rotten wood, for fire (which in the night, at a diſtance reſembles it) whereupon we returned to our packs, and there lay the remainder of the night without fire.

The 13th, in the morning, I deliberated with the officers how to proceed, who were unanimouſly of opinion, that it was beſt to go by land in ſnow-ſhoes, leſt the enemy ſhould diſcover us on the lake; we accordingly

* A ſmall party of the French, as we have ſince heard, had a fire here at this time; but, diſcovering my advanced party, extinguiſhed their fire, and carried the news of our approach to the French fort.

cordingly continued our march on the weſt-ſide, keeping on the back of the mountains that overlooked the French advanced guards. At twelve of the clock we halted two miles weſt of thoſe guards, and there refreſhed ourſelves till three, that the day-ſcout from the fort might be returned home before we advanced; intending at night to ambuſcade ſome of their roads, in order to trepan them in the morning. We then marched in two diviſions, the one headed by Captain Buckley, the other by myſelf: Enſigns White and Wait had the rear-guard, the other officers were poſted properly in each diviſion, having a rivulet at a ſmall diſtance on our left, and a ſteep mountain on our right. We kept cloſe to the mountain, that the advanced guard might better obſerve the rivulet, on the ice of which I imegined they would travel it out, as the ſnow was four feet deep, and very bad traveling on ſnow-ſhoes.

In this manner we marched a mile and an half, when our advanced guard informed me of the enemy being in their view ; and ſoon after, that they had aſcertained their number to be ninety-ſix, chiefly Indians.

We immediately laid down our packs, and prepared for battle, ſuppoſing theſe to be the whole number or main body of the enemy, who were marching on our left up the rivulet, upon the ice. I ordered Enſign M'Donald to the command of the advanced guard, which, as we faced to the left, made

made a flanking party to our right. We marched to within a few yards of the bank, which was higher than the ground we ocupied ; and obferving the ground graduallv to defcend from the bank of the rivulet to the foot of the mountain, we extended our party along the bank, far enough to command the whole of the enemy's at once ; we waited till their front was nearly oppofite to our left wing, when I fired a gun, as a fignal for a general difcharge upon them ; whereupon we gave them the firft fire, which killed above forty Indians; they retreated, and were purfued by about one half of our people. I now imagined the enemy totally defeated, and ordered Enfign M'Donald to head the flying remains of them, that none might efcape ; but we foon found our miftake, and that the party we had attacked were only their advanced guard, their main body coming up, confifting of 600 more, Canadians and Indians ; upon which I ordered our people to retreat to their own ground, which we gained at the expence of fifty men killed; the remainder I rallied, and drew up in pretty gcod order, where they fought with fuch intrepidity and bravery as obliged the enemy (tho' feven to one in number) to retreat a fecond time ; but we not being in a condition to purfue them, they rallied again, and recovered their ground, and warmly pufhed us in front and both wings, while the mountain defended our rear; but they were fowarmly ceived, that their flanking parties foon retreated to their

heir main body with confiderable lofs. This threw he whole again into diforder, and they retreated a third time; but our number being now too far reduced to take advantage of their diforder, they rallied again, and made a frefh attack upon us. About this time we difcovered 200 Indians going up the mountain on our right, as we fuppofed, to get poffeffion of the rifing ground, and attack our rear; to prevent which I fent Lieutenant Philips, with eighteen men, to gain the firft poffeffion, and beat them back; which he did, and being fufpicious that the enemy would go round on our left, and take poffeffion of the other part of the hill, I fent Lieutenant Crafton, with fifteen men, to prevent them there; and foon after defired two Gentlemen, who were there volunteers in the party*, with a few men, to go and fupport him, which they did with great bravery.

The enemy pufhed us fo clofe in front, that the parties

* I had before this defired thefe gentlemen to retire, offering them a Serjeant to conduct them; that as they were not ufed to fnow-fhoes, and were unacquainted with the woods, they would have no chance of efcaping the enemy, in cafe we fhould be broke and put to fight, which I very much fufpected. They at firft feemed to accept the offer, and began to retire; but feeing us fo clofely befet, they undauntedly returned to our affiftance. What befel them after our flight, may be feen by a letter from one of the Gentlemen to the commanding officer, which I have inferted next to this account of our fcout.

parties were not more than twenty yards afunder in general, and fometimes intermixed with each other. The fire continued almoft conftant for an hour and a half from the beginning of the attack, in which time we loft eight officers, and more than 100 private men killed on the fpot. We were at laft obliged to break, and I with about twenty men ran up the hill to Phillips and Crafton, where we ftopped and fired on the Indians who were eagerly pufhing us, with numbers that we could not withftand. Lieutenant Phillips being furrounded by 300 Indians, was at this time capitulating for himfelf and party, on the other part of the hill. He fpoke to me, and faid if the enemy would give them good quarters, he thought it beft to furrender, otherwife that he would fight while he had one man left to fire a gun †.

I now thought it moft prudent to retreat, and bring off with me as many of my party as I poffibly could, which I immediately did; the Indians clofely purfuing us at the fame time, took feveral prifoners. We came to Lake George in the evening, where we found feveral wounded men, whom we took

† This unfortunate officer, and his whole party, after they furrendered, upon the ftrongeft affurances of good treatment from the enemy, were inhumanly tied up to trees, and hewn to pieces, in a moft barbarous and fhocking manner.

took with us to the place where we had left our ſleds, from whence I ſent an expreſs to Fort Edward, deſiring Mr. Haviland to ſend a party to meet us, and aſſiſt us in bringing in the wounded; with the remainder I tarried there the whole night, without fire or blankets, and in the morning we proceeded up the lake, and met with Captain Stark at Hoop Iſland, ſix miles north from Fort William-Henry, and encamped there that night; the next day being the 15th, in the evening, we arrived at Fort Edward.

The number of the enemy was about 700, 600 of which were Indians. By the beſt accounts we could get, we killed 150 of them, and wounded as many more. I will not pretend to determine what we ſhould have done had we been 400 or more ſtrong; but this I am obliged to ſay of thoſe brave men who attended me (moſt of whom are now no more) both officers and ſoldiers in their reſpective ſtations behaved with uncommon reſolution and courage; nor do I know an inſtance during the whole action in which I can juſtly impeach the prndence or good conduct of any one of them.

The following is a L I S T of the Killed, Miſſing, &c.

The Captain and Lieutenant of his Majeſty's regular troops, volunteers in this party, were taken

ken priſoners; the Enſign, another volunteer of the ſame corps, was killed, as were two volunteers, and a Serjeant of the ſaid corps, and one private.

Of Capt. Rogers's Company,
Lieut. Moore — Killed.
Serjeant Parnell — Ditto.
Thirty-ſix privates Ditto.
Of Capt. Shepherd's Company,
Two Serjeants
Sixteen privates

Of Capt. James Rogers's Company,
Enſing M'Donald — Killed.

Of Capt, John Starks's Company,
Two Serjeants — Killed.
Fourteen privates Ditto.
Of Capt. Bulkley's Campany,
Capt. Bulkley — Killed.
Lieut. Pottinger — Ditto.
Enſign White — Ditto.
Forty-ſeven privates — K. and Miſſ.

Of Capt. William Starks's Company,
Enſign Roſs — Killed.

Of Capt. Brewer's Company,
Lieut. Campbell Killed.

A Gentleman of the army, who was a volunteer on

on this party, and who with another fell into the hands of the French, wrote the following letter, ſome time after, to the officer commanding the regiment they belonged to at Fort Edward.

Carillon, March 28, 1758.

" Dear Sir,

As a flag of truce is daily expected here with an anſwer to Monſieur Vaudreuil, I ſit down to write the moment I am able, in order to have a letter ready, as no doubt you and our friends at Fort Edward are anxious to be informed about Mr.—— and me, whom probably you have reckoned amongſt the ſlain in our unfortunate rencounter of the 13th, concerning which at preſent I ſhall not be particular; only to do this juſtice to thoſe who loſt their lives there, and to thoſe who have eſcaped, to aſſure you, Sir, that ſuch diſpoſitions were formed by the enemy, (who diſcovered us long enough before) it was impoſſible for a party ſo weak as ours to hope for even a retreat. Towards the concluſion of the affair, it was cried from a riſing ground on our right, to retire there; where, after ſcrambling with difficulty, as I was unaccuſtomed to ſnow-ſhoes, I found Capt. Rogers, and told him that I ſaw to retire further was impoſſible, therefore earneſtly begged we might collect all the men left, and make a ſtand there. Mr. ———, who was with him, was of my opinion, and Capt. Rogers alſo;

alſo; who therefore deſired me to maintain one ſide of the hill, whilſt he defended the other. Our parties did not exceed above ten or twelve in each, and mine was ſhifting towards the mountain, leaving me unable to defend my poſt, or to labour with them up the hill. In the mean time, Capt. Rogers with his party came to me, and ſaid (as did all thoſe with him) that a large body of Indians had aſcended to our right; he likewiſe added, what was true, that the combat was very unequal, that I muſt retire, and he would give Mr. —— and me a Serjeant to conduct us thro' the mountain. No doubt prudence required us to accept his offer; but, beſides one of my ſnow-ſhoes being untied, I knew myſelf unable to march as faſt as was requiſite to avoid becoming a ſacrifice to an enemy we could no longer oppoſe; I therefore begged of him to proceed, and then leaned againſt a rock in the path, determined to ſubmit to a fate I thought unavoidable. Unfortunately for Mr. —— his ſnow-ſhoes were looſened likewiſe, which obliged him to determine with me, not to labour in a flight we were both unequal to. Every inſtant we expected the ſavages; but what induced them to quit this path, in which we actually ſaw them, we are ignorant of, unleſs they changed it for a ſhorter, to intercept thoſe who had juſt left us. By their noiſe, and making a fire, we imagined they had got the rum in the Rangers packs. This thought, with the

the approach of night, gave us the firſt hopes of retiring; and when the moon aroſe, we marched to the ſouthward along the mountain, about three hours, which brough us to ice, and gave us reaſon to hope our difficulties were almoſt paſt; but we knew not we had enemies yet to combat with more cruel than the ſavages we had eſcaped. We marched all night, and on the morning of the 14th found ourſelves entirely unacquainted with the ice. Here we ſaw a man, who came towards us; he was the ſervant of Capt. Rogers, with whom he had been oftentimes all over the country, and, without the leaſt heſitation whatſoever, he informed us we were upon South-Bay; that Wood-Creek was juſt before us; that he knew the way to Fort Anne extremely well, and would take us to Fort Edward the next day. Notwithſtanding we were diſappointed in our hopes of being upon Lake George, we thought ourſelves fortunate in meeting ſuch a guide, to whom we gave entire confidence, and which he in fact confirmed, by bringing us to a creek, where he ſhewed the tracks of Indians, and the path he ſaid they had taken to Fort Anne. After ſtruggling thro' the ſnow ſome hours, we were obliged to halt to make ſnow-ſhoes, as Mr. ——— and the guide had left theirs at arriving upon the ice. Here we remained all night without any blankets, no coat, and but a ſingle waiſtcoat each, for I gave one of mine to Mr. ——, who had laid aſide his

green

green jacket in the field, as I did likewiſe my furred cap, which became a mark to the enemy, and probably was the cauſe of a ſlight wound in my face; ſo that I had but a ſilk handkerchief on my head, and our fire could not be large, as we had nothing to cut wood with. Before morning we contrived with forked ſticks and ſtrings of leather, a ſort of ſnow-ſhoes, to prevent ſinking entirely; and, on the 15th, followed our guide weſt all day, but he did not fulfil his promiſe; however the next day it was impoſſible to fail; but even then, the 16th, he was unſucceſsful; yet ſtill we were patient, becauſe he ſeemed well acquainted with the way, for he gave every mountain a name, and ſhewed us ſeveral places, where he ſaid his maſter had either killed deer or encamped. The ground, or rather the want of ſun-ſhine, made us incline to the ſouthward, from whence by accident we ſaw ice, at ſeveral miles diſtance, to the ſouth-eaſt. I was very certain, that after marching two days weſt of South Bay, Lake George could not be ſouth-eaſt from us, and therefore concluded this to be the upper end of the bay we had left. For this reaſon, together with the aſſurances of our guide, I adviſed continuing our courſe to the weſt, which muſt ſhortly ſtrike Fort Anne, or ſome other place that we knew. But Mr—— wiſhed to be upon the ice at any rate; he was unable to continue in the ſnow, for the difficulties of our march had overcome him. And really,

ally, Sir, was I to be minute in thoſe we had exprienced already and afterwards, they would almoſt be as tireſome to you to read, as they were to us to ſuffer.

Our ſnow-ſhoes breaking, and ſinking to our middle every fifty paces, the ſcrambling up mountains and acroſs fallen timber, our nights without ſleep or covering, and but little fire, gathered with great fatigue, our ſuſtenance moſtly water, and the bark and berries of trees; for all our proviſions from the beginning was only a ſmall Bologna ſauſage, and a little ginger, I happened to have, and which even now was very much decreaſed; ſo that I knew not how to oppoſe Mr. ———'s intreaties; but as our guide ſtill perſiſted Fort Anne was near, we concluded to ſearch a little longer, and if we made no diſcovery to proceed next day towards the ice; but we ſought in vain, as did our guide the next morning, tho' he returned, confidently aſſerting he had diſcovered freſh proofs, that the fort could not be far off. I confeſs I was ſtill inclined to follow him, for I was almoſt certain the beſt we could hope from deſcending upon this ice to our left was to throw ourſelves into the hands of the French, and perhaps not be able to effect even that; but from the circumſtances I have mentioned, it was a point I muſt yield to, which I did with great reluctancy. The whole day of the 17th we marched a dreadful

road,

road, between the mountains, with but one good ſnow-ſhoe each, the other of our own making being almoſt uſeleſs. The 18th brought us to the ice which tho' we longed to arrive at, yet I ſtill dreaded the conſequence, and with reaſon, for the firſt ſight informed us, it was the very place we had left five days before. Here I muſt own my reſolution almoſt failed me, when fatigue, cold, hunger, and even the proſpect of periſhing in the woods attended us, I ſtill had hopes, and ſtill gave encouragement, but now I wanted it myſelf; we had no reſource but to throw ourſelves into the enemy's hands, or periſh. We had nothing to eat, our ſlender ſtock had been equally ſhared amongſt us three, and we were not ſo fortunate as ever to ſee either bird or beaſt to ſhoot at. When our firſt thoughts were a little calmed, we conceived hopes, that if we appeared before the French fort, with a white flag, the commanding officer would relieve and return us to Fort Edward. This ſerved to palliate our neareſt approach to deſpair, and determined a reſolution, where in fact, we had no choice. I knew Carillon had an extenſive view up South Bay, therefore we concluded to halt during the evening, and march in the night, that we might approach it in the morning, beſides the wind pierced us like a ſword; but inſtead of its abating it increaſed, together with a freezing rain, that incruſted us entirely with ice, and obliged us to remain until morning, the 19th, when we

 fortunately

fortunately got ſome juniper berries, which revived, gave us ſpirits, and I thought ſtrength. We were both ſo firmly of that opinion, that we purpoſed taking the advantage of its being a dark ſnowy day, to approach Carillon, to paſs it in the night, and get upon Lake George. With difficulty we perſuaded the guide to be of our opinion, we promiſed large rewards in vain, until I aſſured him of proviſions hid upon the lake; but we little conſidered how much nature was exhauſted, and how unequal we were to the taſk: however, a few miles convinced us, we were ſoon midway up our legs in the new-fallen ſnow; it drove full in our faces, and was as dark as the fogs upon the banks of Newfoundland. Our ſtrength and our hopes ſunk together, nay, even thoſe of reaching Carillon were doubtful, but we muſt proceed or periſh. As it cleared up a little, we laboured to ſee the fort, which at every turn we expected, until we came to where the ice was gone, and the water narrow. This did not then agree with my idea of South Bay but it was no time for reflection; we quitted the ice to the left, and after marching two miles, our guide aſſured us we ought to be on the other ſide of the water. This was a very diſtreſſing circumſtance, yet we returned to the ice and paſſed to the right, where, after ſtruggling through the ſnow, about four miles, and breaking in every ſecond ſtep, as we had no ſnow-ſhoes, we were ſtopped by a large water-fall. Here I was again

gain aſtoniſhed with appearances, but nothing now was to be thought of only reaching the fort before night; yet to paſs this place ſeemed impracticable: however, I attempted to ford it a litle higher, and had almoſt gained the oppoſite ſhore, where the depth of the water, which was up to my breaſt, and the rapidity of the ſtream, hurried me off the ſlippery rocks, and plunged me entirely into the waters. I was obliged to quit my fuzee, and with great difficulty eſcaped being carried down the fall. Mr.——, who followed me, and the guide, though they held one another, ſuffered the ſame fate; but the hope of ſoon reaching a fire made us think lightly of this: as night approached we laboured exceſſively through the ſnow; we were certain the fort was not far from us, but our guide confeſſed, for the firſt time, that he was at a loſs. Here we plainly obſerved that his brain was affected: he ſaw Indians all around him, and though we have ſince learned we had every thing to fear from them, yet it was a danger we did not now attend to; nay we ſhouted aloud ſeveral times to give information we were there; but we could neither hear nor ſee any body to lead us right, or more likely to deſtroy us, and if we halted a minute we became pillars of ice; ſo that we were reſolved, as it froze ſo hard, to make a fire, although the danger was apparent. Accidently we had one dry cartridge, and in trying with my piſtol if it would flaſh a little of the powder, Mr.—— unfortunately held the cartridge too near, by which it took fire, blew up in our faces, almoſt blinded him, and gave exceſſive pain. This indeed promiſed to be the laſt ſtroke of forune, as hopes of a fire were no more; but although we were not anxious about life, we knew it was more becoming to oppoſe than yield to this laſt misfortune. We made a path round a tree, and there exerciſed all the night, though ſcarcely able to ſtand, or prevent each other from ſleeping. Our guide notwithſtanding repeated cautions, ſtraggled from us where he ſat down and died immediately. On the morning of the 20th, we ſaw the fort, which we approached with a white flag: the officers run violently towards us, and ſaved us from a danger we did not then apprehend; for we were informed, that if the Indians, who were cloſe after them, had ſeized us firſt, it would not have been in the power of the French to have prevented our being hurried to their camp, and perhaps to Montreal the next day, or killed for not being able to march. Monſ. Debecourt and all his officers treated us with humanity and politeneſs, and are ſolicitous in our recovery, which returns ſlowly, as you may imagine, from all theſe difficulties; and though I have omitted many, yet I am afraid you will think me too prolix; but we wiſh, Sir, to perſuade you of a truth, that nothing but the ſituation I have faithfully deſcribed could determine us in a reſolution, which

which appeared only one degree preferable to perishing in the woods.

"I shall make no comments upon these distresses; the malicious perhaps will say, which is very true, we brought them upon ourselves; but let them not wantonly add, we deserved them because we were unsuccessful. They must allow we could not be led abroad, at such a season of snow and ice, for amusement, or by an idle curiosity. I gave you, Sir, my reasons for asking leave, which you were pleased to approve, and I hope will defend them; and the same would make me again, as a volunteer, experience the chance of war to-morrow, had I an opportunity. These are Mr. —— 's sentiments as well as mine; and we both know you, Sir, too well to harbour the least doubt of receiving justice with regard to our conduct in this affair, or our promotion in the regiment; the prospect of not joining that so soon as we flattered ourselves has depressed our spirits to the lowest degree, so that we earnestly beg you will be solicitous with the General to have us restored as soon as possible, or at least to prevent our being sent to France, and separated from you, perhaps, during the war.

I have but one thing more to add, which we learned here, and which perhaps you have already observed from what I have said, that we were upon no other ice than that of Lake George; but by the day overtaking us, the morning of the 14th, in the very place we had, in coming, marched during the night, we were entirely unacquainted with it, and obliged to put a confidence in this guide, whofe head muft have been aftray from the beginning, or he could not fo grofsly have miftaken a place where he had fo often been. This information but added to our diftrefs, until we reflected that our not being entirely loft was the more wonderful. That we had parted from South Bay on the 14th, was a point with us beyond all doubt, and about which we never once hefitated, fo that we acted entirely contrary to what we had eftablifhed as a truth; for if, according to that, we had continued our courfe to the weft, we muft inevitably have perifhed; but the hand of Providence led us back contrary to our judgment; and though even then, and often afterwards, we thought it fevere, yet in the end it faved us, and obliged us to reft fatisfied that we conftrued many things unfortunate, which tended to our prefervation. I am, &c."

Upon my return from the late unfortunate fcout, I was ordered to Albany to recruit my companies, where I met with a very friendly reception from my Lord How, who advanced me cafh to recruit the Rangers, and gave me leave to wait upon General Abercrombie at New York, who had now fucceeded ſucceeded my Lord Loudoun in the chief command, my Lord being at this time about to embark for England. I here received a commiſſion from the General, of which the following is a copy.

"By his Excellency James Abercrombie, Eſq; Colonel of his Majeſty's 44th Regiment of Foot, Colonel in Chief of the 60th or Royal American Regiment, Major General and Commander in Chief of all his Majeſty's Forces raiſed or to be raiſed in North America, &c.

"Whereas it may be of great uſe to his Majeſty's ſervice in the operations now carrying on for recovering his rights in America, to have a number of men employed in obtaining intelligence of the ſtrength, ſituation, and motions of the enemy, as well as other ſervices, for which Rangers, or men acquainted with the woods, only are fit: Having the greateſt confidence in your loyalty, courage and ſkill in this kind of ſervice, I do, by virtue of the power and authority to me given by his Majeſty, hereby conſtitute and appoint you to be Major of the Rangers in his Majeſty's ſervice, and likewiſe Captain of a company of ſaid Rangers. You are therefore to take the ſaid Rangers as Major, and the ſaid Company as Captain, into your care and charge, and duly exercise and instruct, as well the officers as the soldiers thereof, in arms, and to use your best endeavours to keep them in good order and discipline; and I do hereby command them to obey you as their Major and Captain respectively, and you are to follow and observe such orders and directions from time to time as you shall receive from his Majesty, myself, or any other superior officer, according to the rules and discipline of war.

Given at New York, this 6th Day of April 1758, in the thirty-first Year of the reign of our Sovereign Lord George the Second, by the Grace of God, King of Great Britain, France and Ireland, Defender of the Faith, &c.

JAMES ABERCROMBIE.

By his Excellency's command,

J. APPY."

I left New York April 8, and according to orders attended Lord How at Albany for his directions, on the 12th, with whom I had a most agreeable interview, and a long conversation concerning the methods of distressing the enemy, and prosecuting the war with vigour the ensuing campaign. I parted with him, having the strongest assurances of his friendship and influence in my behalf, to wait upon Colonel Grant, commanding officer

officer at Fort Edward, to aſſiſt him in conducting the Rangers, and ſcouting parties, in ſuch a manner as might beſt ſerve the common cauſe, having a letter from my Lord to him. Capt. Stark was immediately diſpatched to Ticonderoga on the weſt-ſide of Lake George. Capt. Jacob, whoſe Indian name was *Nawnawapeteoonks*, on the eaſt-ſide, and Capt. Shepherd betwixt the lakes, with directions to take if poſſible ſome priſoners near Carillon. About the ſame time I marched myſelf with eighteen men for Crown Point. Capt. Burbank was likewiſe diſpatched in queſt of priſoners. Theſe ſcouts being often relieved, were kept out pretty conſtantly, in order to diſcover any parties of the enemy that might ſally out towards our forts or frontiers, and to reconnoitre their ſituation and motions from time to time. The ſucceſs of my own ſcout was as follows.

April 29, 1758, I marched from Fort Edward with a party of eighteen men, up the road that leads to Fort William Henry four miles, then north fou miles, and encamped at Schoon Creek, it having been a very rainy day.

On the 30th we marched north-and-by-eaſt all day, and encamped near South-Bay.

The 1ſt of May we continued the ſame courſe,

 and

and at night encamped near the narrows, north of South Bay.

The 2d, in the morning, made a raft, and crossed the bay over to the east-side, and having distanced the lake about four miles we encamped.

The 3d we steered our course north, and lay at night about three miles from Carillon.

The 4th we marched north-by-east all day, and encamped at night three miles from Crown Point Fort.

The 5th we killed one Frenchman, and took three prisoners.

The 6th, in the morning, began our return homeward, and arrived with our prisoners at Fort Edward the 9th.

One of the prisoners, who appeared to be the most intelligible, reported, "that he was born at "Lorrain in France; that he had been in Ca- "nada eight years, viz. two at Quebec, one at "Montreal, and five at Crown Point; that "at the latter were but 200 soldiers, of which "Mons. le Janong was commander in chief; that "at Ticonderoga there were 400 of the Queen's "regiment, 150 marines 200 Canadians, and about "700

"700 Indians; and that they daily expected 300
"Indians more; that they did not intend to attack
"our forts this summer, but were preparing to re-
"ceive us at Ticonderoga; that they had heard
"that I, with most of my party, was killed in the
"conflict last March; but afterwards by some
"prisoners which a small party of their Indians
"had taken from Dutch Hoosyk, they were in-
"formed that Rogers was yet alive, and was go-
"ing to attack them again, being fully resolved to
"revenge the inhumanity and barbarity with
"which they had used his men, in particular Lieut.
"Philips and his party, who were butchered by
"them, after they had promised them quarters;
"that this was talked of among the Indians, who
"greatly blamed the French for encouraging them
"so to do."

Captains Stark and Jacob returned the day before me; the former brought in with him six prisoners, four of which he took near Ticonderoga; they having escaped from New York and Albany, were in their flight to the French forts. The latter, who had but one white man with him, and eighteen Indians, took ten prisoners, and seven scalps, out of a party of fifty French. An account of these scouts, and the intelligence thereby gained, was transmitted to my Lord How, and by him to the General.

About

About the middle of May, a flag of truce was sent to Ticonderoga, on Col. Schyler's account, which put a stop to all offensive scouts, till its return.

May 28, 1758, I received positive orders from the General, to order all officers and men, belonging to the Rangers, and the two Indian companies, who were on furlow, or recruiting parties, to join their respective companies as soon as possible, and that every man of the corps under my command should be at his post at or before the 10th of next month. These orders were obeyed, and parties kept out on various scouts till the 8th of June, when my Lord Haw arrived at Fort Edward with one half of the army.

His Lordship immediately ordered me out with fifty men in whale-boats, which were carried over in waggons to Lake George, and directed me at all events to take a plan of the landing-place at the north-end with all possible accuracy, and also of the ground from the landing-place to the French fort at Carillon, and of Lake Champlain for three miles beyond it, and to discover the enemy's number in that quarter. Agreeable to these orders, on the 12th in the morning, I marched with a party of fifty men, and encamped in the evening at the place where Fort William-Henry stood.

On

On the 30th we proceeded down the lake in five whale-boats to the first narrows, and so on to the west end of the lake, where I took the plan his Lordship desired. Part of my party then proceeded to reconnoitre Ticonderoga, and discovered a large encampment there, and a great number of Indians. While I was, with two or three others, taking a plan of the fort, encampment &c. I left the remainder of my party at some considerable distance; when I was returning to them, at the distance of about 300 yards, they were fallen upon by a superior number of the enemy who had got between me and them. Capt. Jacobs, with the Mohegon Indians, run off at the first onset, calling to our people to run likewise; but they stood their ground, and discharged their pieces several times, at last broke through the enemy, by whom they were surrounded on all sides except their rear, where a river divided them: they killed three of the enemy, but lost eight of their own party in this skirmish. My party rallied at the boats, where I joined them, and having collected all but the slain together, we returned homewards. On the 20th at Half Way brook, we met my Lord How, advanced with three thousand men, to whom I gave an account of my scout, together with a plan of the landing-place, the fort at Carillon, and the situation of the lakes.

I obtained

I obtained leave of my Lord to go to Fort Edward, where his Excellency Major General Abercrombie was then posted, who ordered me to join my Lord How the next day with all the Rangers, being 600, in order to proceed with his Lordship to the lake.

On the 22d his Lordship encamped at the lake where formerly stood Fort William-Henry, and ordered the Rangers to advance 400 yards on the west-side, and encamp there; from which place, by his Lordship's orders, I sent off next morning three small parties of Rangers, viz. one to the narrows of South Bay, another to the west-side of Lake George, and a third to Ticonderoga Fort, all three parties by land. Another party, consisting of two Lieutenants and seventeen men, proceeded down the lake for discoveries, and were all made prisoners by about 300 French and Indians. This party embarked in whale-boats.

About the 28th of June his Excellency Major General Abercrombie arrived at the lake with the remainder of the army, where he tarried till the morning of the 5th of July, and then the whole army, consisting of near 16,000, embarked in battoes for Ticonderoga.

The

The order of march was a most agreeable sight; the regular troops in the center, provincials on each wing, the light infantry on the right of the advanced guard, the Rangers on the left, with Colonel Broadstreet's battoe-men in the center. In this manner we proceeded, till dusk, down Lake George to Sabbath Day Point, where the army halted and refreshed. About ten o'clock the army moved again, when my Lord How went in the front with his whale-boat, Liutenant Col. Broadstreet's and mine, with Lieutenant Holmes, in another, whom he sent forward to go near the landing-place, and observe if any enemy was posted there.

Holmes returned about day-break, met the army near the Blue Mountains within four miles of the landing place, and reported that there was a party of the enemy at the landing-place, which he discovered by their fires.

As soon as it was light his Lordship, with Col. Broadstreet and myself, went down to observe the landing-place before the army, and when within about a quarter of a mile, plainly discerned that it was but a small detachment of the enemy that was there; whereupon his Lordship said he would return to the General, that the army might land and march to Ticonderoga. About twelve o'clock the whole army landed, the Rangers on the left wing. I imme-

I immediately ſent an officer to wait upon the General for his orders, and received directions from Capt. Abercrombie, one of his Aids de Camps, to gain the top of a mountain that bore north about a mile from the landing-place, and from thence to ſteer eaſt to the river that runs into the falls betwixt the landing and the ſaw-mill, to take poſſeſſion of ſome riſing ground on the enemy's ſide, and there to wait the army's coming. I immediately marched, aſcended to the top of the hill, and from thence marched to the place I was ordered, where I arrived in about an hour, and poſted my party to as good advantage as I could, being within one quarter of a mile of where Monſ. Montcalm was poſted with 1500 men, whom I had diſcovered by ſome ſmall reconnoitring parties ſent out for that purpoſe. About twelve o'clock Colonels Lyman and Fitch of the provincials came to my rear, whom I informed of the enemy's being ſo very near, and inquiring concerning the army, they told me they were coming along. While this converſation paſſed, a ſharp fire began in the rear of Col. Lyman's regiment, on which he ſaid he would make his front immediately, and deſired me to fall on their left flank, which I accordingly did, having firſt ordered Capt. Burbanks with 150 men to remain at the place where I was poſted, to obſerve the motions of the French at the ſaw-mills, and went with the remainder of the Rangers on the left flank of the enemy,

enemy, the river being on their right, and killed several. By this time my Lord Howe, with a detachment from his front, had broke the enemy, and hemmed them in on every side; but advancing himself with great eagerness and intrepidity upon them, was unfortunately shot and died immediately *. There were taken prisoners of the enemy in this action, five officers, two volunteers, and one hundred and sixty men, who were sent to the landing place. Nothing more material was done this day. The next morning, at six o'clock, I was ordered to march to the river that runs into the falls, a place where I was the day before, and there to halt on the west-side till further orders, with four hundred Rangers, while Capt. Stark, with the remainder of the Rangers, marched with Capt. Abercrombie and Mr. Clerk the Engineer, to observe the position of the enemy at the fort, from whence they returned again that evening. The whole army lay the ensuing night under arms. By sun rise next morning, Sir William Johnson joined the army with four hundred and forty Indians. At seven o'clock I received orders to march with my Rangers. A Lieutenant of Captain Stark's led the advanced guard. I was within about three hundred

* This noble and brave officer being universally beloved by both officers and soldiers of the army, his fall was not only most sincerely lamented, but seemed to produce an almost general consternation and languor through the whole.

dred yards of the breaſt-work, when my advanced guard was ambuſhed and fired upon by about 200 Frenchmen. I immediately formed a front, and marched up to the advanced guard, who maintained their ground, and the enemy immediately retreated; ſoon after the battoe-men formed on my left and light infantry on my right. This fire of the enemy did not kill a ſingle man. Soon after three regiments of provincials came up and formed in my rear, at two hundred yards diſtance. While the army was thus forming, a ſcattering fire was kept up between our flying parties and thoſe of the enemy without the breaſt work. About half an hour paſt ten, the greateſt part of the enemy being drawn up, a ſmart fire began on the left wing, where Col. De Lancey's, (the New Yorkers,) and the battoe-men were poſted, upon which I was ordered forward to endeavour to beat the enemy within the breaſt-work, and then to fall down, that the pickets and grenadiers might march through. The enemy ſoon retired within their works; Major Proby marched through with his pickets within a few yards of the breaſt-work, where he unhappily fell, and the enemy keeping up a heavy fire, the ſoldiers haſtened to the right about, when Col. Haldiman came up with the granadiers to ſupport them, being followed by the batalions in brigades for their ſupport. Col. Haldiman advanced very near the breaſt-work, which was

was at leaſt eight feet high ; ſome of the provincials with the Mohocks came up alſo *.

We toiled with repeated attacks for four hours, being greatly embarraſſed by trees that were felled by the enemy without their breaſt-work, when the General thought proper to order a retreat, directing me to bring up the rear which I did in the duſk of the evening. On the ninth in the evening, we arrived at our encampment at the ſouth-end of Lake George, where the army received the thanks of the General for their good behaviour, and were ordered to entrench themſelves ; the wounded were ſent to Fort Edward and Albany. Our loſs both in the regular and provincial troops, was ſomewhat conſiderable. The enemy's loſs was about five hundred, beſides thoſe who were taken priſoners.

July 8, 1758. By order of the General, I this day began a ſcout to South Bay, from which I returned the 16th, having effected nothing conſiderable, except diſcovering a large party of the enemy, ſuppoſed to be near a thouſand, on the eaſt ſide of the lake. This party the next day, viz. the 17th,

* This attack was begun before the General intended it ſhould be, and as it were by accident, from the fire of the New Yorkers in the left wing; upon which Col. Haviland being in or near the center, ordered the troops to advance.

fell

fell upon a detachment of Col. Nicholls's regiment at the half-way brook, killed three captains, and upwards of twenty private men.

The 27th another party of the enemy fell upon a convoy of waggoners between Fort Edward and Half-Way Brook, and killed 116 men, sixteen of which were Rangers. In pursuit of this party, with a design to intercept their retreat, I was ordered to embark the 18th with 700 men; the enemy however escaped me, and in my return home on the 31st, I was met by an express from the General, with orders to march with 700 men to South and East Bay, and return by way of Fort Edward, in the prosecution of which orders nothing very material happened till the 8th of August; in our return, early in the morning of which day, we decamped from the place where Fort Anne stood, and began our march, Major Putnam with a party of Provincials marching in the front, my Rangers in the rear, Capt. Dalyell with the regulars in the center, the other officers suitably disposed among the men, being in number 530, exclusive of officers (a number having by leave returned home the day before.) After marching about three-quarters of a mile, a fire begun with five hundred of the enemy in the front; I brought my people into as good order as possible, Capt Dalyell in the center, and the Rangers on the right, with Col.

Col. Partridge's light infantry; on the left was Capt. Gidding's of the Boston troops with his people, and Major Putnam being in the front of his men when the fire began, the enemy rushing in, took him, one Lieutenant, and two others, prisoners, and considerably disordered others of the party, who afterwards rallied and did good service, particularly Lieutenant Durkee, who notwithstanding two wounds, one in his thigh, the other in his wrist, kept in the action the whole time, encouraging his men with great earnestness and resolution. Capt Dalyell with Gage's light infantry, and Lieut. Eyers of the 44th regiment, behaved with great bravery, they being in the center, where was at first the hottest fire, which afterwards fell to the right where the Rangers were, and where the enemy made four different attacks; in short, officers and soldiers throughout the detachment behaved with such vigour and resolution, as in one hour's time broke the enemy and obliged them to retreat, which they did with such caution in small scattering parties, as gave us no great opportunity to distress them by a pursuit: we kept the field and buried our dead. When the action was over, we had missing fifty-four men, twenty-one of which afterwards came in, being separated from us while the action continued. The enemy's loss was 199 killed on the ſpot, ſeveral of which were Indians*. We arrived at Fort Edward on the 9th, being met at ſome diſtance from it by Col. Provoſt, with a party of 300, and refreſhments for the wounded, which I had deſired by an expreſs ſent before.

I remained at Fort Edward till the 11th of the month, when I received orders from Col. Provoſt, who now ranked as Brigadier, and commanded at Fort Edward, to march and purſue the tracks of a large party of Indians, of which he had received intelligence, down the eaſt-ſide of Hudſon's River, in order to ſecure our convoys from them, and intercept their retreat; but this report which the Colonel had heard being groundleſs, my ſcout was ineffectual. I returned to Fort Edward on the 14th, and went with a detachment directly to the encampment at Lake George.

Aug. 20, 1758. By orders from the General I embarked with five men in a whale-boat, to viſit and reconnoitre Ticonderoga, in which excurſion I obtained ſeveral articles of intelligence concerning the enemy, their ſituation and numbers at different poſts, and returned the 24th to the encampment at Lake George.

I was

* By a detachment that went out afterwards, fifty more of the enemy were found dead near the place of action.

I was employed in various other excurſions towards the enemy's forts and frontiers, and in purſuit of their flying parties till the campaign for this year ended, and our army retired to winter-quarters.

Notwithſtanding little was effected by our late campaign to Ticonderoga; yet the Britiſh army in America were not every where unſucceſsful: for Col. Broadſtreet, with a detachment of 2000 men, reduced the French fort at Cataraqua, called Fort Frontenac*, and General Amherſt, who commanded the Britiſh troops at Cape Breton, had ſucceeded in the reduction of that important fortreſs, and now returned from his conqueſt, with a part of the troops that had been employed there, and was appointed commander in chief of his Majeſty's forces in North America (General Abercrombie embarking for England). The head quarters were now fixed at New York, and I had now new commanders

* This fort was ſquare faced, had four baſtions built with ſtone, and was near three-quarters of a mile in circumference. Its ſituation was very beautiful, the banks of the river preſenting on every ſide an agreeable landſcape, with a fine proſpect of the Lake Ontario, which was diſtant about a league, interſperſed with many iſlands that were well wooded, and ſeemingly fruitful. The French had formerly a great trade at this fort with the Indians, it being erected on purpoſe to prevent their trading with the Engliſh; but it is now totally deſtroyed.

manders to obey, new companions to converſe with, and, as it were, a new apprenticeſhip to ſerve. From Albany where I was ſettling ſome accounts with the Paymaſter, I began my acquaintance by the following letter to Col. Townſhend, Deputy Adjutant General to his Excellency.

" Sir, *Albany, Jan.* 28, 1759.

" Incloſed I ſend you the preſent ſtate of his Majeſty's companies of Rangers at Fort Edward, together with a liſt of the officers, now recruiting in the different parts of New England, who have lately adviſed me, that they have already inliſted near 400 men, which recruits are much wanted at Fort Edward, as it may be expected that the enemy will ſoon ſend their Indians, to endeavour to intercept our convoys between here and Fort Edward.

" To be ſeaſonably ſtrong to prevent their playing their old pranks, I would humbly propoſe, were it conſiſtent with the ſervice and agreeable to General Amherſt, my ſetting out for New England, in order to diſpatch ſuch Rangers as are there with all poſſible ſpeed to Fort Edward, or otherwiſe, as his Excellency ſhall direct. If it ſhould be agreeable to the General that I ſhould go to New-England, I ſhould be glad it might be by way of of New York, that I might have an opportunity to wait upon the General myfelf, and reprefent to him the neceffity of an augmentation of the Rangers now at Fort Edward, and the defire of the Stockbridge Indians to re-enter the fervice.

"The arms of the Rangers are in the hands of Mr. Cunningham at New York, which will be foon wanted at Fort Edward; I fhould therefore be glad they might be forwarded as foon as may be. I have wrote to Mr Cunningham, to make application to you for convenient carriages for the fame, which I fhould be glad you would furnifh him with. And till the time I have an opportunity of paying you my refpects in perfon, I beg leave to fubfcribe myfelf, Sir,

Your moft obedient humble fervant,

Robert Rogers."

"*P. S.* General Stanwix informs me, that a fubaltern officer, and about twenty Rangers, are to be ftationed at No 4; the officer I would recommend for that poft, is Lieut. Stephans, who is well acquainted with the country thereabout. He is now recruiting."

To

To Col. Townſend.

Soon after this I returned to Fort Edward, where I received the Colonel's anſwer, as follows.

" Sir, *Feb.* 5, 1759.

" I received your letter, with the incloſed return. The General commands me to inform you, he can by no means approve of your leaving Fort Edward.

" Your recruiting officers are all ordered to ſend up their recruits to Fort Edward. They are not only wrote to, but an advertiſement is put in all the papers, which was the only method the General had of conveying his intentions to them, as you had not ſent me any return of the officers names, and places where they were to recruit at. In obedience to that order, the recruits will be up ſooner than if they waited your coming down. I have likewiſe repeated the order to every officer, according to your return, by this poſt, and if you are complete by the returns they make, I ſhall order up every individual officer to their poſts.

" Any propoſals for the augmentation of the Rangers, or propoſals from the Stockbridge Indians, you

you would chuse to offer to the General, he desires may be immediately sent down to him.

"The arms for the Rangers, which you mention are in the hands of Mr. Cunningham, shall be sent up to you immediately.

"I have wrote to Lieut. Samuel Stephans, to acquaint him with the General's intentions of leaving him at No 4.

"If the enemy send out any scouting parties this year to pick up intelligence, or attack our convoys, the season of the year is now coming on that we may expect them; you therefore must see the necessity of your remaining at Fort Edward. Your officers and men should join you as fast as possible. The General would at another time comply with your request.

Your obedient humble servant,

R. Townshend, D. A. G."

Feb. 15, 1759.

To Major Rogers.

I wrote to the Colonel, proposing an addition of two new companies of Rangers upon the same

 footing

footing as thoſe already in the ſervice, and the raiſing of three companies of Indians to ſerve the enſuing campaign; and leſt the Indians ſhould be gone out on their hunting parties, and ſo be prevented from joining us, I wrote to three of their Sachems, or chiefs; one of which to King Uncus, head Sachem of the Mohegan Indians (which in ſubſtance is like the others) I will here inſert, as a ſpecimen of the method in which we are obliged to addreſs theſe ſavages.

"Brother Uncus,

"As it is for the advantage of his Majeſty King George, to have a large body of Rangers employed in his ſervice the enſuing campaign, and as I am well convinced of the ſincere attachment you have to him, I therefore carefully obey General Amherſt's orders to me, to engage your aſſiſtance here early in the ſpring.

"I hope you'll continue to ſhew that ardent zeal you have all along expreſſed for the Engliſh, ever ſince you have been allied to them, by raiſing a company of your men with the utmoſt expedition.

"Should you chuſe to come out a Captain, General Amherſt will readily give you the commiſſion

miſſion for it; if not, I ſhall expect Doquipe and Nunnipad. I leave to you the choice of an Enſign and two ſerjeants; but I hope you'll engage the fitteſt men for their ſtations. I would have the company conſiſt of fifty private men, or more, if you can get them; and if thoſe men that deſerted from Capt. Brewer will join you, the General will pardon them. You may employ a Clerk for the company, to whom General Amherſt will allow the uſual pay.

"I heartily wiſh you ſucceſs in raiſing your men, and ſhall be exceeding glad that you join me with all the expedition you poſſibly can. I am,

Brother Uncus,

Your moſt obedient humble ſervant,

To King Uncus. *Robert Rogers.*"

With this letter, or any other wrote to them, in order to give it any credit or influence, muſt go a belt of wampum, ſuitable to the matter and occaſion of it, and upon which the bearer, after having read the letter, interprets it, and then delivers both to the Sachem, or perſon they are directed to.

 The

The latter end of February, about fifty Mohocks, commanded by Captain Lotridge, came from Sir William Johnfon to join me, and proceed to Ticonderoga on a fcout.

March 3, 1759, I received the following orders from Col. Haldiman: "An officer being chofen by the General to make obfervations upon the enemy's fituation, and the ftrength of their forts upon Lake Champlain, you are ordered to march with your Rangers, and the Mohock Indians, under the command of Capt. Lotridge, and take all the meafures and precautions poffible, that he may execute his intentions, and perform the fervice, which the General has much at heart; and to effect this with more fecurity, a body of regulars is likewife ordered to join with you, and you are to have the command of the whole. Lieut. Brheem is to communicate his orders to you; and the fervice being performed, you will endeavour to take a prifoner, or prifoners, or ftrike fuch a ftroke on the enemy, and try to bring us intelligence.

"He recommends it in the ftrongeft manner, that if fome of the enemy fhould fall into your hands to prevent the Indians from exercifing their cruelty

cruelty upon them, as he desires prisoners may be treated with humanity.

Fred. Haldiman,
Commander at
Fort Edward."

Fort Edward,
March 3, 1759.

Pursuant to the above orders, I marched the same day with a party of 358 men, officers included, and encamped the first night at Half-Way-Brook. One Indian, being hurt by accident, returned to Fort Edward. The 4th marched to within one mile and a half of Lake George, and halted till evening, that we might the better pass undiscovered by the enemy, if any were on the hill reconnoitering. We continued our march till two o'clock in the morning, and halted at the first narrows. It being excessive cold, and several of our party being frost-bitten, I sent back twenty-three, under the charge of a careful serjeant, to Fort Edward. We continued here till the evening of the 5th, then marched to Sabbath-day Point, where we arrived about eleven o'clock, almost overcome with the cold. At two o'clock we continued our march, and reached the landing place about eight. I sent out a small party to observe if any of the enemies parties went out. They returned and reported, that none were to be seen on the west-side of the lake, but on the east were two working parties. It now appeared to be a ſuitable time for the engineer to make his obſervations. I left Capt. Williams to remain at this place with the Regulars, and thirty Rangers, while I, with the engineer, forty-nine Rangers, and Capt. Lotridge, with forty-five Indians, went to the iſthmus that overlooks the fort, where he made his obſervations. We returned to our party, leaving five Indians and one Ranger to obſerve what number croſſed the lake in the evening from the eaſt-ſide to the fort, that I might know the better how to attack them next morning. At dark the engineer went again, with Lieut. Tute, and a guard of ten men, to the entrenchments, and returned at midnight without oppoſition, having done his buſineſs to his ſatisfaction. On which I ordered Capt. Williams with the Regulars back to Sabbath-day Point; the party being extremely diſtreſſed with the cold, it appeared to me imprudent to march his men any further, eſpecially as they had no ſnow-ſhoes. I ſent with him Lieut. Tute and thirty Rangers, with directions to kindle fires on the aforeſaid point. At three o'clock I marched with three Lieutenants and forty Rangers, one Regular, and Capt. Lotridge with forty-ſix Indians, in order to be ready to attack the enemy's working parties on the eaſt-ſide of the lake early in the morning. We croſſed South-Bay about eight miles ſouth

ſouth of this fort *; from thence, it being about ſix o'clock, bore down right oppoſite the fort, and within half a mile of where the French parties agreeable to our expectations, were cutting of wood. Here I halted, and ſent two Indians and two Rangers to obſerve their ſituation. They returned in a few minutes, and brought intelligence that the working parties were cloſe to the banks of the lake, and oppoſite the fort, and were about forty in number; upon which we ſtripped off our blankets, and ran down upon them, took ſeveral priſoners, and deſtroyed moſt of the party as they were retreating to the fort, from whence being diſcovered, about eighty Canadians and Indians purſued us cloſely, being backed by about 150 French regulars, and in a mile's march they began a fire in our rear; and as we marched in a line abreaſt, our front was eaſily made; I halted on a riſing ground, reſolving to make a ſtand againſt the enemy, who appeared at firſt very reſolute: but we repulſed them before their reinforcement came up, and began our march again in a line abreaſt; having advanced about half a mile further, they came in ſight again. As ſoon as we could obtain an advantageous poſt, which was a long ridge, we again made a ſtand on the ſide oppoſite the enemy. The Canadians and Indians came very cloſe, but were ſoon ſtopped by a warm

 fire

* Here we found that a party of Indians had gone up the bay towards our forts.

ſire from the Rangers and Mohocks. They broke immediately, and the Mohocks with ſome Rangers purſued, and entirely routed them before their Regulars could come up. After this we marched without any oppoſition. In theſe ſeveral ſkirmiſhes we had two Rangers and one Regular killed, and one Indian wounded, and killed about thirty of the enemy. We continued our march till 12 o'clock at night, and came to Capt. Williams at Sabbath-day Point (fifty miles diſtant from the place we ſet out from in the morning.) The Captain received us with good fires, than which ſcarce any thing could be more acceptable to my party, ſeveral of which had their feet froze, it being exceſſive cold, and the ſnow four feet deep. Next morning marched the whole detachment as far as Long-Iſland in Lake George, and there encamped that night. On our march from Sabbath-day Point to this Iſland, I gave leave to ſome of the Rangers and Indians to hunt near the ſide of the lake, who brought us in great plenty of veniſon for our refreſhment.

I ſent Lieut. Tute, with the following letter, to Col. Haldiman, fearing leſt a party of Indians we had ſome notice of might have gone up South-Bay, and get an opportunity of doing miſchief before I could reach Fort Edward with the whole detachment.

Camp

Camp at Sabbath-day Point, Friday, eight o'clock in the morning.

" SIR,

" I ſend this to let you know that ſixty Indians, in two parties, are gone towards Fort Edward and Saratoga, and I fear will ſtrike ſome blow before this reaches you. Mr. Brheem is ſatisfied he has done his buſineſs agreeable to his orders; ſince which I have taken ſome priſoners from Ticonderoga, and deſtroyed others of the enemy, of the particulars of which the bearer will inform you.

" The Mohocks behaved with great bravery; ſome having been within piſtol-ſhot of the French fort.

" Two-thirds of my detachment have froze their feet (the weather being ſo ſevere that it is almoſt impoſſible to deſcribe it) ſome of which we are obliged to carry. I am, *&c.*

R. ROGERS."

Fort Edward, March 10, 1759.

" Dear Sir,

" I congratulate you heartily on your good ſucceſs, and ſend you twenty-two ſleys to tranſport your ſick. You will by this opportunity, take as many boards as you can conveniently *. My beſt

* Boards left at the place where Fort William Henry ſtood, and now wanted at Fort Edward.

compliments

compliments to Capt. Williams, and to all the gentlemen. I am, Sir,

Your most humble Servant,

FRED. HALDIMAND.

"P. S. I had the signal guns fired to give notice to the different posts. Nothing has appeared as yet †."

We were met by the sleys, and a detachment of 100 men at Lake George, and all arrived safe at Fort Edward, where I received the following letters upon my arrival.

"SIR,

"I yesterday received your letter by Mr. Stark. The general approves of raising the Indian companies; but as he has not heard the Rangers are complete, he cannot agree to the raising more companies, till the present ones are complete at Fort Edward. Mr. Stark sets out to-morrow for New England. I have ordered him to hurry up the recruits of your corps, and repeat my orders to the officers, to join their companies if they are complete. Your arms have been tried and proved by the

† The explosion of these signal-guns (as we afterwards heard) was heard by the party of the enemy, then near Fort Millar, eight miles below Fort Edward, who thereupon supposing themselves discovered, returned with precipitation.

the artillery; they anſwer very well, and are ordered to be ſent to you as faſt as poſſible: The general has ſent to you by Capt. Jacobs. We have choſe out one hundred men from each regiment, and pitched upon the officers to act this year as light infantry; they are cloathed and accoutred as light as poſſible, and, in my opinion, are a kind of troops that has been much wanted in this country. They have what amunition they want, ſo that I don't doubt but they will be excellent markſmen. You may depend upon general Amherſt's intentions to have you; I heard Brigadier Gage mention you to him. From what knowledge I have of the General, I can only ſay that merit is ſure to be rewarded; nor does he favour any recommendation, without the perſon recommended really deſerves his promotion. You will return your companies to me as ſoon as complete.

Your obedient humble ſervant,

New-York, R. TOWNSHEND.

Feb. 26, 1759.

To Major Rogers.

" SIR, *New-York, Feb.* 13, 1759.

" This will be delivered to you by Capt. Jacob Nawnawampeteoonk, who laſt campaign commanded a company of Stockbridge Indians, and who, upon hearing that you had wrote to me concerning him, came to offer me his ſervice for the enſuing campaign:

campaign: But as you have not mentioned to me the terms and conditions on which he was to engage, I have referred him to you to give in his proposals, that you may report to me thereupon, and inform me if you think his service adequate to them; after which I ſhall give you my anſwer. I am, Sir,

Your very humble Servant

JEFF. AMHERST.

To Major Rogers.

Before I received this letter from his Excellency, I had wrote to him, recommending ſeveral officers to the vacancies in the ranging companies, and incloſed a journal of my late ſcout; ſoon after my return from which I went to Albany, to ſettle my accompts with the government, where I waited upon his Excellency the General, by whom I was very kindly received, and aſſured that I ſhould have the rank of Major in the army from the date of my commiſſion under General Abercrombie.

I returned to Fort Edward the 15th of May, where I received the melancholy news, that Capt. Burbank, with a party of thirty men, had in my abſence been ſent out on a ſcout, and were all cut off. This gave me great uneaſineſs, as Mr. Burbank was a gentleman I very highly eſteemed, and one of the beſt officers among the Rangers, and more eſpecially as I judged the ſcout he was ſent

out

out upon by the commanding officer at the fort was needless, and unadvisedly undertaken.

Preparations for the campaign were hastened by his Excellency the General in every quarter; the levies from the several provinces forwarded, the companies of Rangers compleated, and disciplined in the best manner I was capable of, and of which the general was pleased greatly to approve.

In the month of June, part of the army marched with General Gage for the lake. I was ordered to send three companies there with Capt. Stark, and to remain with the General myself with the other three companies, till such time as he marched thither. In this interval, pursuant to his Excellency's orders, I sent out several parties to the French forts, who from time to time discovered the situation of the enemy, and brought satisfactory intelligence.

About the 20th of June, the General with the remainder of the army marched to the lake, the Rangers being in the advanced guard; and here his Excellency was pleased to fulfil his promise to me, by declaring in public orders, my rank of Major in the army, from the date of my commission, as Major of the Rangers. We continued here collecting our strength together, and making necessary preparations, and getting what intelligence we could

of

of the ſtrength and ſituation of the enemy, till July 21, 1759, when the army embarked for Ticonderoga. I was in the front with the Rangers on the right wing, and was the firſt body that landed on July 22, at the north end of Lake George, followed by the grenadiers and light infantry, which Col. Haviland commanded.

I marched, agreeable to orders from the General, acroſs the mountains in the iſthmus; from thence, in a by-way, athwart the woods to the bridge at the Saw-mills; where finding the bridge ſtanding, I immediately croſſed it with my Rangers, and took poſſeſſion of the riſing ground on the other ſide, and beat from thence a party of the enemy, and took ſeveral priſoners, killed others, and put the remainder to flight, before Colonel Haviland with his grenadiers and light infantry got over. The army took poſſeſſion that night of the heights near the Saw-mills, where they lay all this evening.

The enemy kept out a ſcouting-party, with a body of Canadians and Indians, which killed ſeveral of our men, and galled us prodigiouſly.

July 23, The General, early in the morning, put the army in motion; at the ſame time ordered me in the front, with directions to proceed acroſs the

the Chefnut Plain, the nigheft and beft way I could, to Lake Champlain, and do my endeavour to ftrike it near the edge of the cleared ground, between that and the breaft-work, where I was to halt till I received further orders. Having purfued my orders, and halted at the lake, I informed the General of my fituation, and that nothing extraordinary had happened in our march.

The General by this time had appointed and formed a detachment to attack their main breaftwork on the hill, and had got poffeffion of it. I was ordered to fend two hundred men to take poffeffion of a fmall entrenchment next to Lake Champlain; and Captain Brewer, whom I had fent to take poffeffion of this poft, happily fucceeded.

From the time the army came in fight the enemy kept up a conftant fire of cannon from their walls and batteries at our people. The General at this time had left feveral provincial regiments to bring the cannon and ammunition acrofs the Carrying Place, together with provifions, which they did with great expedition *.

July

* About this time fome of the Provincial regiments were fent to Ofwego, to affift in building a fort there.

July 24. All this day the engineers were employed in raifing batteries, as was likewife a great part of the army in that work, and in making and fetching fafcines, till the 26th at night; all which time I had parties out to Crown Point to watch the motions of the enemy there; by which means the General had not only daily, but hourly intelligence from thofe pofts.

I this day received orders from the General to attempt to cut away a boom which the French had thrown acrofs the lake oppofite the fort, which prevented our boats from paffing by, and cutting off their retreat. For the completion of this order I had fixty Rangers in one Englifh flat-bottomed boat, and two whale-boats *, in which, after night came on, I embarked, and paffed over to the other fide of Lake Champlain, oppofite to the Rangers encampment, and from that intended to fteer my courfe along the eaft-fhore, and privately faw off their boom, for which end I had taken faws with me, the boom being made with logs of timber.

About nine o'clock, when I had got about half way

* Thefe boats were carried acrofs the land from Lake George to Lake Champlain, on which day the brave and worthy Colonel Townfhend was killed by a cannon ball from the enemy, whofe fall was much lamented by the General.

way from the place where I had embarked, the enemy, who had undermined their fort, ſprung their mines, which blew up with a loud exploſion, the enemy being all ready to embark on board their boats, and make a retreat. This gave me an opportunity to attack them with ſuch ſucceſs as to drive ſeveral of them aſhore; ſo that next morning we took from the eaſt-ſhore ten boats, with a conſiderable quantity of baggage, and upwards of fifty barrels of powder, and large quantities of ball. About ten o'clock I returned, and made my report to the General.

The 27th I was ordered with my party to the Saw-mills (to wait the flying parties of the enemy which were expected that way) where I lay till the 11th of Auguſt *, on which day I received the following orders from General Amherſt.

" SIR,

" You are this night to ſend a Captain, with a proper proportion of ſubalterns, and two hundred men, to Crown Point, where the officer is to poſt himſelf in ſuch a manner as not to be ſurprized, and to ſeize on the beſt ground for defending himſelf;

* About this time a party of my people diſcovered that the enemy's Fort at Crown Point was likewiſe blown up, and the enemy fled.

ſelf; and if he ſhould be attacked by the enemy, he is not to retreat with his party, but keep his ground till he is reinforced from the army.

I am, Sir,

Your moſt obedient,

To Major Rogers. *Jeff. Amherſt.*"

Capt. Brewer went with a party, and the General followed the 12th with the whole army, and the ſame day arrived at Crown Point, where it was found that Captain Brewer had executed his orders extremely well.

This evening I had orders for encamping, and the ground for each corps being laid out, my camp was fixed in the front of the army. Immediately after the General had got the diſpoſition of his camp ſettled, he began to clear ground, and prepare a place for erecting a new fort, in which ſervice great part of the army was employed. I had orders to ſend Capt. Stark, with two hundred Rangers, to cut a road to No. 4. which party was immediately ſent.

During theſe tranſactions I ſent out (by the General's approbation) ſeveral ſcouting parties againſt the

the enemy *, which brought in prifoners from St. John's Fort, and others penetrated into the back country, the better to learn the nature and fituation of it.

Thus were we employed till the 12th of September, when the General, exafperated at the treatment which Capt. Kennedy had met with, who had been fent with a party as a flag of truce to the St. Francis Indians, with propofals of peace to them, and was by them made a prifoner with his whole party; this ungenerous inhumane treatment determined the General to chaftize thefe favages with fome feverity, and, in order to it, I received from him the following orders, viz.

† "You are this night to fet out with the detachment as ordered yefterday, viz. of 200 men, which you will take under your command, and proceed to Mififquey Bay, from whence you will march

* Captain Tute, and Lieutenant Fletcher, in two different fcouting parties, were taken and carried to Canada.

† That this expedition might be carried on with the utmoft fecrefy after the plan of it was concerted the day before my march, it was put into public orders, that I was to march a different way, at the fame time I had private inftructions to proceed directly to St. Francis.

march and attack the enemy's ſettlements on the ſouth-ſide of the river St. Lawrence, in ſuch a manner as you ſhall judge moſt effectual to diſgrace the enemy, and for the ſucceſs and honour of his Majeſty's arms.

" Remember the barbarities that have been committed by the enemy's Indian ſcoundrels on every occaſion, where they had an opportunity of ſhewing their infamous cruelties on the King's ſubjects, which they have done without mercy. Take your revenge, but don't forget that tho' thoſe villains have daſtardly and promiſcuouſly murdered the women and children of all ages, it is my orders that no women or children are killed or hurt.

" When you have executed your intended ſervice, you will return with your detachment to camp, or to join me wherever the army may be.

Your's, &c.

Camp at Crown Point,
Sept. 13, 1759.

Jeff. Amherſt."

To Major Rogers.

In purſuance of the above orders, I ſet out the ſame

ſame evening with a detachment; and as to the particulars of my proceedings, and the great difficulties we met with in effecting our deſign, the reader is referred to the letter I wrote to General Amherſt upon my return, and the remarks following it.

Copy of my Letter to the General upon my return from St. Francis.

" SIR,

" The twenty-ſecond day after my departure from Crown Point, I came in ſight of the Indian town St. Francis in the evening, which I diſcovered from a tree that I climbed, at about three miles diſtance. Here I halted my party, which now conſiſted of 142 men, officers included, being reduced to that number by the unhappy accident which befel Capt Williams*, and ſeveral ſince tiring, whom I was obliged to ſend back. At eight o'clock this evening I left the detachment, and took with me Lieut. Turner and Enſign Avery, and went to reconnoitre the town, which I did to my ſatisfaction, and

* Capt. Williams of the Royal Regiment was, the fifth day of our march, accidentally burnt with gun-powder, and ſeveral men hurt, which together with ſome ſick, returned back to Crown Point, to the number of forty, under the care of Capt. Williams, who returned with great reluctance.

and found the Indians in a high frolic or dance. I returned to my party at two o'clock, and at three marched it to within five hundred yards of the town, where I lightened the men of their packs, and formed them for the attack.

" At half an hour before sun-rise I surprised the town when they were all fast asleep, on the right, left, and center, which was done with so much alacrity by both the officers and men, that the enemy had not time to recover themselves, or take arms for their own defence, till they were chiefly destroyed, except some few of them who took to the water. About forty of my people pursued them, who destroyed such as attempted to make their escape that way, and sunk both them and their boats. A little after sun-rise I set fire to all their houses, except three, in which there was corn, that I reserved for the use of the party.

" The fire consumed many of the Indians who had concealed themselves in the cellars and lofts of their houses. About seven o'clock in the morning the affair was completely over, in which time we had killed at least two hundred Indians, and taken twenty of their women and children prisoners, fifteen of whom I let go their own way, and five I brought with me, viz. two Indian boys and three

Indian girls. I likewife retook five Englifh captives, which I alfo took under my care.

" When I had paraded my detachment, I found I had Capt. Ogden badly wounded in his body, but not fo as to hinder him from doing his duty. I had alfo fix men flightly wounded, and one Stockbridge Indian killed.

" I ordered my people to take corn out of the referved houfes for their fubfiftence home, there being no other provifion there: and whilft they were loading themfelves I examined the prifoners and captives, who gave the following intelligence: " That a party of 300 French, and fome Indians, were about four miles down the river below us; and that our boats were way-laid, which I had reafon to believe was true, as they told the exact number, and the place where I left them at: that a party of 200 French and fifteen Indians, had, three days before I attacked the town, gone up the river Wigwam Martinic, fuppofing that was the place I intended to attack; whereupon I called the officers together, to confult the fafety of our return, who were of opinion there was no other way for us to return with fafety, but by No. 4. on Connecticut River. I marched the detachment eight days in a body that day; and when provifions grew fcarce, near Ampara Magog Lake, I divided the detachment into ſmall companies, putting proper guides to each, who were to aſſemble at the mouth of Amonſook River*, as I expected proviſions would be brought there for our relief†, not knowing which way I ſhould return.

" Two days after we parted, Enſign Avery, of Fitche's, fell in on my track, and followed in my rear; and a party of the enemy came upon them, and took ſeven of his party priſoners, two of whom that night made their eſcape, and came in to me next morning. Avery, with the remainder of his party joined mine, and came with me to the Cohaſe Intervales, where I left them with Lieut. Grant, from which place I, with Capt. Ogden, and one man more, put down the river on a ſmall raft to this place, where I arrived yeſterday; and in half an hour after my arrival diſpatched proviſions up the river to Lieut. Grant in a canoe, which I am pretty certain will reach him this night, and next morning ſent two other canoes up the river for the relief

* Amonſook River falls into Connecticut River about ſixty miles above No 4.

† An officer upon ſome intelligence that I had when going out, was ſent back to Crown Point from Miſiſquey Bay, to deſire that proviſions might be conveyed to this place, as I had reaſon to believe we ſhould be deprived of our boats, and conſequently be obliged to return this way.

relief of the other parties, loaded with provisions, to the mouth of Amonsook River.

"I shall set off to go up the river myself to-morrow, to seek and bring in as many of our men as I can find, and expect to be back in about eight days, when I shall, with all expedition, return to Crown Point. As to other particulars relative to this scout, which your Excellency may think proper to inquire after, I refer you to Capt. Ogden, who bears this, and has accompanied me all the time I have been out, behaving very well. I am, Sir, with the greatest respect,

Your Excellency's most obedient servant,

No. 4. *R. Rogers.*"
Nov. 5, 1759.

To General Amherst.

I cannot forbear here making some remarks on the difficulties and distresses which attended us, in effecting this enterprize upon St. Francis, which is situated within three miles of the river St. Lawrence, in the middle of Canada, about half way between Montreal and Quebec. It hath already been mentioned, how our party was reduced by the accident which befel Capt. Williams, the fifth day after our departure, and ſtill farther by numbers tiring and falling ſick afterwards. It was extremely difficult while we kept the water (and which retarded our progreſs very much) to paſs undiſcovered by the enemy, who were then cruizing in great numbers upon the lake; and had prepared certain veſſels, on purpoſe to decoy any party of ours, that might come that way, armed with all manner of machines and implements for their deſtruction; but we happily eſcaped their ſnares of this kind, and landed (as hath been mentioned) the tenth day at Miſiſquey Bay. Here, that I might with more certainty know whether my boats (with which I left proviſions ſufficient to carry us back to Crown Point) were diſcovered by the enemy, I left two truſty Indians to lie at a diſtance in ſight of the boats, and there to ſtay till I came back, except the enemy found them; in which latter caſe they were with all poſſible ſpeed to follow on my track, and give me intelligence. It happened the ſecond day after I left them, that theſe two Indians came up to me in the evening, and informed me that about 400 French had diſcovered and taken my boats, and that about one half of them were hotly purſuing on my track. This unlucky circumſtance (it may well be ſuppoſed) put us into ſome conſternation. Should the enemy overtake us, and we get the better of them in an encounter; yet being ſo far advanced into their country, where no reinforcement could

could possibly relieve us, and where they could be supported by any numbers they pleased, afforded us little hopes of escaping their hands. Our boats being taken, cut off all hope of a retreat by them; besides the loss of our provisions left with them, of which we knew we should have great need at any rate, in case we survived, was a melancholy consideration. It was, however, resolved to prosecute our design at all adventures, and, when we had accomplished it, to attempt a retreat (the only possible way we could think of) by way of No 4; and that we might not be destroyed by famine in our return, I dispatched Lieut. M'Mullen by land to Crown Point, to desire of the General to relieve me with provision at Amonsook River, at the end of Cohase Intervales on Connecticut River, that being the way I should return, if at all, and the place appointed being about sixty miles from No. 4. then the most northerly English settlement. This being done, we determined if possible to outmarch our pursuers, and effect our design upon St. Francis before they could overtake us. We marched nine days through wet sunken ground; the water most of the way near a foot deep, it being a spruce bog. When we encamped at night, we had no way to secure ourselves from the water, but by cutting the boughs of trees, and with them erecting a kind of hammocks. We commonly began our march a little before day, and continued it till after dark at night.

The tenth day after leaving Misisquey Bay, we came to a river about fifteen miles above the town of St. Francis to the South of it; and the town being on the oppofite or eaft fide of it, we were obliged to ford it, which was attended with no fmall difficulty, the water being five feet deep, and the current fwift. I put the talleft men up the ftream, and then holding by each other, we got over with the lofs of feveral of our guns, fome of which were recovered by diving to the bottom for them. We had now good dry ground to march upon, and difcovered and deftroyed the town as before related, which in all probability would have been effected with the lofs of no man but the Indian who was killed in the action, had not my boats been difcovered, and our retreat that way cut off.

This nation of Indians was notorioufly attached to the French, and had for near a century paft harraffed the frontiers of New England, killing people of all ages and fexes in a moft barbarous manner, at a time when they did not in the leaft fufpect them; and to my own knowledge, in fix years time, carried into captivity, and killed, on the before-mentioned frontiers, 400 perfons. We found in the town hanging on poles over their doors, 600 fcalps, moftly Englifh.

The

The circumſtances of our return are chiefly related in the preceding letter; however it is hardly poſſible to deſcribe the grief and conſternation of thoſe of us who came to Cohaſe Intervales. Upon our arrival there (after ſo many days tedious march over ſteep rocky mountains, or through wet dirty ſwamps with the terrible attendants of fatigue and hunger) to find that here was no relief for us, where we had encouraged ourſelves that we ſhould find it, and have our diſtreſſes alleviated; for notwithanding the officer I diſpatched to the general diſcharged his truſt with great expedition, and in nine days arrived at Crown Point, which was an hundred miles through the woods, and the General, without delay, ſent Lieut. Stephans to No. 4, with orders to take proviſions up the river to the place where I had appointed, and there wait as long as there was any hopes of my returning; yet the officer that was ſent being an indolent fellow, tarried at the place but two days, when he returned, taking all the proviſions back with him, about two hours before our arrival. Finding a freſh fire burning in his camp, I fired guns to bring him back, which guns he heard, but would not return, ſuppoſing we were an enemy *.

 Our

* This Gentleman, for this piece of conduct, was broke by a general court-martial, and rendered incapable of ſuſtaining any office in his Majeſty's ſervice for the future: a poor reward however

Our diſtreſs upon this occaſion was truly inexpreſſible; our ſpirits, greatly depreſſed by the hunger and fatigues we had already ſuffered, now almoſt entirely ſunk within us, ſeeing no reſource left, nor any reaſonable ground to hope that we ſhould eſcape a moſt miſerable death by famine. At length I came to a reſolution to puſh as faſt as poſſible towards No. 4, leaving the remains of my party, now unable to march further, to get ſuch wretched ſubſiſtence as the barren wilderneſs could afford *, till I could get relief to them, which I engaged to do within ten days. I, with Captain Ogden, one Ranger, and a captive Indian boy, embarked upon a raft we made of dry pine trees. The current carried us down the ſtream in the middle of the river, where we endeavoured to keep our wretched veſſel by ſuch paddles as we had made out of ſmall trees, or ſpires ſplit and hewed. The ſecond day we reached White River Falls, and very narrowly eſcaped being carried over them by the current. Our little remains of ſtrength however enabled us to land, and to march by them. At the bottom of theſe

ever, for the diſtreſſes and anguiſh thereby occaſioned to ſo many brave men, to ſome of which it proved fatal, they actually dying with hunger.

* This was ground-nuts and lilly roots, which being cleaned and boiled will ſerve to preſerve life, and the uſe and method of preparing which I taught to Lieut. Grant commander of the party.

these falls, while Capt. Ogden and the Ranger hunted for red squirrels for a refreshment, who had the good fortune likewise to kill a partridge, I attempted forming a new raft for our further conveyance. Being not able to cut down trees, I burnt them down, and then burnt them off at proper lengths. This was our third day's work after leaving our companions. The next day we got our materials together, and compleated our raft, and floated with the stream again till we came to Wattockquitchey Falls, which are about fifty yards in length: here we landed, and by a weath made of hazel bushes, Capt. Ogden held the raft, till I went to the bottom, prepared to swim in and board it when it came down, and if possible paddle it ashore this being our only resource for life, as we were not able to make a third raft in case we had lost this. I had the good fortune to succeed, and the next morning we embarked and floated down the stream to within a small distance of No. 4, where we found some men cutting of timber, who gave us the first relief, and assisted us to the fort, from whence I dispatched a canoe with provisions, which reached the men at Cohase four days after, which (agreeable to my engagement) was the tenth after I left them.

Two days after my arrival at No. 4 I went with other canoes, loaded with provisions, up the river myſelf, for the relief of others of my party that might be coming in that way*, having hired ſome of the inhabitants to aſſiſt me in this affair. I likewiſe ſent expreſſes to Suncook and Pennecook upon Merrimack river, that any that ſhould chance to ſtraggle that way might be aſſiſted; and proviſions were ſent up ſaid rivers accordingly.

On my return to No. 4, I waited a few days to refreſh ſuch of my party as I had been able to collect together, and during my ſtay there received the following letter from General Amherſt, in anſwer to mine of No. 5.

" SIR, *Crown Point, Nov.* 8, 1759.

" Captain Ogden delivered me your letter of the 5th inſtant, for which I am not only to thank you, but to aſſure you of the ſatisfaction I had on reading it; as every ſtep you informed me you have taken, has been very well judged, and deſerves may full approbation. I am ſorry Lieut. Stephens judged ſo ill in coming away with the proviſions from the place where I ſent him to wait for you. An

* I met ſeveral different parties; as Lieut- Curgill, Lieut. Campbell, Lieut. Farrington, and Serjeant Evans, with their reſpective diviſions, and ſent canoes further up for the relief of ſuch as might be ſtill behind, and coming this way. Some I met who eſcaped from Dunbar's and Turner's party, who were overtaken (being upwards of twenty in number) and were moſtly killed or taken by the enemy.

" An Indian is come in last night, and said he had left some of your party at Otter River. I sent for them; they are come in. ' This afternoon four Indians, two Rangers, a German woman, and three other prisoners; they quitted four of your party some days since, and thought they had arrived here*. I am in hopes all the rest will get in very safe. I think there is no danger but they will, as you quited them not till having marched eight days in a body; the only risk after that will be meeting hunting parties. I am, Sir,

Your humble servant,

To Major Rogers.

JEFF. AMHERST."

As soon as my party were refreshed, such as were able I marched to Crown Point, where I arrived Dec. 1, 1759, and upon examination found, that, since our leaving the ruins of St. Francis, I had lost three Officers, viz. Lieut. Dunbar of Gage's Light Infantry, Lieut. Turner of the Rangers, and Lieut. Jenkins of the Provincials, and forty-six serjeants and privates.

The Rangers at that place were all dismissed before my return, excepting two companies, commanded by Captains Johnson and Tute†, with whom I found

* Upon our seperation, some of the divisions were ordered to make for Crown point, that being the best route for hunting.

† Capt. Tute who had been taken prisoner, was returned by a flag of truce, while I was gone to St, Francis.

I found orders left by the General for me to continue at that garrison during the winter, but had leave, however, to go down the country, and to wait upon his Excellency at New York.

After giving in my return to the General, and what intelligence I could of the enemy's situation, he desired me, when I had leisure, to draw a plan of my march to St. Francis; and then by his order, I returned by the way of Albany; which place I left the 6th of February 1760, with thirteen recruits I had inlisted; and the 13th, on my way between Ticonderoga and Crown Point, from whence I would have pursued them immediately; but Col. Haviland, the commanding officer there, judged it not prudent, by reason the garrison at that time was very sickly *, I continued at Crown Point the remainder of the winter.

On the 31st of march, Capt. James Tute, with two regular officers and six men, went out a scouting, and were all made prisoners; the enemy was not pursued, on account of the sickness of the garrison.

The

* My own sley was taken with 1196l. York currency in cash, besides stores and other necessaries; 800l. of this money belonged to the crown, which was afterwards allowed me, the remaining 396l. was my own, which I entirely lost.

The ſame day I received from General Amherſt the following letter.

"SIR, *New York, March* 1, 1760.

"The command I have received from his Majeſty, to purſue the war in this country, has determined me, if poſſible, to complete the companies of Rangers that were on foot laſt campaign; and as Captain Wait called upon me yeſterday, and repreſented that he could eaſily complete the one he commands in the colony of Connecticut and the Province of the Maſſachuſet's Bay, I have furniſhed him with beating orders for that purpoſe, as alſo with a warrant for 800 dollars on account of that ſervice.

"This day I have wrote to Capt. John Stark in New Hampſhire, and Capt. David Brewer in the Maſſachuſet's Bay, incloſing to each of them a beating order for the reſpective provinces; and I herewith ſend you a copy of the inſtructions that accompany the ſame, by which you will ſee they are ordered, as faſt as they get any number of men, to ſend them to Albany. I am, SIR,

Your humble ſervant,

To Major Rogers. *Jeff. Amherſt.*"

My

My anſwer to the above.

"Sir, *Crown Point, March* 15, 1760.

"I received your Excellency's letter, dated the 1ſt inſtant, together with a copy of your inſtructions to Capt. John Stark and Capt. David Brewer, whereby I learn that they are to be at Albany by the 1ſt of May next with their companies. Since I received intelligence from your Excellency that the Rangers are to be raiſed again, I have wrote to ſeveral of my friends in New England, who will aſſiſt them in compleating their companies; and as many of the men belonging to the two companies here were froſt-bitten in the winter, and others ſick, many of whom I judged would not be fit for ſervice the enſuing campaign, I employed Lieut. M'Cormack, of Capt. William Stark's company (that was with Major Scott) Lieut. John Fletcher, and one Holmes, and ſent them recruiting the 20th of February for my own and Captain Johnſon's company, and advanced them 1100 dollars. Theſe three recruiters I do not doubt will bring good men enough to complete us here; ſo that thoſe who are froſt-bitten may be ſent to hoſpitals, and thoſe unfit for duty diſcharged, or otherwiſe diſpoſed of, as your Excellency ſhall direct.

There

There being ſo few Rangers fit for duty here, and thoſe that are much wanted at this place, has prevented me from propoſing any tour to the French and Indian ſettlements in purſuit of a priſoner, which may, I believe, be eaſily got at any time, if ſent for. I am, SIR,

Your Excellency's

moſt obedient humble ſervant,

R. Rogers."

To General Amherſt.

A letter from General Amherſt,

" SIR, *New York*, 9th *March*, 1760.

" As I have not heard that either of the Jacobuſes, who each commanded a company of Stockbridge Indians the laſt campaign, are returned from their captivity, I would have you write (if you think Lieut. Solomon capable of and fit for ſuch a command) to him, to know if he chuſes to accept of the ſame; but it muſt be upon condition of bringing to the field none but good men, that are well inclined, and that are hale and ſtrong. Whatever number he or any of his friends can raiſe that will anſwer this deſcription, I will readily employ

this

this ſummer, and they ſhall meet with all the encouragement their ſervices ſhall merit. All others that are too old or too young, I ſhall reject, nor ſhall I make them any allowance of payment, altho' they ſhould join the army; ſo that, in order to prevent his having any difference with theſe people, it will behove him to engage none but what ſhall be eſteemed fit for the ſervice; he muſt alſo obſerve to be aſſembled with them at Albany by the 1ſt of May at furtheſt, from which day he and they ſhall be entitled to their pay, that is, for ſo many as ſhall be muſtered there, and for no more; he muſt likewiſe take care that every man comes provided with a good firelock, and that they be always ready to march at a moment's warning, wherever they are ordered to, in default of which they ſhall forfeit their pay that ſhall be due to them at that time. All this you will explain to him particularly, and ſo ſoon as you receive his anſwer, inform me thereof. As an encouragement to enter the ſervice upon the foregoing conditions, you may aſſure him alſo, that if he conforms to them in every reſpect, and that he and his men prove uſeful, they ſhall be better rewarded than they have yet been.

" Capt. Ogden having ſolicited me for a company of Rangers, aſſured me that he could raiſe and complete a very good one in the Jerſies; I have given

given him a beating order for that purpofe, and inftructions fimilar to thofe I fent you a copy of in my laft for Captains Stark and Brewer, and have alfo granted him a warrant for four hundred dollars, on account of the bounty-money, to be as ufual ftopped out of the firft warrant for the fubfiftence of that company. I am, SIR,

Your humble fervant,

To Major Rogers. *Jeff. Amherft.*"

My Letter to the General.

Crown Point, 20th *March*, 1760.

" SIR,

" I obferve the contents of your Excellency's letter of the 19th, and fhall take particular care to let Lieut. Solomon know every circumftance relative to his being employed the next fummer, and to advife your Excellency as foon as I hear from him. He has already informed me he would be glad to engage with fome Indians.

" Mr. Stuart, the Adjutant of the Rangers, who is at Albany, I have defired to go to Stockbridge, to deliver Solomon his orders, and to explain them properly to him.

" I am

"I am heartily glad that your Excellency hath been pleaſed to give to Capt. Ogden a company of the Rangers, who, from the good character he bears, I doubt not will anſwer your expectations.

"Incloſed is a ſketch of my travels to and from St. Francis. I am, Sir,

Your Excellency's moſt humble ſervant,

To General Amherſt. *R. Rogers.*"

The General's Letter to me.

"Sir, *New York*, 9th *April*, 1760.

"I am to own the receipt of your letters of the 15th and 20th ultimo, and to approve what you therein mention to have done for completing your and Capt. Johnſon's company; as alſo your having ſent Adjutant Stuart to Stockbridge, to deliver Solomon his orders, and to explain them properly to him. This will avoid all miſtakes, and enable you the ſooner to inform me of Solomon's intentions, which I ſhall be glad to know as ſoon as poſſible.

"I thank you for your ſketch of your travels to and from St. Francis, and am, Sir,

Your very humble ſervant,

To Major Rogers. *Jeff. Amherſt.*"

Soon

Soon after this I had the pleasure of informing the General that the Stockbridge Indians determined to enter the service this year; but as many of them were out a hunting, that they could not be collected at Albany before the 10th of May; and that the recruits of the ranging companies began to assemble at Crown Point.

May 4, 1760. This day Serjeant Beverly, who had been taken prisoner, and made his escape, came in seven days from Montreal to Crown Point. He had lived at the Governor's (Monsieur de Vaudreuil) house, and brought the following intelligence, which I immediately transmitted to the General, viz.

"That about the 10th of April, the enemy withdrew all their troops from Nut Island, excepting 300, which they left there to garrison the place, under the command of Monsieur Bonville: that the enemy also brought from the island one half of the ammunition they had there, and half of the cannon: that the enemy had two frigates, one of 36 guns, the other of 20 guns, that lay all winter in the river St. Lawrence, and some other small vessels, such as row-galleys, &c. that all the troops of France in Canada went down to Jecorty the 20th of April, except those left to garrison their

their fort, which was very ſlenderly done, together with all the militia that could be ſpared out of the country, leaving only one man to two females to ſow their grain, where they were aſſembled by Monſieur Levy, their General, with an intent to retake Quebec *: that ninety ſix men of the enemy were drowned going down to Jecorty: that he ſaw a man who was taken priſoner the 15th of April, belonging to our troops at Quebec: that this man told him our garriſon there was healthy; and that Brigadier General Murray had 4000 men fit for duty in the city, beſides a poſt of 300 men at Point Levy, which the enemy attempted to take poſſeſſion of in the month of February laſt, with a conſiderable body of troops, and began to fortify a church at or near the Point, but that General Murray ſent over a detachment of about 1000 men, which drove the enemy from the poſt, and took a Captain, with about thirty French ſoldiers, priſoners, and fortified the church for his own conveniency: that the General has another poſt on the north-ſide of the river at Laurat, a little diſtance from the town, in which he keeps 300 men: that there is a line of block-houſes well fortified all round the land-ſide of the town, under cover of the cannon:

* This place, the capital of all Canada, had been taken by the Engliſh troops laſt year, under the command of General Wolfe.

non: that a breaſt-work of fraziers is extended from one block-houſe to another, as far as thoſe houſes extend: that they heard at Quebec of the enemy's coming, but were not in the leaſt concerned: that a detachment from Quebec ſurpriſed two of the enemy's guards, at a place called Point de Treamble, each guard conſiſting of fifty men, and killed or took the moſt part of them. One of thoſe guards were all grenadiers."

He moreover reports, "That two more of our frigates had got up the river, and that two more men of war were near the Iſland of Orleans: that the French told him that there was a fleet of ten ſail of men of war ſeen at Gaſpee Bay, with ſome tranſports, but put back to ſea again on account of the ice; but as they had up different colours, they could not tell whether they were French or Engliſh: that the beginning of May the enemy was to draw off 2000 of their men to Nut Iſland, and as many more to Oſwagotchy: he heard that they did not intend to attack Quebec, except the French fleet gets up the river before ours: that 100 Indians were to come this way, and ſet out about the fifth of May; the remainder of the Indians were at preſent gone to Jecorty: that General Levy, the Attawawas, and Cold Country Indians, will all be in Canada by the beginning of June, ten Sachems being ſent by the French laſt fall, to call thoſe nations

tions to their aſſiſtance: that a great number had deſerted to the French from the battalion of Royal Americans at Quebec, which the French have engaged in their ſervice; but that they were to be ſent off, under the care of Monſieur Boarbier, up to Attawawas River, to the French colony betwixt the lakes and the Miſſiſſipi River: that the moſt part of the enemies Indians are intent on going there; and that a great number of French, eſpecially thoſe who have money, think to ſave it by carrying it to New Orleans: that he ſaw at Montreal two Rangers, Reynolds and Hall, that were returned by Col. Haviland deſerted laſt fall: that they were taken priſoners near River-head Block-houſe, when after cattle: that two more Rangers are to be here in ten days with freſh intelligence from Montreal, if they can poſſibly make their eſcape: that Monſieur Longee, the famous partiſan, was drowned in the river St. Laurence, a few days after he returned with the party that took Captain Tute: that the Indians have a great eye to No. 4. roads, as they ſay they can get ſheep and oxen coming here from that place: that he heard Gen. Murray had hanged ſeveral Canadians lately, that were carrying ammunition out of Quebec to the enemy: that the two Captains Jacobs are ſtill in Canada; the one taken with Capt. Kennedy is on board a veſſel in irons, the other ran away laſt fall, but

but returned, having froze his feet, and is at Montreal."

A few days after this, I went down the Lake Champlain, to reconnoitre Nut Island, and the garrison there, the landing places, &c. On my return from that service to Crown Point, I had an order from Gen. Amherst to repair to Albany, the head-quarters, as fast as possible.

I set out, in obedience to this order, the 19th of May, and waited upon the General at Albany the 23d, and gave him all the information I could, in regard to the passage into Canada by the Island de Noix, or Nut Island, and likewise that by Oswego and La Galette.

The General being acquainted by an express, that Quebec was then besieged by the French, informed me of his intentions of sending me with a party into Canada, and if the siege of Quebec was continued, to destroy their country as far as possible, and by constantly marching from one place to another, try to draw off the enemy's troops, and prolong the siege till our vessels got up the river. He strongly recommended, and ordered me to govern myself according to the motions of the French army; to retreat if they had raised the siege; and in case, by prisoners or otherwise, I should find the

the ſiege ſtill going on, to harraſs the country, tho' it were at the expence of my party. I had at the ſame time the following inſtructions from him in writing.

" Major Rogers, you are to take under your command a party of 300 men, compoſed of 275 Rangers, with their proper officers, and a ſubaltern, two ſerjeants, and twenty-five men of the Light Infantry regiments; with which detachment you will proceed down the lake, under convoy of the brig, where you will fix upon the ſafeſt and beſt place for laying up your boats, which I imagine one of the iſlands will beſt anſwer, while you are executing the following ſervices.

" You will with 250 men land on the weſt-ſide, in ſuch manner that you may get to St. John's (without the enemy at the Iſle au Noix having any intelligence of it) where you will try to ſurprize the fort, and deſtroy the veſſels, boats, proviſions, or whatever elſe may be there for the uſe of the troops at the Iſle au Noix. You will then march to Fort Chamble, where you will do the ſame, and you will deſtroy every magazine you can find in that part, ſo as to diſtreſs the enemy as much as you can. This will ſoon be known at the Iſle au Noix, and you muſt take care not to be cut off in

your

your retreat; for which reaſon, when you have done all you think practicable on the weſtern ſide; I judge your beſt and ſafeſt retreat will be, to croſs the river and march back the eaſt-ſide of Iſle au Noix. When you land on the weſt-ſide, you will ſend ſuch officer with the fifty Rangers, as you think will beſt anſwer their intended ſervice, which is, to march for Wigwam Martinique, to deſtroy what he may find there and on the eaſt-ſide of the river, and afterwards to join you, or to retreat in ſuch manner as you will direct him. You will take ſuch proviſions as you judge neceſſary with you, and fix with Capt. Grant (who ſhall have orders to wait for your return) the places where he may look out for you when you come back.

" You will take your men as light with you as poſſible, and give them all the neceſſary caution for the conduct, and their obedience to their officers; no firing without order, no unneceſſary alarms, no retreating without an order; they are to ſtick by one another and nothing can hurt them; let every man whoſe fire-lock will carry it have a bayonet; you are not to ſuffer the Indians to deſtroy women or children, no plunder to be taken to load your men, who ſhall be rewarded at their return as they deſerve.

May 25, 1760. *Jeff. Amherſt.*"

H With

With the above inſtructions the General delivered me a letter directed to General Murray at Quebec, deſiring me to convey it to him in ſuch manner as I thought would be quickeſt and ſafeſt.

Having received theſe inſtructions I returned to Crown-Point as faſt as poſſible, and about the begining of June ſet out from thence with a party of two hundred and fifty men* down Lake Champlain, having four veſſels, on board of which this detachment embarked, putting our boats and proviſions into them, that the enemy might have leſs opportunity of diſcovering our deſigns.

The 3d, I landed Lieut. Holmes with fifty men in Miſiſquey Bay, and gave him proper directions agreeable to my orders from the General, informing him that one of the ſloops ſhould cruiſe for him till his return, which upon ſignals that were given him would take him on board, upon which he was to join me or wait on board 'till my return, as the ſituation of affairs might direct him. Here likewiſe I ſent the letter I had received from the General

* The Stockbridge Indians who had been muſtered at, and now marched from Albany, and who were to be a part of the detachment of 300, agreeable to the General's orders, had not arrived at Crown Point at the time of my embarkation, but were ordered to follow after and join me.

neral to Brigadier Murray, through the woods, and gave the following inſtructions to the Officer I intruſted with it, viz.

Inſtructions for Serjeant Beverly of his Majeſty's Rangers.

"You are hereby directed to take under your command, theſe three men, viz. John Shute, Luzford Goodwin, and Joſeph Eaſtman, and march them from Miſiſquey Bay, to which place you will be convoyed by Lieut. Holmes with a party I have ſent there for a particular purpoſe; you are to land in the night time, as otherwiſe you may be diſcovered by a party from the Iſle au Noix; you will ſteer your courſe about north-eaſt, and make all the diſpatch you poſſibly can with the letter in your charge to Quebec, or to the Engliſh army at or near that place, and deliver it to Brigadier Murray, or to the officer commanding his Majeſty's forces in or upon the river St. Lawrence. A ſketch of the country will be delivered you with theſe orders, that you may the better know the conſiderable rivers you have to croſs, betwixt Miſiſquey Bay and Quebec. The Diſtances are marked in the draught, as is the road I travelled in laſt fall, from Miſiſquey Bay to St. Francis, which road you will croſs ſeveral times, if you will keep the courſe I before directed. The rivers are ſo plainly deſcribed in the plan, that you will know them when you come to them. The river St. Francis is about half way of your journey, and is very ſtill water, and may be eaſily rafted where you croſs it; but lower down it is ſo ſwift and rapid that you muſt not attempt it. Shedoir River you will likewiſe be obliged to paſs on a raft; it is ſwift water for ſome miles from its mouth; you had better examine it well before you attempt to croſs it. As ſoon as you paſs this river, ſteer your courſe about eaſt, leaving Point Levy on your left hand, and fall in with the river St. Lawrence, near the lower end of the iſland of Orleans, as it may be poſſible that General Murray may have encamped the army either at the iſle of Orleans or the iſle of Quodoa; therefore you are not to depend on finding at once the exact place of his encampment, but are poſitively ordered to look out for the Engliſh fleet, and the firſt line of battle ſhip you ſee, you are to venture on board, as I think it not poſſible the enemy ſhould have any large ſhips there, and whatever Engliſh ſhip you get on board of, will convoy you directly to General Murray, when you will deliver him the verbal meſſage I told you. You may apply to the general for fifty pounds who will pay it to you, and alſo give you proper directions to join me as ſoon as you have reſted yourſelf from your march. I wiſh you a good journey, and am, Your's, &c.

To Serjeant Beverley. *Robert Rogers.*"

As

As ſoon as I had diſpatched the two parties before-mentioned, I, with the remainder, croſſed Lake Champlain to the weſt-ſide, and the 4th in the morning got into my boats, and landed with about 200 men, about twelve miles ſouth of the iſland Noix, with an intent to put in execution the General's orders to me of May 5th with all ſpeed. Capt. Grant ſent the two ſloops to attend, which I ordered to cruiſe further down the lake than where I landed, and nearer to their fort, to command the attention of the enemy till I could get into their country. I lay ſtill all the 5th, there being a heavy rain, and the buſhes ſo wet that both we and our proviſions would have been greatly expoſed by a march.

In the afternoon of this day, ſeveral French boats appeared on the Lake, which were diſcovered by the two ſloops, as well as by my party on the ſhore. Theſe boats continued as near as they could to our veſſels without endangering themſelves, till after dark. Concluding their boats would cruize the whole night to watch the motions of our ſloops, I imagined it would be a prudent ſtep to ſend the ſloops back to Capt. Grant, the commander of theſe veſſels, who lay near Mott Iſland; I accordingly went to the ſloops in a boat after dark, and ordered them to return. The enemy, who kept all night in their boats, having by a ſtrict look-out, diſcovered where I landed, ſent a detachment from the iſland next morning to cut off my party. I difcovered their intentions by my reconnoitring parties, who counted them as they croffed from the fort in the morning in their boats, to the weft-fhore, and informed me that they were 350 in number. I had intelligence again when they were about a mile from us. Half after eleven they attacked me very brifkly on my left, having on my right a bog, which they did not venture over, thro' which, however, by the edge of the lake, I fent feventy of my party to get round and attack them in the rear. This party was commanded by Lieut. Farrington. As foon as he began his attack, I pufhed them in the front, which broke them immediately. I purfued them with the greateft part of my people about a mile, where they retired to a thick cedar fwamp, and divided into fmall parties. By this time it rained again very hard. I called my party immediately together at the boats, where I found that Enfign Wood of the 17th regiment was killed, Capt. Johnfon wounded through the body, a fecond fhot thro' his left arm, and a third in his head. I had two men of the Light Infantry, and eight Rangers, wounded, and fixteen Rangers killed. We killed forty of the enemy, and recovered about fifty firelocks. Their commanding officer, Monfieur la Force, was mortally hurt, and feveral of the party were likewife wounded. After the action I got the killed and maimed of my detachment together in battees, battoes, returned with them to the Isle a Mot, near which the brig lay. I dispatched one of the vessels to Crown Point, on board of which was put the corpse of Mr. Wood, but Capt. Johnson died on his passage thither; this vessel I ordered to bring more provisions. I buried the rest of the dead on an island, and then began to prepare for a second landing; being joined about this time by the Stockbridge Indian Company, I was determined at all adventures to pursue my orders, settled the plan of landing, and left the following instructions with Capt. Grant, viz.

"You will be so good as to fall down the lake with your vessels as soon as possible, as far as the Wind Mill Point, or near where you lay at anchor the last time I was with you, and cruize near it for two or three days, which will be the only method I can think of that has any appearance of attracting the attention of the enemy till I get into their country; as soon as I observe or think you pretty near the Wind Mill Point, I shall land with my party on the west side opposite to the north-end of the Isle a Mot, in the river that runs into the bay which forms itself there, and from thence proceed to execute the General's orders. If they do not attack me in my march till I compleat my design, you may be certain I shall come back on the east-side, and endeavour to join you near the Wind

Mill Point, or betwixt that and the Iſle a Mot. When I arrive, the ſignal that I will make for your diſcovering me, will be a ſmoak and three guns, at a minute's interval each from the other, and repeated a ſecond time, in half an hour after the firſt; but if the enemy ſhould attack me on my march before I get to the place I am ordered, which I believe they will do, in caſe I am worſted I ſhall be obliged to come back on the weſt-ſide, and ſhall make the before mentioned ſignals betwixt the Iſle a Mot and the place where I had the battle with the enemy the 6th inſtant. It is uncertain when I ſhall be at either ſhore; ſo that I would recommend it to you not to come back ſouth of the Iſle a Mot till my return, as a contrary wind might prevent your getting in with your veſſels to relieve me. I ſend you Serjeant Hacket and ten Rangers, to be with you in my abſence, as we this day agreed. If Lieutenant Darcy comes down in ſeaſon to go with me, I ſhall leave Enſign Wilſon with you; but if Darcy ſhould not come till after I land, you'll be pleaſed to take him under your direction, as well as all thoſe that may come with him to join me; tho' I would recommend it not to ſend any party to the iſland, to take a priſoner, till the fifth day after my landing, as the loſs of a man from us may be of very bad conſequence. Lieut. Holmes has appointed between the eleventh and ſixteenth day after his landing for his return to Miſiſquey Bay, and from the

the eleventh to the ſixteenth, as before mentioned; I ſhould be glad the ſloop might cruize for him at the place he appointed to meet her. I am, Sir,

Your humble ſervant,

R. Rogers."

I cannot but obſerve with pleaſure, that Mr. Grant, like an able officer, very diligently did all that could be expected of him for the good of the ſervice, carefully attending with his veſſels till my return from this ſecond excurſion, on which I embarked with two hundred and twenty men, officers included, and landed the 9th of June, about midnight, on the weſt ſhore oppoſite the Iſle a Mot, from thence marched as faſt as poſſible to St. John's, and came to the road that leads from it to Montreal, about two miles from the fort, the evening of the 15th. At eleven o'clock this night, I marched with an intent to ſurpriſe the fort, to within four hundred yards of it, where I halted to reconnoitre; which I did, and found they had more men than I expected. The number of the centries within the fort were ſeventeen, and ſo well fixed, that I thought it was impoſſible for me to take the place by ſurpriſe, eſpecially as they had ſeen me, and fired ſeveral guns accordingly. I left it at two o'clock, and marched down the river to St. d'Etrefe; at break of day I reconnoitred this place, and found that the enemy had in it a ftockaded fort, defenfible againft fmall arms. I obferved two large ftore-houfes in the infide, and that the enemy were carting hay into the fort. I waited for an opportunity when the cart had juft entered the gate-way, run forward, and got into the fort before they could clear the way for fhutting the gate. I had at this time fent different parties to the feveral houfes, about fifteen in number, which were near the fort, and were all furprifed at the fame inftant of time, and without firing a fingle gun. We took in the fort twenty-four foldiers, and in the houfes feventy-eight prifoners, women and children included; fome young men made their efcape to Chamblee. I examined the prifoners, and found I could not proceed to Chamblee with any profpect of fuccefs; therefore concluded my beft way was to burn the fort and village, which I did, together with a confiderable magazine of hay, and fome provifions, with every battoe and canoe, except eight battoes which I kept to crofs the river, and thefe we afterwards cut to pieces: we alfo killed their cattle, horfes &c. deftroyed their waggons, and every other thing which we thought could ever be of fervice to the enemy. When this was done, I fent back the women and children, and gave them a pafs to go to Montreal, directed to the feveral officers of the different detachments under my com-

mand.

mand. I continued my march on the east side of Lake Champlain, and when passing by Missisquey Bay, opposite the Isle au Noix, my advance-party, and the advance-party of about 800 French, that were out after me from their fort, engaged with each other; but the body of the enemy, being about a mile behind their advance-party, retreated, to my great satisfaction. I pursued my march with all possible speed: and the same day, being the 20th day of June, arived at the lake opposite where the vessels lay; and as I had sent a few men forward to repeat the signals, the boats met us at the shore. We directly put on board, the enemy soon after appeared on the shore where we embarked. I had not at this time any account from Lieutenant Holmes, either by prisoners or otherways.

Upon examination the prisoners reported, some of them had been at the siege of Quebec) " that the French had lost five hundred men there; and that they retreated after twelve days bombarding and cannonading, and came to Jack's quarters, where General Levy left five hundred men, being composed of a picquet of each battalion of the army, and that there were four hundred Canadians who staid voluntarily with them; that the rest of the army was quartered by two's and three's on the inhabitants, from there to St. John's. In Montreal there are about a hundred and fifty troops, and the inhabitants do duty. That in Chamblee

Fort

Fort are about one hundred and fifty men, including workmen; and the remnant of the Queen's regiment are in the village. That there are twelve cannon at St. John's, and about three hundred men, including workmen, who are obliged to take arms on any alarm. That at the Isle au Noix are about eight hundred stationed, besides the scouts between that and Montreal. That there are about an hundred pieces of cannon there." This is the substance of their report, in which they all agree, and which, with an account of my proceedings, I transmitted to the General.

On the 21st I put the twenty-six prisoners on board one of the vessels, with fifty men of my detachment, and ordered her to proceed to Crown Point, and tarried with the other vessels to cover Mr. Holmes's retreat, who joined us the same evening, without having succeeded in his enterprise, missing his way by following down a river that falls into Sorrel, instead of that called Wigwam Martinic, which empties itself into St Lawrence at Lake St. Francis. I arrived at Crown Point the 23d of June, and encamped my Rangers on the east-shore, opposite the fort.

The following letter I received from General Amherst, dated at Canijoharry, June 26, 1760.

"Sir,

"Colonel Haviland sent me your letter of June

21,

21, which I received laſt night, and ſaw with pleaſure, you was returned without the loſs of a man of your party, and that you had done every thing that was prudent for you to attempt with the number of men you had under your command. From the ſituation the enemy is now in, by being forced back to their former quarters, on Governor Murray's having obliged them to abandon their cannon, and raiſe the ſiege of Quebec, I hope Lieutenant Holmes will return with equal ſucceſs as you have done. I am, Sir,

Your humble ſervant,

To Major Rogers. *Jeff. Amherſt.*"

I remained at Crown point with my people without effecting any thing conſiderable, more than in ſmall parties reconnoitring the country about the fort, while every thing was got in readineſs for embarking the army the 16th of Auguſt; which was done accordingly, having one brig, three ſloops, and four rideaus, which latter were occupied by the royal train of artillery, commanded by Lieut. Colonel Ord. Our order of march was as follows, viz.

Six hundred Rangers and ſeventy Indians in whale-boats in the front, commanded by Major Rogers as an advance-guard for the whole army, all

all in a line a-breaſt, about half a mile a-head of the main body, followed by the light infantry and grenadiers in two columns, two boats a-breaſt in each column, commanded by Col. Darby. The right wing was compoſed of Provincials, commanded by Brigadier Ruggles, who was ſecond in command of the whole army. The left was made up of New Hampſhire and Boſton troops, commanded by Col. Thomas. The ſeventeenth and twenty-ſeventh regiments, with ſome few of the Royals, that formed the center column, were commanded by Major Campbell of the 17th regiment. Col. Haviland was in the front of theſe diviſions, between that and the light infantry, and grenadiers. The royal artillery followed the columns, and was commanded by Colonel Ord, who had for his eſcort, one Rhode Iſland regiment of Provincials. The ſutlers, &c. followed the artillery. In this manner we rowed down the lake forty miles the firſt day, putting aſhore where there was good landing on the weſt-ſide, and there encamped.

The day following we lay by. The 18th, the wind blowing freſh at ſouth, orders were given for embarking, and the ſame day reached a place on the weſt ſhore, within ten miles of the Iſle a Mot, where the army encamped. It having blown a freſh gale moſt part of the day, ſome of my boats ſplit

by

by the violence of the waves, and ten of my Rangers were thereby drowned.

The 19th we ſet ſail again early in the morning, and that night encamped on the north-end of the Iſle a Mot.

The 20th, before day, the army was under way, with intention to land; having but twenty miles to go, and having the advantage of a fair wind, we ſoon came in ſight of the French fort, and about ten in the morning Col. Darby, with the granadiers and Light Infantry, and myſelf with the Rangers, landed on the eaſt-ſhore, and marched and took poſſeſſion of the ground oppoſite the fort on that ſide, without the leaſt oppoſition. Having done this, an officer was ſent to acquaint Col. Haviland (who, with the remainder of the army, was at the place where we landed) that there was not the leaſt danger to apprehend from the enemy. The next day we began to raiſe batteries, and ſoon after to throw ſome ſhells into the garriſon. About the 24th a propoſal was made for taking the enemy's veſſels, three of which were at anchor a little below the fort, and ſome of their rideaus likewiſe. It was introduced by Col. Darby, who was ordered to take the command of the party appointed for this ſervice, which conſiſted of two companies of Regulars,

gulars, and four companies of my rangers, with the Indians. We carried with us two haubitzers and one ſix-pounder, and ſilently conveying them along thro' the trees, brought them oppoſite the veſſels, and began a briſk fire upon them, before they were in the leaſt appriſed of our deſign, and, by good fortune, the firſt ſhot from the ſix pounder cut the cable of the great rideau, and the wind being weſt, blew her to the eaſt-ſhore, where we were, and the other veſſels weighed anchor and made for St. John's, but got all a-ground, in turning a point about two miles below the fort. I was, by Col. Darby, ordered down to the eaſt-ſhore with my Rangers, and croſſed a river about thirty yards wide, which falls into Lake Champlain from the eaſt. I ſoon got oppoſite the veſſels, and, by firing from the ſhore, gave an opportunity to ſome of my party to ſwim on board with their tomahawks, and took one of the veſſels; in the mean time Col. Darby had got on board the rideau, and had her manned, and took the other two; of which ſucceſs he immediately acquainted Col. Haviland, who ſent down a ſufficient number of men to take charge of and man the veſſels, and ordered the remainder of the Rangers, Light Infantry and Grenadiers, to join the army that night, which was accordingly done; and about midnight the night following the French troops left the iſland, and landed

landed ſafe on the main; ſo that next morning nothing of them was to be ſeen but a few ſick, and Col. Haviland took poſſeſſion of the fort.

The ſecond day after the departure of Monſieur Bonville and his troops from the iſland, Mr. Haviland ſent me with my Rangers to purſue him as far as St. John's Fort, which was about twenty miles further down the lake, and at that place I was to wait the coming of the army, but by no means to follow further than the fort, nor run any riſk of advancing further to Montreal. I went in boats, and about day-light got to St. John's, and found it juſt ſet on fire. I purſued, and took two priſoners, who reported, "That Monſieur Bonville was to encamp that night about half-way on the road to Montreal; and that he went from St John's about nine o'clock the night before; but that many of their men were ſick, and that they thought ſome of the troops would not reach the place appointed till the middle of the afternoon." It being now about ſeven in the morning, I ſet all hands to work, except proper guards, to fortify the loghouſes that ſtood near the lake ſide, in order that part of my people might cover the battoes, while I, with the remainder, followed Monſieur Bonville, and about eight o'clock I got ſo well fortified, that I ventured our boats and baggage under

der the care of 200 Rangers, and took with me 400, together with the two companies of Indians, and followed after the French army, which consisted of about 1500 men, and about 100 Indians, they had to guard them. I was resolved to make his dance a little the merrier, and pursued with such haste, that I overtook his rear-guard about two miles before they got to their encamping ground. I immediatly attacked them, who, not being above 200, suddenly broke, and then stood for the main body, which I very eagerly pursued, but in good order, expecting Monsieur Bonville would have made a stand, which however he did not chuse, but pushed forward to get to the river, where they were to encamp, and having crossed it, pulled up the bridge, which put a stop to my march, not judging it prudent to cross at a disadvantage, inasmuch as the enemy had a good breast-work on the other side, of which they took possession; in this pursuit, however, we considerably lessened their number, and returned in safety.

In the evening Mr. Haviland came in sight, and landed at St. John's. As soon as he came on shore, I waited upon him, and acquainted him with what I had done, &c. and that I had two prisoners for him; he said it was very well, and ordered his troops there that night, and next day went down the

the river Sorriel, as far as St. d'Etrefe, where he encamped, and made a ftrong breaft-work, to defend his people from being furprifed. I was fent down the river Sorriel, to bring the inhabitants under fubjection to his Britannick Majefty, and went into their fettled country in the night, took all their priefts and militia officers, and fent fome of them for the inhabitants. The firft day I caufed all the inhabitants near Chamblee to take the oaths of allegiance, &c. who appeared glad to have it in their power to take the oaths and keep their poffeffions, and were all extreamly fubmiffive. Having obliged them to bring in their arms, and fulfilled my inftructions in the beft manner I could, I joined Col. Darby at Chamblee, who came there to take the fort, and had brought with him fome light cannon. It foon furrendered, as the garrifon confifted only of about fifty men. This happened on the firft of September.

On the 2d, our army having nothing to do, and having good intelligence both from Gen. Amherft and Gen. Murray, Mr. Haviland fent me to join the latter, while he marched with the reft of the army for La Pierre. The 5th in the morning I got to Longville, about four miles below Montreal, oppofite where Brigadier Murray lay, and gave him notice

notice of my arrival, but not till the morning of the 26th, by reafon of my arrival fo late.

By the time I came to Longville the army under the command of Gen. Amherft, had landed about two miles from the town, where they encamped; and early this morning Monfieur de Vaudreuil, the governor and commander in chief of all Canada, fent out to capitulate with our General, which put a ftop to all our movements, till the 8th of September, when the articles of capitulation were agreed to, and figned, and our troops took poffeffion of the town-gates that night. Next morning the Light Infantry, and Granadiers of the whole army, under the command of Col. Hald.man, with a company of the royal artillery, with two pieces of cannon, and fome haubitzers, entered the town, retaking the Englifh colours belonging to Pepperel's, and Shirley's regiments which had been taken by the French at Ofwego.

Thus at length, at the end of the fifth campaign, Montreal and the whole country of Canada was given up, and became fubject to the King of Great Britain; a conqueft perhaps of the greateft importance that is to be met with in the Britifh annals, whether we confider the prodigious extent of country we are hereby made mafters of, the vaft addition it muft make to trade and navigation, or the fecurity ſecurity it muſt afford to the northern provinces of America, particularly thoſe flouriſhing ones of New England and New York the irretrievable loſs France ſuſtains hereby, and the importance it muſt give the Britiſh crown among the ſeveral ſtates of Europe: all this, I ſay, duly conſidered, will, perhaps, in its conſequences render the year 1760 more glorious than any preceding.

And to this acquiſition, had we, during the late war, either by conqueſt or treaty, added the fertile and extenſive country of Louiſiana, we ſhould have been poſſeſſed of perhaps the moſt valuable territory upon the face of the globe, attended with more real advantages than the ſo-much-boaſted mines of Mexico and Peru, and would have for ever deprived the French, thoſe treacherous rivals of Britain's glory, of an oppportunity of acting hereafter the ſame perfidious parts they have already ſo often repeated.

On the 9th General Amherſt informed me of his intention of ſending me to Detroit, and on the 12th in the morning, when I waited upon him again, I received the following orders.

By his Excellency Jeffery Amherſt, Eſq; Major General and commander in chief of all his Majeſty's forces in North America, &c. &c. &c.

To

To Major Rogers, commanding his Majeſty's independent companies of Rangers.

"You will upon receipt hereof, with Capt. Waite's and Capt, Hazen's companies of Rangers under your command, proceed in whale-boats from hence to Fort William-Auguſtus, taking along with you one Joſeph Poupao, alias La Fleur, an inhabitant of Detroit, and Lieut. Brehme, Aſſiſtant Engineer.

"From Fort William-Auguſtus you will continue your voyage by the north-ſhore to Niagara, where you will land your whale-boats, and tranſport them acroſs the Carrying-place into Lake Erie, applying to Major Walters, or the officer commanding at Niagara, for any aſſiſtance you may want on that or any other occaſion, requeſting of him at the ſame time to deliver up to you Monſieur Gamelin, who was made priſoner at the reduction of ſaid fort, and has continued there ever ſince, in order to conduct him, with the above-mentioned Poupao, to their habitations at Detroit, where, upon taking the oath of allegiance to his moſt ſacred Majeſty, whoſe ſubjects they are become by the capitulation of the 8th inſtant; they ſhall be protected in the peaceable and quiet poſſeſſion of their properties and ſo long as they behave as becometh good and faithful ſubjects, ſhall partake of all the other privileges

privileges and immunities granted unto them by the ſaid capitulation.

" With theſe, and the detachment, under your command, you will proceed in your whale-boats acroſs Lake Erie to Preſque Iſle, where, upon your arrival, you will make known the orders I have given to the officer commanding that poſt; and you will leave ſaid whale-boats and party, taking only a ſmall detachment of your party, and marching by land, to join Brigadier General Monkton, where-ever he may be

" Upon your arrival with him, you will deliver into his hands the diſpatches you ſhall herewith receive for him, and follow and obey ſuch orders as he ſhall give you for the relief of the garriſons of the French poſts at Detroit, Michlimakana, or any others in that diſtrict, for gathering in the arms of the inhabitants thereof, and for adminiſtering to them the oath of allegiance already mentioned; when you will likewiſe adminiſter, or ſee adminiſtered, the ſame to the before mentioned Gamelin and Poupao; and when this is done, and that you have reconnoitered and explored the country as much as you can, without loſing time unneceſſarily you are to bring away the French troops and arms, to ſuch a place as you ſhall be directed by General Monkton.

" And

"And when the whole of this ſervice is compleated, you will march back to your detachment to Preſquiſle, or Niagara, according to the orders you receive from Brigadier Monkton, where you will embark the whole, and in like manner as before, tranſport your whale-boats acroſs the Carrying place into Lake Ontario, where you will deliver over your whale-boats into the care of the commanding officer marching your detachment by land to Albany, or wherever I may be, to receive what further orders I may have to give you.

"Given under my hand at the head quarters in the camp Montreal, 12th Sept. 1760.

Jeff. Amherſt."

By his Excellency's command.

J. Appy."

An additional order was given, which was to be ſhewn only to the commanding officers of the different poſts I might touch at, the expedition being intended to be kept a profound ſecret for fear the march ſhould be impeded by the enemy Indians through whoſe country I was obliged to march.

This order was as follows, viz.

" Major

" Major Walters, or the officer commanding at Niagara, will judge whether or not there is provision sufficient at Presque Isle; and Major Rogers will accordingly take provisions from Niagara. Eight days provision will take him from Montreal to Fort William-Augustus; there he will apply to the commanding officer for a sufficient quantity to proceed to Niagara. Major Rogers knows where he is going, and the provisions he will want; some should be in store likewise at Presque Isle, for the party Brigadier General Monkton will send.

Jeff. Amherst.

Montreal, 12th Sept. 1760.

In pursuance of these orders I embarked at Montreal the 13th Sept. 1760 (with Captain Brewer, Captain Wait, Lieutenant Brheme, Assistant Engineer, Lieut. Davis of the royal train of artillery, and two hundred Rangers) about noon, in fifteen whale-boats; and that night we encamped at la Chine; next morning we reached Isle de Praires, and took a view of the two Indian settlements at Coyhavagu and Conesadagu.

On the 16th we got up to an island in the Lake of St. Francis, and the next night encamped on the western shore, at the lower end of the upper rifts. We ascended these rifts the day following, and con-

 tinued

tinued all night on the ſhore, oppoſite a number of iſlands.

In the evening of the 19th we came to the Iſle de Gallettes, and ſpent the 20th in repairing our whale-boats, which had received ſome damage in aſcending the rifts.

This morning I ſent off ten ſick Rangers to Albany, by the way of Oſwego, recommending them to the care of Col. Fitch, commanding at Oſwego, who was to give them ſuitable directions.

We left Iſle de Gallettes on the 21ſt; about twelve o'clock, the wind being unfavourable, we paſſed Oſwegachi, and encamped but three miles above it on the northern ſhore.

On the 22d we continued our courſe up the river, the wind blowing freſh at ſouth, and halted in the evening at the narrow paſſes near the iſlands; but, upon the winds abating at midnight, we embarked and rowed the remainder of that night, and the whole day following, till we came to the place where formerly ſtood the old Fort of Frontiniac, where we found ſome Indian hunters from Oſwegachi. We were detained here all the next day by the tempeſtuouſneſs of the weather, which was very windy, attended with ſnow and rain: we, however

ever, improved the time in taking a plan of the old fort, ſituated at the bottom of a fine ſafe harbour

There were about five hundred acres of cleared ground about it which, tho' covered with clover ſeemed bad and rocky, and interſperſed with ſome pine-trees. The Indians here ſemed to be well pleaſed with the news we brought them of the ſurrender of all Canada, and ſupplied us with great plenty of veniſon and wild fowl.

We left this the 25th, about ten in the morning, ſteering a ſouth-courſe two miles, then weſt ſix miles, which brought us to the mouth of a river thirty feet wide; then ſouth four miles, where we halted to refreſh the party.

About four in the afternoon we rowed for the mountain bearing ſouth-weſt, which we did not come up to till ſome time in the night, and found it to be a ſteep rock, about one hundred feet high. It now grew foggy, and miſtaking our way about ſix miles, we rowed all night, and till 8 o'clock next morning, before we put aſhore; which we then did on a point, where we breakfaſted, and then proceeded on our voyage, rowing till 8 o'clock at night (being about one hundred miles, as we imagined, from Frontiniac) we landed. This evening we paſſed two ſmall iſlands at the end of

a point

a point extending far into the lake; the darkneſs and fog prevented us from taking ſuch a ſurvey of them as to be able to give a particular deſcription of them.

The 27th of September, being very windy, we ſpent the time in deer-hunting, there being great plenty of them there, tho' the land is rocky, the timber bad, chiefly hemlock and pine; and I believe it is generally ſo on the north-ſide of Lake Ontario.

We embarked very early on the 28th, ſteering ſouth-weſt, leaving a large bay on the right, about twenty miles wide; the weſtern ſide of which terminates in a point, and a ſmall iſland: having paſſed both, about twenty miles on a courſe weſt by ſouth we entered the chops of a river, called by the Indians *Grace of Man*; there we encamped, and found about 50 Meſſiſſagua Indians fiſhing for ſalmon. At our firſt appearance they ran down, both men and boys, to the edge of the lake, and continued firing their pieces, to expreſs their joy at the ſight of the Engliſh colours, till ſuch time as we had landed.

They preſented us with a deer juſt killed and ſplit in halves, with the ſkin on, but the bowels taken out, which, with them, in a moſt elegant and polite preſent,

ſent, and ſignificant of the greateſt reſpect. I told them of the ſucceſs of their Engliſh brethren, againſt their fathers the French; at which they either were, or pretended to be, very well pleaſed.

Some of us fiſhed with them in the evening being invited by them, and filled a bark-canoe with ſalmon in about half an hour. Their method of catching the fiſh is very extraordinary. One perſon hold a lighted pine-torch, while a ſecond ſtrikes the fiſh with a ſpear. This is the ſeaſon in which the ſalmon ſpawn on theſe parts, contrary to what they do in any other place I ever knew them before.

I found the ſoil near this river very good and level. The timber is chiefly oak and maple, or the ugar-tree.

At ſeven o'clock the next morning we took our departure from this river, the wind being a-head. About fifteen miles further, on a weſt-ſouth-weſt courſe, we put into another river, called the Life of Man. The Meſſiſſaguas, who were hunting here, about thirty in number, paid us the ſame compliments with thoſe we juſt before received from their countrymen, and inſtead of a deer, ſplit up a young bear and preſented me with it. Plenty of fiſh was catched here alſo. The land continued good and level, the ſoil of blackiſh colour, and the banks of the lake were low.

The wind being fair the 30th, we embarked at the firſt dawn of day, and with the aſſiſtance of ſails and oars, made great way on a ſouth-weſt courſe, and in the evening reached the river Toronto, haing run ſeventy miles. Many points extending far into the lake, occaſioned a frequent alteration of our courſe. We paſſed a bank of twenty miles in length, but the land behind it ſeemed to be level, well-timbered with large oaks, hickaries, maples, and ſome poplars. No mountain appeared in ſight. There was a track of about 300 acres of cleared ground, round the place where formerly the French had a fort, that was called Fort Toronto. The ſoil here is principally clay. The deer are extremely plenty in this country. Some Indians were hunting at the mouth of the river, who run into the woods at our approach, very much frightened. They came in, however, in the morning and teſtified their joy at the news of our ſucceſs againſt the French. They told us "that we could eaſilyaccompliſh our journey from thence to Detroit in eight days: that when the French traded at that place, the Indians uſed to come with their poultry from Michlimakana, down the river Toronto : that the partage was but twenty miles from that to a river falling into Lake Huron, which had ſome falls, but none veryconſiderable: they added, that there was a carrying-place of fifteen miles from ſome weſterly part of Lake Erie, to a river running without any falls thro' ſeveral Indian towns into Lake St. Clair.

I think Toronto a moſt convenient place for a factory, and that from thence we may very eaſily ſettle the north-ſide of Lake Erie.

We left Toronto the 1ſt of October, ſteering ſouth, right acroſs the weſt-end of Lake Ontario. At dark we arrived at the ſouth-ſhore, five miles weſt of Fort Niagara, ſome of our boats being now become exceeding leaky and dangerous.

This morning, before we ſet out, I directed the following order of march:

"The boats in a line. If the wind roſe high, the red flag hoiſted, and the boats to croud nearer, that they might be ready to give mutual aſſiſtance in caſe of a leak or other accident;" by which means we ſaved the crew and arms of the boat commanded by Lieutenant M'Cormack, which ſprung a leak and ſunk, loſing nothing except their packs.

We halted all the next day at Niagara, and provided ourſelves with blankets, coats, ſhirts, ſhoes, magaſſins, &c.

I received from the commanding officer eighty barrels of proviſions, and changed two whale-boats for as many battoes, which proved leaky.

In the evening ſome of my party proceeded with the proviſions to the falls, and in the morning marched the reſt there, and began the portage of the proviſions and boats. Meſſ. Brheme and Davis took a ſurvey of the great cataract of Niagara.

As the winter-ſeaſon was now advancing very faſt in this country, and I had orders to join Brig. Monkton from Preſque Iſle, wherever he might be, to receive his directions, I ſet out this evening, the 5th of October, in a bark-canoe, with Lieutenants Brheme and Holmes, and eight Rangers, leaving the command of my party to Capt. Brewer, with inſtructions to follow to Preſque Iſle, and encamped eight miles up the ſtream iſſuing out of Lake Erie. The land appeared to be good on both ſides the river.

Next morning embarked early, and ſteered a ſouth-weſt courſe. About noon opened Lake Erie, and leaving a bay to the left, we arrived by ſunſet at the ſouthern ſhore of the lake; we then ſteered weſt till eight o'clock at night, and drew up our boats on a ſandy beach, forty miles diſtant from where we embarked in the morning.

The wind was very freſh next day, which prevented our ſetting out till 11 o'clock; ſo that we made no further progreſs than about twenty-eight miles

miles on a weſt-ſouth-weſt courſe. A little after noon, on the 8th of October, we arrived at Preſque Iſle, having kept a ſoutherly courſe all the morning; I tarried there till 3 o'clock, when, having ſent back my party to aſſiſt Captain Brewer, Mr. Brheme, Lieutenant Holmes, and myſelf, took leave of Colonel Bouquet, who commanded at Preſque Iſle, and with three other men, in a bark-canoe, proceeded to French Creek, and at night encamped on the road, half way to Fort du Bouf. We got to this fort about 10 o'clock next day, and after three hours reſt launched our canoe into the river, and paddled down about ten miles below the fort.

On the 10th we encamped at the ſecond croſſings of the river, the land on both ſides appeared to be good all the way. The 11th we reached the Mingo Cabbins, and the night of the 12th we lodged at Venango; from thence went down the River Ohio; and on the morning of the 17th I waited upon Brigadier Monkton at Pittſburgh, and delivered him General Amherſt's diſpatches, and my own inſtructions.

I left Pittſburgh the 20th, at the requeſt of General Monkton, who promiſed to ſend his orders after me to Preſque Iſle, by Mr. Croghan, and to forward Capt. Campbell immediately with a company of the Royal Americans; I got back to Presque Isle the 30th of October, Captain Campbell arrived the day after; Captain Brewer was got there before us, with the Rangers from Niagara, having lost some of the boats, and part of the provisions.

We immediately began to repair the damaged boats; and, as there was an account that a vessel, expected with provisions from Niagara, was lost, I dispatched Capt. Brewer by land to Detroit, with a drove of forty oxen, supplied by Col. Bouquet. Capt. Wait was about the same time sent back to Niagara for more provisions, and ordered to cruise along the north-coast of Lake Erie, and halt about twenty miles to the east of the streight between the Lakes Huron and Erie, till further orders. Brewer had a battoe to ferry his party over the Creeks, two horses, and Capt. Monter with twenty Indians, composed of the Six Nations, Delawares and Shawanese, to protect him from the insults of the enemy Indians.

My order of march over from Presque Isle was as follows:

“ The boats to row two deep; first, Major Rogers’s boat, abreast of him Captain Croghan; Captain Campbell follows with his company, the Rangers

Rangers next; and laftly, Lieutenant Holmes, who commands the rear-guard, with his own boat, and that of Enfign Wait's, fo as to be ready to affift any boat that may be in diftrefs. Boats in diftrefs are to fire a gun, when Mr. Holmes with the other boats under his command are immediately to go to their relief, take them to the fhore, or give fuch other affiftance as he thinks may be beft. When the wind blows hard, fo that the boats cannot keep their order, a red flag will be hoifted in the Major's boat; then the boats are not to mind their order, but put after the flag as faft as poffible to the place of landing, to which the flag-boat will always be a guide.

"It is recommended to the foldiers as well as officers, not to mind the waves of the lake; but when the furf is high to ftick to their oars, and the men at helm to keep the boat quartering on the waves, and brifkly follow, then no mifchief will happen by any ftorm whatever. Ten of the beft fteerfmen amongft the Rangers are to attend Captain Campbell and company in his boats. It is likewife recommended to the officers commanding in thofe boats, to hearken to the fteerfmen in a ftorm or bad weather, in managing their boats. At evening, (if it is thought neceffary to row in the night time) a blue flag will be hoifted in the Major's boat, which is the fignal for the boats to drefs,

drefs, and then proceed in the following manner: the boats next the hindermoft, are to wait for the two in the rear, the two third boats for the fecond two; and fo on to the boats leading a-head, to prevent feparation, which in the night would be hazardous.

"Mr. Bhreme is not to mind the order of march, but to fteer as is moft convenient for him to make his obfervations; he is however defired never to go more than a league a-head of the detachment, and is to join them at landing or encamping.

"On landing, the Regulars are to encamp in the center, and Lieutenant Holmes's divifion on the right wing with Mr. Croghan's people, Lieut. M'Cormick on the left wing with his divifion; Mr. Jequipe to be always ready with his Mohegan Indians, which are the picquet of the detachment, part of which are always to encamp in the front of the party; Capt. Campbell will mount a guard confifting of one Subaltern, one Serjeant, and thirty privates, immediately on landing, for the fecurity of his own encampment and battoes; Lietenant Holmes's divifion to keep a guard of one Serjeant and ten Rangers on the right, and Lieutenant M'Cormick the like number on the left, and likewife to act as Adjutant to the detachment,

ment, and the orderly drum to attend him, to be at the Serjeant's call. The general to beat when ordered by the Major, at which time the whole party is to prepare for embarking, the troops half an hour after, when all the guards are to be called in, and the party embark immediately after.

" There is to be no firing of guns in this detachment without permiſſion from the commanding officer, except when in diſtreſs on the lake. No man to go without the centries, when in camp, unleſs he has orders ſo to do ; great care to be taken of the arms, and the officers to review them daily. Captain Campbell will order a drum to beat, for the regulation of his company when landed, at any time he thinks proper for parading his men, or reviewing their arms, &c.

" It is not doubted but due attention will be paid to all orders given.

" Mr. Croghan will, at landing always attend the Major for orders, and to give ſuch intelligence as he may have had from the Indians, throughout the day."

We left Preſque Iſle the 4th of November, kept a weſtern courſe, and by night had advanced twenty miles.

The

The badneſs of the weather obliged us to lie by all the next day; and as the wind continued very high, we did not advance more than ten or twelve miles the 6th, on a courſe weſt-ſouth-weſt.

We ſet out very early on the 7th, and came to the mouth of Chogage River; here we met with a party of Attawawa Indians, juſt arrived from Detroit. We informed them of our ſucceſs in the total reduction of Canada, and that we were going to bring off the French garriſon at Detroit, who were included in the capitulation. I held out a belt, and told them I would take my brothers by the hand, and carry them to Detroit, to ſee the truth of what I had ſaid. They retired, and held a council, and promiſed an anſwer next morning. That evening we ſmoaked the calamet, or pipe of peace, all the Indians ſmoaking by turns out of the ſame pipe. The peace thus concluded, we went to reſt, but kept good guards, a little diſtruſting their ſincerity.

The Indians gave their anſwer early in the morning, and ſaid their young warriors ſhould go with me, while the old ones ſtaid to hunt for their wives and children.

I gave them ammunition at their requeſt, and a ſtring of wampum in teſtimony of my approbation, and

and charged them to ſend ſome of their ſachems, or chiefs, with the party who drove the oxen along ſhore; and they promiſed to ſpread the news, and prevent any annoyance from their hunters.

We were detained here by unfavourable weather till the 12th, during which time the Indians held a plentiful market in our camp of veniſon and turkies.

From this place we ſteered one mile weſt, then a mile ſouth, then four miles weſt, then ſouth-weſt ten miles, then five miles weſt-and-by-ſouth, then ſouth-weſt eight miles, then weſt-and-by-ſouth ſeven miles, then four miles weſt, and then ſouth-weſt ſix miles, which brought us to Elk River, as the Indians call it, where we halted two days on account of bad weather and contrary winds.

On the 15th we embarked, and kept the following courſes; weſt-ſouth-weſt two miles, weſt-north-weſt three miles, weſt-by-north one mile, weſt two miles; here we paſſed the mouth of a river, and then ſteered weſt one mile, weſt-by-ſouth two miles, weſt-by-north four miles, north weſt three miles, weſt-north-weſt two miles, weſt-by-north ten miles, where we encamped at the mouth of a river twenty-five yards wide.

The

The weather did not permit us to depart till the 18th, when our courſe was weſt-by-ſouth ſix miles, weſt-by-north four miles, weſt two miles; here we found a river about fifteen yards over, then proceeded weſt half a mile, weſt-ſouth-weſt ſix miles and a half, weſt two miles and an half, north-weſt two miles, where we encamped, and diſcovered a river ſixteen yards broad at the entrance.

We left this place the next-day, ſteering north-weſt four miles, north-north-weſt ſix miles, which brought us to Sanduſky Lake; we continued the ſame courſe two miles, then north-north-eaſt half a mile, north-weſt a quarter of a mile, north the ſame diſtance, north-weſt half a mile, north-by-eaſt one furlong, north-weſt-by-north one quarter of a mile, north-weſt-by-weſt one mile, weſt-north-weſt one mile, then weſt half a mile, where we encamped near a ſmall river, on the eaſt-ſide.

From this place I detached Mr. Brheme with a letter to Monſieur Beleter, the French commandant at Detroit, in theſe words:

To Capt. Beleter, *or the Officer commanding at* Detroit.

" Sir,

" That you may not be alarmed at the approach of the Engliſh troops under my command, when they come to Detroit, I ſend forward this by Lieut.

Lieut. Brheme, to acquaint you, that I have Gen. Amherſt's orders to take poſſeſſion of Detroit, and ſuch other poſts as are in that diſtrict, which, by capitulation, agreed to and ſigned by the Marquis de Vaudreuil, and his Excellency Major General Amherſt, the 8th of September laſt, now belong to the King of Great Britain.

" I have with me the Marquis de Vaudreuil's letters to you directed, for your guidance on this occaſion, which letters I ſhall deliver you when I arrive at or near your poſt, and ſhall encamp the troops I have with me at ſome diſtance from the fort, till you have reaſonable time to be made acquainted with the Marquis de Vaudreuil's inſtructions, and the capitulation, a copy of which I have with me likewiſe. I am,

SIR,

Your humble ſervant,

Robert Rogers."

The land on the ſouth-ſide of Lake Erie, from Preſque Iſle, puts on a very fine appearance; the country level, the timber tall, and of the beſt ſort, ſuch as oak, hickerie and locuſt; and for game, both

both for plenty and variety, perhaps exceeded by no part of the world.

I followed Mr. Brheme on the 20th, and took a courſe north-weſt four miles and an half, ſouth-weſt two, and weſt three, to the mouth of a river in breadth 300 feet.

Here we found ſeveral Huron ſachems, who told me, "that a body of 400 Indian warriors was collected at the entrance into the great ſtreight, in order to obſtruct our paſſage; and that Monſieur Beleter had excited them to defend their country: that they were meſſengers to know my buſineſs, and whether the perſon I had ſent forward had reported the truth that Canada was reduced." I confirmed this account, and that the fort at Detroit was given up by the French Governor. I preſented them a large belt, and ſpoke to this effect:

"Brothers,

"With this belt I take you by the hand. You are to go directly to your brothers aſſembled at the mouth of the river, and tell them to go to their towns till I arrive at the fort. I ſhall call you there as ſoon as Monſieur Beleter is ſent away, which ſhall be in two days after my arrival. We will

will then fettle all matters. You live happily in your own country. Your brothers have long defired to bring this about. Tell your warriors to mind their fathers (the French) no more, for they are all prifoners to your brothers (the Englifh), who pitied them, and left them their houfes and goods, on their fwearing by the Great One who made the world, to become as Englifhmen for ever. They are now your brothers; if you abufe them, you affront me, unlefs they behave ill. Tell this to your brothers the Indians. What I fay is truth. When we meet at Detroit I will convince you it is all true."

Thefe fachems fet out in good temper the next morning, being the 21ft; but as the wind was very high, we did not move from this place.

On the 22d we encamped on a beach, after having fteered that day north-weft fix miles, north-north-weft four, to a river of the breadth of twenty yards, then north-weft-by-weft two miles, weft-north-weft one, weft four, and weft north-weft five; it was with great difficulty we could procure any fuel here, the weft-fide of the Lake Erie abounding with fwamps.

We rowed ten miles the next day, on a courfe north-weft and by weft, to Point Cedar, and then

formed

formed a camp; here we met ſome of the Indian meſſengers, to whom we had ſpoken two days before: they told us, their warriors were gone up to Monſieur Beleter, who, they ſaid, is a ſtrong man, and intends to fight you; a ſachem of Attawawas was amongſt them. All their Indians ſet out with us. The 24th we went north-weſt and by north ten miles, and fourteen miles north-eaſt, to a long point; this night ſixty of the Indian party came to our camp, who congratulated us on our arrival in their country, and offered themſelves as an eſcort to Detroit, from whence they came the day before. They informed me, that Mr. Bhreme, and his party were confined; and that Monſieur Beleter had ſet up an high flag-ſtaff, with a wooden effigy of a man's head on the top, and upon that a crow; that the crow was to repreſent himſelf, the man's head mine, and the meaning of the whole, that he would ſcratch out my brains. This artifice, however, had no effect; for the Indians told him (as they ſaid) that the reverſe would be the true explanation of the ſign.

After we had proceeded ſix miles north-eaſt, we halted at the requeſt of the Indians, who deſired me to call in the chief Captains of the party at the Streight's mouth. I did ſo, and ſpent the 26th at the ſame place, in conciliating their ſavage minds to peace and friendſhip.

The

The morning of the 27th, Monfieur Beleter fent me the following letter by Monfieur Babee.

"MONSIEUR,

"J'ai recu la lettre que vous m'avez ecrite par un de vos Officiers; comme je n'ai point d'interprete, je ne puis faire la reponfe amplement.

L'Officier qui m'a remife la votre, me fait favoir qu'il etoit detache afin de m'anoncer votre arrive, pour prendre poffeffion de cette garifon, felon la capitulation fait et Canada, que vous avez conjointement avec un lettre de Monfieur de Vaudreuil a mon addreffe. Je vous prie, Monfieur, d'arreter vos troupes a l'entrance de la riviere, jufques a ce que vous m'envoyes la capitulation & la lettre de Monfeigneur le Marquis de Vaudreuil, afin de pouvoir y conformer.

Je fuis bien furpris qu'on ne m'a pas envoye un Officier Francois avec vous, felon la coutume.

J'ai l'honneur d'etre, &c. &c.

De Beleter."

A Monfieur Monfieur *Rogers*,
Major, & commandant le
detachment Anglois."

In

In Engliſh thus.

" Sir,

I received the letter you wrote me by one of your Officers; but as I have no interpreter, cannot fully anſwer it.

The Officer that delivered me yours, gives me to underſtand, that he was ſent to give me notice of your arrival to take poſſeſſion of this garriſon, according to the capitulation made in Canada; that you have likewiſe a letter from Monſ Vaudreuil, directed to me. I beg, Sir, you'll halt your troops at the entrance of the river, till you ſend me the capitulation and the Marquis de Vaudreuil's letter, that I may act in conformity thereto.

I am ſurpriſed there is no French Officer ſent to me along with you, as is the cuſtom on ſuch occaſions. I have the honour to be &c. &c.

De Beleter."

To Mr. *Rogers*, Major and Commander of the Engliſh detachment."

Shortly after a French party, under Captain Burrager, beat a parley on the weſt-ſhore; I ſent Mr.

Mr. M'Cormick to know his businefs, who returned with the Officer and the following letter:

Detroit, le 25me Novembre, 1760.

MONSIEUR,

"Je vous ai deja marque par Monfieur Burrager les raifons pourquoi je ne puis repondre en detail a la lettre qui m'a ete remife le 22me de courant, par l' Officier que vous m'avez detache.

J'ignore les raifons pourquoi il n'a pas voulu retourner aupres de vous. J'ai envoye mon interprete Huron chez cettre nation, que l'on me dit etre attroupe fur le chemin de les contenir, ne fachant pofitivement fi c'eft a vous ou a nous qu'ils en veuillent, & pour leur dire de ma part, qu'ils ayent a fe tenir tranquilement; que je favois ce que je devois a mon General,& que de lorfque l'acte de la capitula tion feroit regle, j'etois oblige d'obeir. Le dit interprete aordre de vous attendre, & de vous remettre la prefent. Ne foyez point furpris, Monfieur, fi fur le long de la cote vous trouverez nos habitans fur leur garde; on leur a annonce qu'il y avoit beaucoup de nations a votre fuite, a qui on avois promis le pillage, & que lefdites nations etoient meme determinees a vous le demander; je leur ai permis de regarder, c'eft pour votre converfation & furete ainfi que pour la notre, en cas que les dites nations devenoient

devenoient a faire les insolents, vous seul ne seriez peut-etre pas dans les circonstances presentes en etat de les require. Je me flatte, Monsieur, que si tot que la present vour sera parvenue, vous voudriez bien m'envoyer par quel qu'un de vos Messieurs, & la capitnlation la lettre de Monsieur Vaudreuil. J'ai l'honneurd'ettre,

MONSIEUR,

Votre tres-humble & obeissant serviteur,

Pign. de Beletere."

A Monsieur Monsieur *Rogers*,
Major, commandant le detachment Anglois au bas de la riviere.

In English thus:

" SIR, Detroit, 25th Nov. 1760.

" I have already by Mr. Burrager acquainted you with the reasons why I could not answer particularly the letter which was delivered me the 22d instant by the Officer you sent to me.

" I am

" I am entirely unacquainted with the reaſons of his not returning to you. I ſent my Huron interpreter to that nation, and told him to ſtop them, ſhould they be on the road, not knowing poſitively whether they were inclined to favour you or us, and to tell them from me they ſhould behave peaceably; that I knew what I owed to my General, and that when the capitulation ſhould be ſettled I was obliged to obey. The ſaid interpreter has orders to wait on you, and deliver you this.

" Be not ſurpriſed, Sir, if along the coaſt you find the inhabitants upon their guard; it was told them you had ſeveral Indian nations with you, to whom you had promiſed permiſſion to plunder, nay, that they were even reſolved to force you to it. I have therefore allowed the ſaid inhabitants to take to their arms, as it is for your ſafety and preſervation as well as ours; for ſhould theſe Indians become inſolent, you may not perhaps, in your preſent ſituation, be able to ſubdue them alone.

" I flatter myſelf, Sir, that, as ſoon as that ſhall come to hand, you will ſend me by ſome of the Gentlemen you have with you, both the capitulation and Monſieur Vaudreuil's letter. I have the honour to be,

SIR,

Your very humble and obedient ſervant,

To Major Rogers.

Pign. Beletere."

We encamped the next day five miles up the river, having rowed againſt the wind; and on the 29th I diſpatched Captain Campbell, with Meſſieurs Burrager and Babce, and their parties, with this letter.

"SIR,

"I acknowledge the receipt of your two letters, both of which were delivered to me yeſterday. Mr. Brheme has not yet returned. The incloſed letter from the Marquis de Vaudreuil will inform you of the ſurrender of all Canada to the King of Great Britain, and of the great indulgence granted to the inhabitants; as alſo of the terms granted to the troops of his Moſt Chriſtian Majeſty. Captain Campbell, whom I have ſent forward with this letter, will ſhew you the capitulation. I deſire you will not detain him, as I am determined, agreeable

greeable to my inſtructions from General Amherſt, ſpeedily to relieve your poſt. I ſhall ſtop the troops I have with me at the hither end of the town till four o'clock, by which time I expect your anſwer; your inhabitants under arms will not ſurpriſe me, as yet I have ſeen no other in that poſition, but ſavages waiting for my orders. I can aſſure you, Sir, the inhabitants of Detroit ſhall not be moleſted, they and your complying with the capitulation, but be protected in the quiet and peaceable poſſeſſion of their eſtates; neither ſhall they be pillaged by my Indians, nor by your's that have joined me.

I am, &c.

To Capt. Beletere, *commanding at* Detroit.

R. Rogers."

I landed at half a mile ſhort of the fort, and fronting it, where I drew up my detachment on a field of graſs. Here Captain Campbell joined me, and with him came a French officer, to inform me that he bore Monſieur Beletere's compliments, ſignifying he was under my command. From hence I ſent Lieutenants Leſlie and M'Cormick, with thirty-ſix Royal Americans, to take poſſeſſion of the fort. The French garriſon laid down their arms, Engliſh colours were hoiſted, and the French

 taken

taken down, at which about 700 Indians gave a ſhout, merrily exulting in their prediction being verified, that the crow repreſented the Engliſh.

They ſeemed amazed at the ſubmiſſive ſalutations of the inhabitants, expreſſed their ſatisfaction at our generoſity in not putting them to death, and ſaid they would always for the future fight for a nation thus favoured by Him that made the world.

I went into the fort, received a plan of it, with a liſt of the ſtores, from the commanding officer, and by noon of the 1ſt of December we had collected the militia, diſarmed them, and to them alſo adminiſtered the oaths of allegiance.

The interval from this time to the 9th was ſpent in preparing to execute ſome meaſures that appeared to be neceſſary to the ſervice we were upon. I put Monſieur Beletere and the other priſoners under the care of Lieut. Holmes and thirty Rangers, to be carried to Philadelphia; and ordered Capt. Campbell and his company to keep poſſeſſion of the fort. Lieut. Butler, and Enſign Wait were ſent with a detached party of twenty men, to bring French troops from the forts Miamie and Gatanois. I ordered, that, if poſſible, a party ſhould ſubſiſt at the former this winter, and give the earlieſt notice

at

at Detroit of the enemy's motions in the country of the Illinois. I ſent Mr. M'Gee, with a French officer, for the French troops at the Shawaneſe town on the Ohio. And as proviſions were ſcarce, directed Capt. Brewer to repair with the greateſt part of the Rangers to Niagara, detaining Lieutenant M'Cormack with thirty-ſeven more, to go with me to Michlimakana.

I made a treaty with the ſeveral tribes of Indians living in the neighbouring country; and having directed Capt. Wait, juſt arrived from Niagara, to return again thither immediately, I ſet out for Lake Huron, and on the night of the 10th encamped at the north-end of the little Lake St. Clair, and the next evening on the weſt-ſide of the ſtreight, at the entrance of a conſiderable river, where many Indians were hunting. We opened Lake Huron the day following, and ſaw many Indian hunters on both ſides of the mouth of the ſtreights. We coaſted along the weſt-ſhore of the Lake, about twenty miles north-and-by-weſt, the next day being the 13th forty, and the 15th thirty-eight miles, paſſing the cakes of ice with much difficulty. We could not advance all the 16th, a heavy north-wind ſetting the cakes of ice on the ſouth-ſhore in ſuch quantities, that we could find no paſſage between them. I conſulted the Indians

 about

about a journey to Michlimakana acrofs by land; but they declared it impracticable at this feafon without fnow-fhoes, and to our great mortification we were obliged to return to Detroit; the ice obftructing us fo much, that, with the greateft diligence and fatigue, we did not arrive there till the 21ft.

I delivered the ammunition to Capt. Campbell, and on the 23d fet out for Pittfburg, marching along the weft-end of Lake Erie, till the fecond of January 1761, when we arrived at Lake Sandufky.

I have a very good opinion of the foil from Detroit to this place; it is timbered principally with white and black oaks, hickerie, locufts, and maple. We found wild apples along the weft-end of Lake Erie, fome rich favannahs of feveral miles extent, without a tree, but cloathed with jointed grafs near fix feet high, which, rotting there every year, adds to the fertility of the foil. The length of Sandufky is about fifteen miles from eaft to weft, and about fix miles acrofs it. We came to a town of the Windot Indians, where we halted to refrefh.

On January 3d, fouth-eaft-by-eaft three miles, eaft-by-fouth one mile and a half, fouth-eaft a mile through a meadow, croffed a fmall creek about fix yards

yards wide, running eaſt, travelled ſouth-eaſt-by-eaſt one mile, paſſed thro' Indian houſes, ſouth-eaſt three quarters of a mile, and came to a ſmall Indian town of ten houſes. There is a remarkable fine ſpring at this place, riſing out of the ſide of a ſmall hill with ſuch force, that it boils above the ground in a column three feet high. I imagine it diſcharges ten hogſheads of water in a minute. From this town our courſe was ſouth-ſouth-eaſt three miles, ſouth two miles, croſſed a brook about five yards wide, running eaſt ſouth eaſt travelled ſouth one mile, croſſed a brook about four yards wide, running eaſt-ſouth-eaſt, travelled ſouth-ſouth-eaſt two miles, croſſed a brook about eight yards wide. This day we killed plenty of deer and turkies on our march, and encamped.

On the 4th we travelled ſouth-ſouth-eaſt one mile, and came to a river about twenty-five yards wide, croſſed the river, where are two Indian houſes, from thence ſouth-by-eaſt one mile, ſouth-ſouth-eaſt one mile and a half, ſouth-eaſt two miles, ſouth-ſouth-eaſt one mile, and came to an Indian houſe, where there was a family of Windots hunting, from thence ſouth-by-eaſt a quarter of a mile, ſouth five miles, came to the river we croſſed this morning; the courſe of the river here is weſt-north-weſt. This day killed ſeveral deer and other game, and encamped.

On

On the 5th travelled ſouth-ſouth-weſt half a mile, ſouth one mile, ſouth-ſouth-weſt three quarters of a mile, ſouth half a mile, croſſed two ſmall brooks running eaſt, went a ſouth-ſouth-weſt courſe half a mile, ſouth half a mile, ſouth-eaſt half a mile, ſouth two miles, ſouth-eaſt one mile, ſouth half a mile, croſſed a brook running eaſt-by-north, travelled ſouth-by-eaſt half a mile, ſouth-ſouth-eaſt two miles, ſouth-eaſt three quarters of a mile, ſouth ſouth-eaſt one mile, and came to Maſkongom Creek, about eight yards wide, croſſed the creek, and encamped about thirty yards from it. This day killed deer and turkies in our march.

On the 6th we travelled about fourteen or fifteen miles, our general courſe being about eaſt-ſouth-eaſt, killed plenty of game, and encamped by a very fine ſpring.

The 7th our general courſe about ſouth-eaſt, travelled about ſix miles, and croſſed Maſkongom Creek, running ſouth, about twenty yards wide. There is an Indian town about twenty yards from the creek, on the eaſt-ſide, which is called the Mingo Cabbins. There were but two or three Indians in the place, the reſt were hunting. Theſe Indians have plenty of cows, horſes, hogs, &c.

The

The 8th, halted at this town to mend our mogasons, and kill deer, the provisions I brought from Detroit being entirely expended. I went a-hunting with ten of the Rangers, and by ten o'clock got more venison than we had occasion for.

On the 9th travelled about twelve miles, our general course being about south-east, and encamped by the side of a long meadow, where there were a number of Indians hunting.

The 10th, about the same course, we travelled eleven miles, and encamped, having killed in our march this day three bears and two elks.

The 11th, continuing near the same course, we travelled thirteen miles and encamped, where were a number of Wiandots and Six Nation Indians hunting.

The 12th, travelled six miles, bearing rather more to the east, and encamped. This evening we killed several beavers.

The 13th, travelled about north-east six miles, and came to the Delaware's town, called Beaver Town. This Indian town stands on good land, on the weſt-ſide of the Maſkongom River; and oppoſite to the town, on the eaſt-ſide, is a fine river, which diſcharges itſelf into it. The latter is about thirty yards wide, and the Maſkongom about forty; ſo that when they both join, they make a very fine ſtream, with a ſwift current, running to the ſouth-weſt. There are about 3000 acres of cleared ground round this place. The number of warriors in this town is about 180. All the way from the Lake Sanduſky I found level land, and a good country. No pine-trees of any ſort; the timber is white, black, and yellow oak, black and white walnut, cyprus, cheſnut, and locuſt trees. At this town I ſtaid till the 16th in the morning to refreſh my party, and procured ſome corn of the Indians to boil with our veniſon.

On the 16th we marched nearly an eaſt courſe about nine miles, and encamped by the ſide of a ſmall river.

On the 17th kept much the ſame courſe, croſſing ſeveral rivulets and creeks. We travelled about twenty miles, and encamped by the ſide of a ſmall river.

On the 18th we travelled about ſixteen miles an eaſterly courſe, and encamped by a brook.

The 19th, about the ſame general courſe, we croſſed two conſiderable ſtreams of water, and ſome large hills timbered with cheſnut and oak, and having travelled about twenty miles, we encamped by the ſide of a ſmall river, at which place were a number of Delawares hunting.

On the 20th, keeping ſtill an eaſterly courſe, and having much the ſame travelling as the day before, we advanced on our journey about nineteen miles, which brought us to Beaver Creek, where are two or three Indian houſes on the weſt ſide of the creek, and in ſight of the Ohio.

Bad weather prevented our journeying on the 21ſt, but the next day we proſecuted our march. Having croſſed the creek, we travelled twenty miles, nearly ſouth-eaſt, and encamped with a party of Indian hunters.

On the 23d we came again to the Ohio, oppoſite to Fort Pitt, from whence I ordered Lieutenant

M'Cormack

M'Cormack to march the party acroſs the country to Albany, and, after tarrying there till the 26th, I came the common road to Philadelphia, from thence to New York, where, after this long, fatiguing tour, I arrived February 14, 1761.

F I N I S.

AN
Hiſtorical ACCOUNT
OF THE
EXPEDITION
AGAINST THE
OHIO INDIANS,
IN THE YEAR MDCCLXIV,
UNDER THE COMMAND OF
HENRY BOUQUET, Eſq.

Colonel of foot, and now Brigadier General in America. Including his Tranſactions with the Indians, Relative to the Delivery of the Priſoners, and the Preliminaries of Peace. With an Introductory Account of the Preceding Campaign, and Battle at Buſhy-Run.

To which are annexed

MILITARY PAPERS,

CONTAINING

Reflections on the War with the Savages; a Method of forming Frontier Settlements; ſome Account of the Indian Country; with a Liſt of Nations, Fighting Men, Towns, Diſtances, and different Routes.

Publiſhed, from authentic Documents, by a Lover of his Country.

DUBLIN.

Printed for JOHN MILLIKEN, at (No 10,) in *Skinner-Row*, MDCCLXIX.

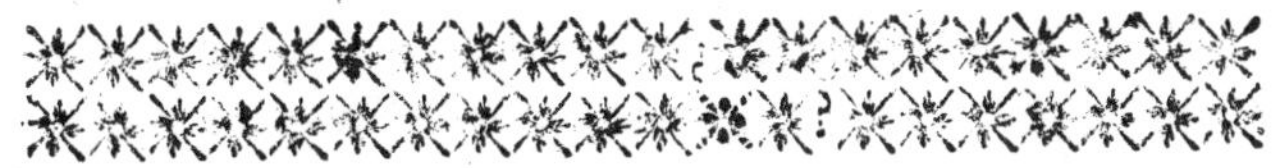

INTRODUCTION.

THE general peace, concluded between Great-Britain, France and Spain, in the year 1762, although viewed in different lights by persons variously affected in the mother country, was nevertheless universally considered as a most happy event in America.

To behold the French, who had so long instigated and supported the Indians, in the most destructive wars and cruel depredations on our frontier settlements at last compelled to cede all Canada, and restricted to the western side of Mississippi, was what we had long wished, but scarcely hoped an accomplishment of in our own days. The precision with which our boundaries were expressed, admitted of no ground for future disputes, and was matter of exultation to every one who understood and regarded the interest of these colonies. We had now the pleasing prospect of "entire * security from all molestation of the Indians, since French intrigue could no longer be employed to seduce, or French force to support them."

* The several quotations in this introduction are taken from the Annual Register, 1763, which is written with great elegance and truth, so far as the author appears to have been furnished with materials.

"UNHAPPILY, however, we were disappointed in this expectation. Our danger arose from that very quarter, in which we imagined ourselves in the most perfect security; and just at the time when we concluded the Indians to be entirely awed, and almost subjected by our power, they suddenly fell upon the frontiers of our most valuable settlements, and upon all our out-lying forts, with such unanimity in the design, and with such savage fury in the attack, as we had not experienced, even in the hottest times of any former war."

SEVERAL reasons have been assigned for this perfidious conduct on their part; such as an omission of the usual presents, and some settlements made on lands not yet purchased from them. But these causes, if true, could only affect a few tribes, and never could have formed so general a combination against us. The true reason seems to have been a jealousy of our growing power, heightened by their seeing the French almost wholly driven out of America, and a number of forts now possessed by us, which commanded the great lakes and rivers communicating with them, and awed the whole Indian country. They probably imagined that they beheld "in every little garrison the germ of a future colony," and thought it incumbent on them to make one general and timely effort to crush our power in the birth.

BY the papers in the Appendix, a general idea may be formed of the strength of the different Indian nations surrounding our settlements, and their situation with respect to each other.

THE Shawanese, Delawares and other Ohio tribes, took the lead in this war, and seem to have

have begun it rather too precipitately, before the other tribes in confederacy with them, were ready for action.

THEIR ſcheme appears to have been projected with much deliberate miſchief in the intention, and more than uſual ſkill in the ſyſtem of execution. They were to make one general and ſudden attack upon our frontier ſettlements in the time of harveſt, to deſtroy our men, corn, cattle, &c. as far as they could penetrate, and to ſtarve our out-poſts, by cutting off their ſupplies, and all communication with the inhabitants of the Provinces.

IN purſuance of this bold and bloody project, they fell ſuddenly upon our traders whom they had invited into their country, murdered many of them, and made one general plunder of their effects, to an immenſe value.

THE frontiers of Pennſylvania, Maryland and Virginia, were immediately over-run with ſcalping parties, marking their way with blood and devaſtation wherever they came, and all thoſe examples of ſavage cruelty, which never fail to accompany an Indian war.

ALL our out-forts, even at the remoteſt diſtances, were attacked about the ſame time; and the following ones ſoon fell into the enemies hands—viz. Le Boeuf, Venango, Preſqu' Iſle, on and near lake Erie; La Bay upon lake Michigan; St. Joſeph's, upon the river of that name; Miamis upon the Miamis river; Ouachtanon upon the Ouabache; Sanduſky upon lake Junundat; and Michilimackinac.

BEING but weakly garriſoned, truſting to the ſecurity of a general peace ſo lately eſtabliſhed, unable to obtain the leaſt intelligence from the colonies, or from each other, and being ſeparately persuaded by their treacherous and savage assailants that they had carried every other place before them, it could not be expected that these small posts could hold out long; and the fate of their garrisons is terrible to relate.

THE news of their surrender, and the continued ravages of the enemy, struck all America with consternation, and depopulated a great part of our frontiers. We now saw most of those posts, suddenly wrested from us, which had been the great object of the late war, and one of the principal advantages acquired by the peace. Only the forts of Niagara, the Detroit and Fort-Pitt, remained in our hands, of all that had been purchased with so much blood and treasure. But these were places of consequence, and we hope it will ever remain an argument of their importance, and of the attention that should be paid to their future support, that they alone continued to awe the whole power of the Indians, and balanced the fate of the war between them and us!

THESE forts, being larger, were better garrisoned and supplied to stand a siege of some length, than the places that fell. Niagara was not attacked, the enemy judging it too strong.

THE officers who commanded the other two deserved the highest honour for the firmness with which they defended them, and the hardships they sustained rather than deliver up places of such importance.

MAJOR GLADWIN, in particular, who commanded at the Detroit, had to withstand the united and vigorous attacks of all the nations living upon the Lakes

THE design of this publication, and the materials in my hands, lead me more immediately-

ly

ly to ſpeak of the defence and relief of Fort Pitt.

THE Indians had early ſurrounded that place, and cut off all communication from it, even by meſſage. Tho' they had no cannon, nor underſtood the methods of a regular ſiege, yet, with incredible boldneſs, they poſted themſelves under the banks of both rivers † by the walls of the fort, and continued as it were buried there, from day to day, with aſtoniſhing patience; pouring in an inceſſant ſtorm of muſquetry and fire arrows; hoping at length, by famine, by fire, or by harraſſing out the garriſon, to carry their point.

CAPTAIN ECUYER, who commanded there, tho' he wanted ſeveral neceſſaries for ſuſtaining a ſiege, and the fortifications had been greatly damaged by the floods, took all the precautions which art and judgment could ſuggeſt for the repair of the place, and repulſing the enemy. His garriſon, joined by the inhabitants, and ſurviving traders who had taken refuge there, ſeconded his efforts with reſolution. Their ſituation was alarming, being remote from all immediate aſſiſtance, and having to deal with an enemy from whom they had no mercy to expect.

GENERAL AMHERST, the commander in chief, not being able to provide in time for the ſafety of the remote poſts, bent his chief attention to the relief of the Detroit, Niagara, and Fort-Pitt. The communication with the two former was chiefly by water, from the province of New-York; and it was on that account the

† The Ohio and Monongahela, at the junction of which ſtands Fort Pitt.

more easy to throw succours into them. The detachment sent to the Detroit arrived there on the 29th of July, 1763; but Captain Dalyell, who commanded that detachment, and seventy of his men, lost their lives in a rencounter with the Indians near the fort. Previous to this disaster he had passed thro' Niagara, and left a reinforcement there.

Fort Pitt remained all this while in a most critical situation. No account could be obtained from the garrison, nor any relief sent to it, but by a long and tedious land march of near 200 miles beyond the settlements; and through those dangerous passes where the fate of Braddock and others still rises on the imagination.

Col. Bouquet was appointed to march to the relief of this fort, with a large quantity of military stores and provisions, escorted by the shattered remainder of the 42d and 77th regiments, lately returned in a dismal condition from the West-Indies, and far from being recovered of their fatigues at the siege of the Havannah. General Amherst, having at that time no other troops to spare, was obliged to employ them in a service which would have required men of the strongest constitution and vigour.

Early orders had been given to prepare a convoy of provisions on the frontiers of Pennsylvania, but such were the universal terror and consternation of the inhabitants, that when Col. Bouquet arrived at Carlisle, nothing had yet been done. A great number of the plantations had been plundered and burnt by the savages; many of the mills destroyed, and the full-ripe crops stood waving in the field, ready for the sickle, but the reapers were not to be found!

The

THE greateſt part of the county of Cumberland, thro' which the army had to paſs, was deſerted, and the roads were covered with diſtreſſed families, flying from their ſettlements, and deſtitute of all the neceſſaries of life.

IN the midſt of that general confuſion, the ſupplies neceſſary for the expedition became very precarious, nor was it leſs difficult to procure horſes and carriages for the uſe of the troops.

THE commander found that, inſtead of expecting ſuch ſupplies from a miſerable people, he himſelf was called by the voice of humanity to beſtow on them ſome ſhare of his own proviſions to relieve their preſent exigency. However, in 18 days after his arrival at Carliſle, by the prudent and active meaſures which he purſued, joined to his knowledge of the country, and the diligence of the perſons he employed, the convoy and carriages were procured with the aſſiſtance of the interior parts of the country, and the army proceeded.

THEIR march did not abate the fears of the dejected inhabitants. They knew the ſtrength and ferocity of the enemy. They remembered the former defeats even of our beſt troops, and were full of diffidence and apprehenſions on beholding the ſmall number and ſickly ſtate of the regulars employed in this expedition. Without the leaſt hopes, therefore, of ſucceſs, they ſeemed only to wait for the fatal event, which they dreaded, to abandon all the country beyond the Suſquehannah.

IN ſuch deſpondency of mind, it is not ſurpriſing, that tho' their whole was at ſtake, and depended intirely upon the fate of this little army, none of them offered to aſſiſt in the defence of the country, by joining the expedition; in which they would have been of infinite ſervice, being in general well acquainted with the woods, and excellent markſmen.

IT cannot be conteſted that the defeat of the regular troops on this occaſion, would have left the province of Pennſylvania in particular, expoſed to the moſt imminent danger, from a victorious, daring, and barbarous enemy; for (excepting the frontier people of Cumberland county) the bulk of its induſtrious inhabitants is compoſed of merchants, tradeſmen and farmers, unaccuſtomed to arms, and without a militia law.

THE legiſlature ordered, indeed, 700 men to be raiſed for the protection of the frontiers during the harveſt; but what dependence could be placed in raw troops, newly raiſed and undiſciplined? Under ſo many diſcouraging circumſtances, the Colonel (deprived of all aſſiſtance from the provinces, and having none to expect from the General, who had ſent him the laſt man that could be removed from the hoſpitals) had nothing elſe to truſt to, but about 500 ſoldiers of approved courage and reſolution indeed, but infirm, and intire ſtrangers to the woods, and to this new kind of war. A number of them were even ſo weak, as not to be able to march, and ſixty were carried in waggons to reinforce the garriſons of the ſmall poſts on the communication.

MEANWHILE Fort-Ligonier ſituated beyond the Allegheney-Mountains, was in the greateſt danger of falling into the hands of the enemy, before the army could reach it. The ſtockade being very bad, and the garriſon extremely weak, they had attacked it vigorouſly, but had been repulſed by the bravery and good conduct of Lieutenant Blane who commanded there.

THE

THE preservation of that post was of the utmost consequence, on account of its situation and the quantity of military stores it contained, which if the enemy could have got possession of, would have enabled them to continue their attack upon Fort-Pitt, and reduced the army to the greatest streights. For an object of that importance, every risk was to be run; and the Colonel determined to send through the woods, with proper guides, a party of thirty men to join that garrison. They succeeded by forced marches in that hazardous attempt, not having been discovered by the enemy till they came within sight of the Fort, into which they threw themselves, after receiving some running shot.

PREVIOUS to that reinforcement of regulars, 20 voluntiers, all good woodsmen, had been sent to Fort-Ligonier by Capt. Ourry, who commanded at Fort-Bedford another very considerable magazine of provisions, and military stores, the principal and centrical stage between Carlisle and Fort-Pitt, being about 100 miles distance from each. This fort was also in a ruinous condition, and very weakly garrisoned, although the two small intermediate posts, at the crossings of the Juniata and of Stony Creek, had been abandoned to strengthen it.

HERE the distressed families, scattered for 12 or 15 miles round, fled for protection, leaving most of their effects a prey to the savages.

ALL the necessary precautions were taken by the commanding officer, to prevent surprize, and repel open force, as also to render ineffectual the enemies fire arrows. He armed all the fighting men, who formed two companies of voluntiers, and did duty with the garrison till the arrival of

two

two companies of light infantry, detached as ſoon as poſſible from Colonel Bouquet's little army.

THESE two magazines being ſecured, the Colonel advanced to the remoteſt verge of our ſettlements, where he could receive no ſort of intelligence of the number, poſition, or motions of the enemy. Not even at Fort-Bedford, where he arrived with his whole convoy on the 25th of July, for tho' the Indians did not attempt to attack the fort, they had by this time killed, ſcalped, and taken eighteen perſons in that neighbourhood, and their ſculking parties were ſo ſpread, that at laſt no expreſs could eſcape them. "This" (want of intelligence) "is often a very embarraſſing circumſtance in the conduct of a campaign in America. The Indians had better intelligence, and no ſooner were they informed of the march of our Army, than they broke up the ſiege of Fort-Pitt, and took the route by which they knew we were to proceed, reſolved to take the firſt advantageous opportunity of an attack on the march."

IN this uncertainty of intelligence under which the Colonel laboured, he marched from Fort-Bedford the 28th of July, and as ſoon as he reached Fort-Ligonier, he determined very prudently to leave his waggons at that poſt, and to proceed only with the pack horſes. Thus diſburdened, the army continued their route. Before them lay a dangerous defile at Turtle Creek, ſeveral miles in length, commanded the whole way by high and craggy hills. This defile he intended to have paſſed the enſuing night, by a double or forced march; thereby, if poſſible, to elude the vigilance of ſo alert an enemy, propoſing only to make a ſhort halt in his way, to refreſh the Troops, at Buſhy-Run.

WHEN

When they came within half a mile of that place, about one in the afternoon, (August 5th, 1763) after an harrassing march of seventeen miles, and just as they were expecting to relax from their fatigue, they were suddenly attacked by the Indians, on their advanced guard; which being speedily and firmly supported, the enemy was beat off, and even pursued to a considerable distance.

'† But the flight of these barbarians must 'often be considered as a part of the engagement, '(if we may use the expression) rather than a 'dereliction of the field. The moment the pur-'suit ended, they returned with renewed vigour 'to the attack. Several other parties, who had 'been in ambush in some high grounds which 'lay along the flanks of the army, now started 'up at once, and falling with a resolution equal 'to that of their companions, galled our troops 'with a most obstinate fire.

'It was necessary to make a general charge 'with the whole line to dislodge them from these 'heights. This charge succeeded; but still the 'success produced no decisive advantage; for as 'soon as the savages were driven from one post, 'they still appeared on another, till by constant 'reinforcements they were at length able to sur-'round the whole detachment, and attack the 'convoy which had been left in the rear.

† The above quotation is from the writer already mentioned, and seems so accurately and elegantly drawn up, from the account of this engagement, sent to his Majesty's ministers, that nothing better can be inserted in its room. There are but one or two small mistakes in it, which are here corrected.

'This

'THIS manœuvre obliged the main body to 'fall back in order to protect it. The action, 'which grew every moment hotter and hotter, 'now became general. Our troops were attack-'ed on every side; the savages supported their 'spirit throughout; but the steady behaviour of 'the English troops, who were not thrown into 'the least confusion by the very discouraging na-'ture of this service, in the end prevailed; they 'repulsed the enemy, and drove them from all 'their posts with fixed bayonets.

'THE engagement ended only with the day, 'having continued from one without any inter-'mission.

'THE ground, on which the action ended, 'was not altogether inconvenient for an encamp-'ment. The convoy and the wounded were in 'the middle, and the troops, disposed in a circle, 'incompassed the whole. In this manner, and 'with little repose, they passed an anxious night, 'obliged to the strictest vigilance by an enter-'prizing enemy who had surrounded them.

'THOSE who have only experienced the se-'verities and dangers of a campaign in Europe, 'can scarcely form an idea of what is to be done 'and endured in an American war. To act in 'a country cultivated and inhabited, where 'roads are made, magazines are established, and 'hospitals provided; where there are good towns 'to retreat to in case of misfortune; or, at the 'worst, a generous enemy to yield to, from 'whom no consolation, but the honour of vic-'tory, can be wanting; this may be considered 'as the exercise of a spirited and adventurous 'mind, rather than a rigid contest where all is 'at stake, and mutual destruction the object: 'and as a contention between rivals for glory,

'rather

'rather than a real ſtruggle between ſanguinary 'enemies. But in an American campaign every 'thing is terrible; the face of the country, the 'climate, the enemy. There is no refreſhment 'for the healthy, nor relief for the ſick. A vaſt 'unhoſpitable deſart, unſafe and treacherous, 'ſurrounds them, where victories are not deci-'ſive, but defeats are ruinous; and ſimple death 'is the leaſt misfortune which can happen to 'them. This forms a ſervice truly critical, in 'which all the firmneſs of the body and mind is 'put to the ſevereſt trial; and all the exertions 'of courage and addreſs are called out. If the 'actions of theſe rude campaigns are of leſs dig-'nity, the adventures in them are more intereſt-'ing to the heart, and more amuſing to the 'imagination, than the events of a regular war.

'But to return to the party of Engliſh, whom 'we left in the woods. At the firſt dawn of 'light the ſavages began to declare themſelves, 'all about the camp, at the diſtance of about '500 yards; and by ſhouting and yelling in the 'moſt horrid manner, quite round that exten-'ſive circumference, endeavoured to ſtrike terror 'by an oſtentation of their numbers, and their 'ferocity.

'After this alarming preparative, they at-'tacked our forces, and, under the favour of an 'inceſſant fire, made ſeveral bold efforts to pe-'netrate into the camp. They were repulſed in 'every attempt, but by no means diſcouraged 'from new ones. Our troops, continually vic-'torious, were continually in danger. They 'were beſides extremely fatigued with a long 'march, and with the equally long action, of 'the preceding day; and they were diſtreſſed to 'the

'the last degree by a total want of water, much 'more intolerable than the enemy's fire.

'TIED to their convoy, they could not lose 'sight of it for a moment, without exposing, 'not only that interesting object, but their 'wounded men, to fall a prey to the savages, 'who pressed them on every side. To move 'was impracticable. Many of the horses were 'lost, and many of the drivers, stupefied by 'their fears, hid themselves in the bushes, and 'were incapable of hearing or obeying orders.

'THEIR situation became extremely critical 'and perplexing, having experienced that the 'most lively efforts made no impression upon an 'enemy, who always gave way when pressed; 'but who, the moment the pursuit was over, 'returned with as much alacrity as ever to the 'attack. Besieged rather than engaged; attack-'ed without interruption, and without decision; 'able neither to advance nor to retreat, they 'saw before them the most melancholy prospect 'of crumbling away by degrees, and entirely 'perishing without revenge or honour, in the 'midst of those dreadful desarts. The fate of 'Braddock was every moment before their eyes; 'but they were more ably conducted.

'THE commander was sensible that every 'thing depended upon bringing the savages to a 'close engagement, and to stand their ground 'when attacked. Their audaciousness, which 'had increased with their success, seemed fa-'vourable to this design. He endeavoured, 'therefore, to increase their confidence as much 'as possible.

'FOR that purpose he contrived the following 'stratagem. Our troops were posted on an emi-'nence, and formed a circle round their convoy from

'from the preceding night, which order they 'still retained. Col. BOUQUET gave directions, 'that two companies of his troops, who had 'been posted in the most advanced situations, 'should fall within the circle; the troops on the 'right and left immediately opened their files, and 'filled up the vacant space, that they might 'seem to cover their retreat. Another company 'of light infantry, with one of grenadiers, were 'ordered "to lie in ambuscade," to support 'the two first companies of grenadiers, who 'moved on the feigned retreat, and were in-'tended to begin the real attack. The dispositi-'ons were well made, and the plan executed 'without the least confusion.

'THE savages gave entirely into the snare. 'The thin line of troops, which took possession 'of the ground which the two companies of light 'foot had left, being brought in nearer to the 'center of the circle, the barbarians mistook 'those motions for a retreat, abandoned the 'woods which covered them, hurried headlong 'on, and advancing with the most daring intre-'pidity, galled the English troops with their 'heavy fire. But at the very moment when, 'certain of success, they thought themselves 'masters of the camp, the two first companies 'made a sudden turn, and sallying out from a 'part of the hill, which could not be observed, 'fell furiously upon their right flank.

'THE savages, though they found themselves 'disappointed and exposed, preserved their re-'collection, and resolutely returned the fire 'which they had received. Then it was the su-'periority of combined strength and discipline 'appeared. On the second charge they could 'no longer sustain the irresistible shock of the

'regular

'regular troops, who rushing upon them, killed 'many, and put the rest to flight.

'At the instant when the savages betook 'themselves to flight, the other two companies, 'which had been ordered to support the first, 'rose "from the ambuscade," marched to the 'enemy, and gave them their full fire. This ac-'complished their defeat. The four companies 'now united, did not give them time to look be-'hind them, but pursued the enemy till they 'were totally dispersed.

'The other bodies of the savages attempted 'nothing. They were kept in awe during the 'engagement by the rest of the British troops, 'who were so posted as to be ready to fall on 'them upon the least motion. Having been wit-'nesses to the defeat of their companions, with-'out any effort to support or assist them, they 'at length followed their example and fled.

'This judicious and successful manœuvre res-'cued the party from the most imminent danger. 'The victory secured the field, and cleared all 'the adjacent woods. But still the march was 'so difficult, and the army had suffered so much, 'and so many horses were lost, that before they 'were able to proceed, they were reluctantly 'obliged to destroy such part of their convoy of 'provisions as they could not carry with them 'for want of horses. Being lightened by this sa-'crifice, they proceeded to Bushy-Run, where 'finding water, they encamped."

The enemy lost about sixty men on this occasion, some of them their chief warriors; which they reputed a very severe stroke. They had likewise many wounded in the pursuit. The English lost about fifty men and had about sixty wounded.

The

THE ſavages, thus ſignally defeated in all their attempts to cut off this reinforcement upon its march, began to retreat with the utmoſt precipitation to their remote ſettlements, wholly giving up their deſigns againſt Fort-Pitt; at which place Col. Bouquet arrived ſafe with his convoy, four days after the action; receiving no further moleſtation on the road, except a few ſcattered ſhot from a diſheartened and flying enemy.

HERE the Colonel was obliged to put an end to the operations of this campaign, not having a ſufficient force to purſue the enemy beyond the Ohio and take advantage of the victory obtained over them; nor having any reaſon to expect a timely reinforcement from the provinces in their diſtreſſed ſituation. He was therefore forced to content himſelf with ſupplying Fort-Pitt, and other places on the communication, with proviſions, ammunition, and ſtores; ſtationing his ſmall army to the beſt advantage he could, againſt the approach of winter.

THE tranſactions of the ſucceeding campaign, will be the ſubject of the following work, and we ſhall conclude this introduction, by ſhewing the ſenſe which his Majeſty was pleaſed to entertain, of the conduct and bravery of the officers and army, on this trying occaſion.

HEAD-

HEAD-QUARTERS, NEW-YORK, Jan. 5, 1764.

ORDERS.

" HIS Majesty has been graciously pleased
" to signify to the commander in chief,
" his royal approbation of the conduct and bra-
" very of Col. BOUQUET, and the officers and
" troops under his command, in the two actions
" of the 5th and 6th of August; in which, not-
" withstanding the many circumstances of dif-
" ficulty and distress they laboured under, and
" the unusual spirit and resolution of the Indians,
" they repelled and defeated the repeated attacks
" of the Savages, and conducted their convoy
" safe to Fort-Pitt.

" Signed MONCRIEF,
" Major of Brigade."

To Colonel BOUQUET,
or officer commanding at Fort-Pitt.

AN

Hiſtorical ACCOUNT

OF

COLONEL BOUQUET's EXPEDITION

Againſt the OHIO INDIANS in the Year 1764.

IN the preceding introduction, ſome account hath been given of the ſudden, treacherous and unprovoked attack, made by the Indians upon the frontiers of Pennſylvania, Maryland, and Virginia, ſoon after the publication of the general Peace, at a time when we were but juſt beginning to reſpire from our former calamities, and looked for an approach of quiet on every ſide. The principal tranſactions of the campaign 1763 have likewiſe been briefly recapitulated, and the reader informed by what means the editor became poſſeſſed of the valuable papers, which have enabled him to bring the hiſtory of this Indian war to a concluſion, and furniſhed the materials of the following ſheets.

COLONEL BOUQUET, as before mentioned, not having a ſufficient number of troops to garriſon the different poſts, under his command, and at the ſame time to croſs the Ohio and take advantage of the dejection into which he had thrown the enemy, by the defeat at Buſhy-Run, was obliged

liged to reſtrain his operations to the ſupplying the forts with proviſions, ammunition and other neceſſaries.

IN the execution of this ſervice, he received no annoyance from the enemy, for they now ſaw themſelves not only forced to give up their deſigns againſt FORT-PITT; but, retreating beyond the Ohio, they deſerted their former towns, and abandoned all the country between Preſque-Iſle and Sanduſki; not thinking themſelves ſafe till they arrived at Muſkingam.

HERE they began to form new ſettlements, and remained quiet during the winter. But, in the mean time, having ſupplied themſelves with powder, &c. from the French traders, (and now flattering themſelves that the great diſtance of their ſettlements would render them inacceſſible to our troops) the enſuing ſpring 1764 preſented theſe ſavage enemies afreſh on our frontiers; ravaging and murdering with their uſual barbarity.

To chaſtiſe them for their perfidy, General Gage reſolved to attack them on two different ſides, and to force them from our frontiers; by carrying the war into the heart of their own country. With this view, he deſtined a corps of troops to proceed under Col. Bradſtreet, to act anainſt the Wiandots, Ottawas, Chipwas and other nations, living upon or near the lakes; while another corps, under the command of Col. Bouquet, ſhould attack the Delawares, Shawaneſe, Mingoes, Mohickons, and other nations, between the Ohio and the lakes.

THESE two corps were to act in concert; and as that of Col. Bradſtreet could be ready much ſooner than the other, he was to proceed to Detroit, Michilimackinac and other places.

On

On his return, he was to encamp and remain at Sanduſki, to awe, by that poſition, the numerous tribes of weſtern Indians, ſo as to prevent their ſending any aſſiſtance to the Ohio Indians, while Colonel Bouquet ſhould execute his plan of attacking them in the heart of their ſettlements.

Col. Bouquet's expedition was to proceed altogether by land, and was on that account attended with great difficulties. His men were to penetrate through a continued depth of woods, and a ſavage unexplored country; without roads, without poſts, and without a retreat if they failed of ſucceſs. When once engaged in theſe deſerts, they had no convoy, nor any kind of aſſiſtance to expect. Every thing was to be carried with them—their ammunition, baggage, tools, ſtores, and proviſions neceſſary for the troops during the whole expedition. And beſides, they were liable to many embarraſſments, and difficulties which no prudence could foreſee, ſcarce any caution prevent; ſo that, in this account, ſundry things, which, in the uſual method of conducting military operations, might not be thought worthy of a detail, may nevertheleſs be found highly ſerviceable to thoſe who may afterwards be employed in this ſpecies of war, which is new to Europeans, who muſt ſubmit to be inſtructed in it by experience, and in many articles even by the ſavages themſelves.

Part of the 42d and 60th regiments were ordered on this expedition, and were to be joined by two hundred friendly Indians, and the troops required of Virginia and Pennſylvania. The Indians never came, and the Virginians pleaded their inability to raiſe men, having already in pay about 700 militia for the defence of their own frontier,

frontier. In Pennsylvania, a bill for raising 1000 men was passed May 30th; but, with the utmost diligence that could be used, the number could not be compleated till the beginning of August.

On the 5th of that month, the men being assembled at Carlisle, one hundred and eighteen miles to the westward of Philadelphia, Governor Penn, who had accompanied Col. Bouquet to that place, acquainted the two Pennsylvania battalions with the necessity we were laid under of chastising the Indians "for their repeated and "unprovoked barbarities on the inhabitants of "the Province; a just resentment of which, "added to a remembrance of the loyalty and "courage of our provincial troops on former oc-"casions, he did not doubt, would animate "them to do honour to their country; and that "they could not but hope to be crowned with "success, as they were to be united with the "same regular troops, and under the same able "commander, who had by themselves, on that "very day, the memorable 5th of August in "the preceding year, sustained the repeated at-"tacks of the savages, and obtained a compleat "victory over them."—He also reminded them "of the exemplary punishments that would be "inflicted on the grievous crime of desertion, if "any of them were capable of so far forgetting "their solemn oath and duty to their king and "country, as to be involved in it."

Col. Bouquet then assumed the command of the regular and provincial troops; and the four following days were spent in the necessary preparations for their march; the Colonel giving the most express orders to the officers and men to observe strict discipline, and not to commit the least violation of the civil rights or peace of the inhabitants.

inhabitants.—He, at the ſame time, made the moſt prudent regulations for a ſafe and commodious carriage of the baggage, taking care to rid himſelf of all unneceſſary incumbrances.

THE 13th of Auguſt this ſmall army got to Fort Loudoun; but notwithſtanding all the precautions taken to prevent deſertion, the Pennſylvania troops were now reduced to about 700 men. The Colonel was therefore under a neceſſity to apply to the government of that province to enable him to compleat their number to the full complement; which was generouſly granted by a reſolve of the Governor and Commiſſioners Auguſt 16th; and the army advancing now beyond the ſettled parts of Pennſylvania, he made application to the colony of Virginia, where (under the countenance of Governor Fauquier the men wanted were ſoon raiſed, and joined) the army at Pittſburgh, about the latter end of September.

NOTHING material happened in their march from Fort Laudoun to Fort Pitt, (formerly Fort Du Queſne) on the Ohio, three hundred and twenty miles weſt from Philadelphia; at which place Col. Bouquet arrived the 17th of September.

DURING this interval, ſeveral large convoys were forwarded under ſtrong eſcorts; and though the enemy continued their ravages all that time on the frontiers, they durſt not attack any of thoſe convoys, which all arrived ſafe at Fort Pitt.

WHILE Col. Bouquet was at Fort Loudoun, he received diſpatches by expreſs from Colonel, Bradſtreet, dated from Preſque-Iſle Auguſt 14th acquainting him that he (Colonel Bradſtreet) had concluded a peace with the Delawares and Sha-

 waneſe;

wanese; but Colonel Bouquet perceiving clearly that they were not sincere in their intentions, as they continued their murders and depredations, he determined to prosecute his plan without remission, till he received further instructions from General Gage; who, upon the same principles, refused to ratify the treaty, and renewed his orders to both armies to attack the enemy.

About the time of Colonel Bouquet's arrival at Fort Pitt, ten Indians appeared on the north side of the Ohio, desiring a conference; which stratagem the savages had made use of before, to obtain intelligence of our numbers and intentions. Three of the party consented, though with apparent reluctance, to come over to the Fort; and as they could give no satisfactory reason for their visit, they were detained as spies, and their associates fled back to their towns.

On the 20th of September Colonel Bouquet sent one of the above three Indians after them with a message, in substance as follows—" I have " received an account from Colonel Bradstreet " that your nations had begged for peace, which " he had consented to grant, upon assurance that " you have recalled all your warriors from our " frontiers; and in consequence thereof, I would " not have proceeded against your towns, if I " had not heard that, in open violation of your " engagements, you have since murdered several " of our people.

" As soon as the rest of the army joins me, " which I expect immediately, I was therefore " determined to have attacked you, as a people " whose promises can no more be relied on. But " I will put it once more in your power to save " yourselves and your families from total destruction, by giving us satisfaction for the hostilities

" against

" againſt us. And firſt you are to leave the path " open for my expreſſes from hence to Detroit; " and as I am now to ſend two men with diſ- " patches to Colonel Bradſtreet who commands " on the lakes, I deſire to know whether you " will ſend two of your people with them to bring " them ſafe back with an anſwer? And if they " receive any injury either in going or coming, " or if the letters are taken from them, I will " immediately put the Indians now in my power " to death, and will ſhew no mercy for the fu- " ture to any of your nations that ſhall fall into " my hands. I allow you ten days to have my " letters delivered at Detroit, and ten days to " bring me back an anſwer."

He added "that he had lately had it in his pow- " er, while they remained on the other ſide of " the river, to have put their whole party to " death, which puniſhment they had deſerved " by their former treachery; and that if they " did not improve the clemency now offered to " them, by returning back as ſoon as poſſible " with all their priſoners, they might expect to " feel the full weight of a juſt vengeance and " reſentment."—

We have been the more particular in our account of this firſt tranſaction with the Indians; becauſe the Colonel's firm and determined conduct in opening the campaign, had happy effects in the proſecution of it, and ſhews by what methods theſe faithleſs ſavages are to be beſt reduced to reaſon.

On the 1ſt of October, two of the Six Nation tribes, an Onondago and Oneida Indian, came to Fort Pitt, and under colour of our ancient friendſhip with them, and their pretended regard to the Engliſh, endeavoured to diſſuade the Colonel from proceeding with the army. They told him that his force was not ſufficient to withſtand the power of the numerous nations through whoſe countries he was to paſs, and aſſured him that if he would wait a little, they would all come and make peace with him; at the ſame time recommending it particularly to him to ſend back the two Indians detained as ſpies. Theſe little arts being clearly made uſe of to ſpin out the ſeaſon till the approach of winter ſhould render it impoſſible to proceed, they made but little impreſſion. He told them that he could not depend on the promiſes of the Delawares and Shawaneſe; and was determined to proceed to Tuſcarowas, where, if they had any thing to ſay, he would hear them.

In the mean time, he was uſing the utmoſt diligence to prepare for his march, and was obliged to enforce the ſevereſt diſcipline. One woman belonging to each corps, and two nurſes for the general hoſpital, were all that were permitted to follow the army. The other women in the camp, and thoſe unneceſſary in the garriſon, were ordered immediately down the country into the ſettlements. Two ſoldiers were ſhot for deſertion; an example which became abſolutely neceſſary to ſuppreſs a crime which, in ſuch an expedition, would have been attended with fatal conſequences, by weakening an army already too ſmall.

Colonel Bouquet, having at length, with great difficulty, collected his troops, formed his magazines, and provided for the ſafety of the poſts he was to leave behind him, was ready on the 2d of October to proceed from Fort Pitt, with about

1500 men, including drivers and other neceſſary followers of the army.

THE Colonel, expreſſing the greateſt confidence in the bravery of the troops, told them, "he did not doubt but this war would ſoon be "ended, under God, to their own honor, and "the future ſafety of their country, provided the "men were ſtrictly obedient to orders, and guard- "ed againſt the ſurprizes and ſudden attacks of "a treacherous enemy, who never dared to face "Britiſh troops in any open field; that the diſ- "tance of the enemy's towns, and the clearing "roads to them, muſt neceſſarily require a con- "ſiderable time; that the troops in thoſe deſerts, "had no other ſupplies to expect but the ammu- "nition and proviſions they carried with them; "and that therefore the utmoſt care and frugality "would be neceſſary in the uſe of them." He publiſhed the ſeveral penalties againſt thoſe who ſhould be found guilty of ſtealing or embezzling any part of them, and ordered his march in the following manner.—

A CORPS of Virginia * volunteers advanced before the whole; detaching three ſcouting parties. One of them, furniſhed with a guide, marched in the center path, which the army was to follow. The other two extended themſelves in a line a-breaſt, on the right and left of the aforeſaid party, to reconnoitre the woods.

UNDER cover of this corps, the ax-men, conſiſting of all the artificers, and two companies of light infantry, followed in three diviſions, under the direction of the chief engineer, to clear three

* Theſe were the men raiſed in Virginia to compleat the Pennſylvania troops, and were in the pay of the laſt mentioned province.

different paths, in which the troops and the convoy followed, viz.—

THE front-face of the square, composed of part of the 42d regiment, marched in a column, two deep, in the center path.

THE right face of the square, composed of the remainder of the 42d and of the 60th regiment, marched in a single file in the right-hand path.

THE first battalion of Pennsylvanians composed the left face, marching in like manner in the path to the left of the center.

THE corps de reserve, composed of two platoons of grenadiers, followed the right and left faces of the square.

THE 2d battalion of Pennsylvanians formed the rear face of the square, and followed the corps de reserve, each in a single file on the right and left hand paths; all these troops covering the convoy, which moved in the center path.

A PARTY of light horse-men marched behind the rear-face of the square, followed by another corps of Virginia volunteers, forming the rear-guard.

THE Pennsylvania volunteers, dividing themselves equally, and marching in a single file, at a proper distance, flanked the right and left faces of the square.

THIS was the general order of march. Nor was less attention paid to particular matters of a subordinate nature. The ammunition and tools were placed in the rear of the first column, or front face of the square, followed by the officers' baggage, and tents. The oxen and sheep came after the baggage, in separate droves, properly guarded. The provisions came next to the baggage, in four divisions, or brigades of pack-horses, each conducted by a horse master.

THE

THE troops were ordered to obſerve the moſt profound ſilence, and the men to march at two yards diſtance from one another. When the line or any part of it halted, the whole were to face outwards; and if attacked on their march, they were to halt immediately, ready to form the ſquare when ordered. The light horſe were then to march into the ſquare, with the cattle, proviſions, ammunition and baggage. Proper diſpoſitions were likewiſe made in caſe of an attack in the night; and for encampments, guards, communications between the centries, ſignals, and the like.

THINGS being thus ſettled, the army decamped from Fort-Pitt on Wedneſday October 3d, and marched about one mile and an half over a rich level country, with ſtately timber, to camp No. 2. a ſtrong piece of ground, pleaſantly ſituated, with plenty of water and food for cattle.

THURSDAY October 4th, having proceeded about two miles, they came to the Ohio, at the beginning of the narrows, and from thence followed the courſe of the river along a flat gravelly beech, about ſix miles and a quarter; with two iſlands on their left, the lowermoſt about ſix miles long, with a riſing ground running acroſs, and gently ſloping on both ſides to its banks, which are high and upright. At the lower end of this iſland, the army left the river, marching through good land, broken with ſmall hollows to camp No. 3; this day's march being nine miles and a quarter.—

FRIDAY October 5th. In this day's march the army paſſed through Loggs-towns, ſituated ſeventeen miles and an half, fifty ſeven perches, by the path, from Fort-Pitt. This place was noted before the laſt war for the great trade carried on there by the Engliſh and French; but its inhabitants, the Shawaneſe and Delawares, abandoned it in the year 1750. The lower town extended about ſixty perches over a rich bottom to the foot of a low ſteep-ridge, on the ſummit of which, near the declivity, ſtood the upper town, commanding a moſt agreeable proſpect over the lower, and quite acroſs the Ohio, which is about 500 yards wide here, and by its majeſtic eaſy current adds much to the beauty of the place. Proceeding beyond Logg's-town, through a fine country, interſperſed with hills and rich valleys, watered by many rivulets, and covered with ſtately timber, they came to camp No. 4; on a level piece of ground, with a thicket in the rear, a ſmall precipice round the front, with a run of water at the foot, and good food for cattle. This day's march was nine miles, one half, and fifty three perches.

SATURDAY October 6th, at about three miles diſtance from this camp, they came again to the Ohio, purſuing its courſe half a mile farther, and then turning off, over a ſteep ridge, they croſſed Big Beaver-creek, which is twenty perches wide, the ford ſtony and pretty deep. It runs through a rich vale, with a pretty ſtrong current, its banks high, the upland adjoining it very good, the timber tall and young.——About a mile below its confluence with the Ohio, ſtood formerly a large town, on a ſteep bank, built by the French of ſquare logs, with ſtone chimneys, for ſome of the Shawaneſe, Delaware and Mingo tribes, who abandoned it in the year 1758, when the French deſerted Fort Du Queſne. Near the fording of Beaver-creek alſo ſtood about ſeven houſes, which were deſerted and deſtroyed by the Indians, after their

their defeat at Buſhy-run, when they forſook all their remaining ſettlements in this part of the country, as has been mentioned above.

ABOUT two miles before the army came to Beaver-creek, one of our people who had been made priſoner by ſix Delawares about a week before, near Fort Bedford, having made his eſcape from them, came and informed the Colonel that theſe Indians had the day before fallen in with the army, but kept themſelves concealed, being ſurpriſed at our numbers. Two miles beyond Beaver-creek, by two ſmall ſprings, was ſeen the ſcull of a child, that had been fixed on a pole by the Indians. The Tracts of 15 Indians were this day diſcovered. The camp No. 5 is ſeven miles one quarter and fifty ſeven perches from big Beaver-creek; the whole march of this day being about twelve miles.

SUNDAY 7th October, paſſing a high ridge, they had a fine proſpect of an extenſive country to the right, which in general appeared level, with abundance of tall timber. The camp No. 6 lies at the foot of a ſteep deſcent, in a rich valley, on a ſtrong ground, three ſides thereof ſurrounded by a hollow, and on the fourth ſide a ſmall hill, which was occupied by a detached guard. This day's march was ſix miles ſixty-five perches.

MONDAY 8th October, the army croſſed little Beaver-creek, and one of its branches. This creek is eight perches wide, with a good ford, the country about it interſperſed with hills, rivulets and rich valleys, like that deſcribed above. Camp No. 7 lies by a ſmall run on the ſide of a hill, commanding the ground about it, and is diſtant eleven miles one quarter and forty nine perches from the laſt encampment.

TUESDAY October 9th. In this day's march, the path divided into two branches, that to the southwest leading to the lower towns upon the Muskingam. In the forks of the path stand several trees painted by the Indians, in a hieroglyphic manner, denoting the number of wars in which they have been engaged, and the particulars of their success in prisoners and scalps. The camp No. 8. lies on a run, and level piece of ground, with Yellow-creek close on the left, and a rising ground near the rear of the right face. The path after the army left the forks was so brushy and entangled, that they were obliged to cut all the way before them, and also to lay several bridges, in order to make it passable for the horses; so that this day they proceeded only five miles, three quarters and seventy perches.

WEDNESDAY 10th. Marched one mile with Yellow-creek on the left at a small distance all the way, and crossed it at a good ford fifty feet wide; proceeding through an alternate succession of small hills and rich vales, finely watered with rivulets, to camp No. 9. seven miles and sixty perches in the whole.

THURSDAY 11th. Crossed a branch of Muskingam river about fifty feet wide, the country much the same as that described above, discovering a good deal of free stone. The camp No. 10. had this branch of the river parallel to its left face, and lies ten miles one quarter and forty perches from the former encampment.

FRIDAY 12th. Keeping the aforesaid creek on their left, they marched through much fine land, watered with small rivers and springs; proceeding likewise through several savannahs or cleared spots, which are by nature extremely beautiful; the second which they passed being, in particular, one

one continued plain of near two miles, with a fine riſing ground forming a ſemicircle round the right hand ſide, and a pleaſant ſtream of water at about a quarter of a mile diſtant on the left. The camp No. 11. has the abovementioned branch of Muſkingam on the left, and is diſtant ten miles and three quarters from the laſt encampment.

SATURDAY 13th. Croſſed Nemenſhehelas creek, about fifty feet wide, a little above where it empties itſelf into the aforeſaid branch of Muſkingam, having in their way a pleaſant proſpect over a large plain, for near two miles on the left. A little further, they came to another ſmall river which they croſſed about fifty perches above where it empties into the ſaid branch of Muſkingam. Here a high ridge on the right, and the creek cloſe on the left, form a narrow defile about ſeventy perches long. Paſſing afterwards over a very rich bottom, they came to the main branch of Muſkingam, about ſeventy yards wide, with a good ford. A little below and above the forks of this river is Tuſcarowas, a place exceedingly beautiful by ſituation, the lands rich on both ſides of the river; the country on the north-weſt ſide being an entire level plain, upwards of five miles in circumference. From the ruined houſes appearing here, the Indians who inhabited the place and are now with the Delawares, are ſuppoſed to have had about one hundred and fifty warriors. This camp No. 12. is diſtant eight miles nineteen perches from the former.

SUNDAY 14th. The army remained in camp; and two men who had been diſpatched by Colonel Bouquet from Fort-Pitt, with letters for Colonel Bradſtreet, returned and reported? — " That, within a few miles of this place, they

" had

" had been made prisoners by the Delawares, " and carried to one of their towns sixteen miles " from hence, where they were kept, till the " savages, knowing of the arrival of the army " here, set them at liberty, ordering them to " acquaint the Colonel that the head men of the " Delawares and Shawanese were coming as soon " as possible to treat of peace with them."

MONDAY 15th. The army moved two miles forty perches further down the Muskingam to camp No. 13, situated on a very high bank, with the river at the foot of it, which is upwards of 100 yards wide at this place, with a fine level country at some distance from its banks, producing stately timber, free from underwood, and plenty of food for cattle.

THE day following, six Indians came to inform the Colonel that all their chiefs were assembled about eight miles from the camp, and were ready to treat with him of peace, which they were earnestly desirous of obtaining. He returned for answer that he would meet them the next day in a bower at some distance from the camp. In the mean time, he ordered a small stockaded fort to be built to deposite provisions for the use of the troops on their return; and to lighten the convoy.

As several large bodies of Indians were now within a few miles of the camp, whose former instances of treachery, although they now declared they came for peace, made it prudent to trust nothing to their intentions, the strictest orders were repeated to prevent a surprise.

WEDNESDAY 17th. The Colonel, with most of the regular troops, Virginia volunteers and light horse, marched from the camp to the bower erected for the congress. And soon after the

the troops were ſtationed, ſo as to appear to the beſt advantage, the Indians arrived, and were conducted to the bower. Being ſeated, they began, in a ſhort time, to ſmoak their pipe or calumet, agreeable to their cuſtom. This ceremony being over, their ſpeakers laid down their pipes, and opened their pouches, wherein were their ſtrings and belts of wampum. The Indians preſent were,

SENECAS.	DELAWARES.	SHAWANESE.
Kiyaſhuta, chief with 15 warriors.	Cuſtalogo, chief of the Wolfe-tribe, Beaver, chief of the Turky-tribe, with 20 warriors.	Keiſſinautchtha, a chief, and 6 warriors.

Kiyaſhuta, Turtle Heart, Cuſtaloga and Beaver, were the ſpeakers.

THE general ſubſtance of what they had to offer, conſiſted in excuſes for their late treachery and miſconduct, throwing the blame on the raſhneſs of their young men and the nations living to the weſtward of them, ſuing for peace in the moſt abject manner, and promiſing ſeverally to deliver up all their priſoners. After they had concluded, the Colonel promiſed to give them an anſwer the next day, and then diſmiſſed them, the army returning to the camp.—The badneſs of the weather, however, prevented his meeting them again till the 20th, when he ſpoke to them in ſubſtance as follows, viz.

" THAT their pretences to palliate their guilt
" by throwing the blame on the weſtern nations,
" and the raſhneſs of their young men, were
" weak and frivolous, as it was in our power to
" have

" have protected them against all these nations, " if they had solicited our assistance, and that " it was their own duty to have chastised their " young men when they did wrong, and not " to suffer themselves to be directed by them."

He recapitulated to them many instances of their former perfidy—" their killing or captivat-" ing the traders who had been sent among them " at their own request, and plundering their ef-" fects; — their attacking Fort-Pitt, which had " been built with their express consent; their " murdering four men that had been sent on a " public message to them, thereby violating the " customs held sacred among all nations, how-" ever barbarous; ——their attacking the King's " troops last year in the woods, and after being " defeated in that attempt, falling upon our fron-" tiers, where they had continued to murder " our people to this day, &c."—

He told them how treacherously they had violated even their late engagements with Colonel Bradstreet, to whom they had promised to deliver up their prisoners by the 10th of September last, and to recall all their warriors from the frontiers, which they had been so far from complying with, that the prisoners still remained in their custody, and some of their people were even now continuing their depredations; adding, that these things which, he had mentioned, were only " a small " part of their numberless murders and breaches " of faith; and that their conduct had always " been equally perfidious.——You have, said he, " promised at every former treaty, as you do " now, that you would deliver up all your pri-" soners, and have received every time, on that " account, considerable presents, but have never " complied with that or any other engagement.

" I am

" I am now to tell you, therefore, that we will " be no longer impoſed upon by your promiſes. " This army ſhall not leave your country till " you have fully complied with every condition " that is to precede my treaty with you.

" I HAVE brought with me the relations of " the people you have maſſacred, or taken pri- " ſoners. They are impatient for revenge; and " it is with great difficulty that I can protect you " againſt their juſt reſentment, which is only " reſtrained by the aſſurances given them, that " no peace ſhall ever be concluded till you have " given us full ſatisfaction."—

" YOUR former allies, the Ottawas, Chip- " was, Wyandots, and others, have made their " peace with us. The Six Nations have joined " us againſt you. We now ſurround you, hav- " ing poſſeſſion of all the waters of the Ohio, " the Miſſiſippi, the Miamis, and the lakes. " All the French living in thoſe parts are now " ſubjects to the king of Great-Britain, and dare " no longer aſſiſt you. It is therefore in our " power totally to extirpate you from being a " people——But the Engliſh are a merciful and " generous nation, averſe to ſhed the blood, even " of their moſt cruel enemies; and if it was " poſſible that you could convince us, that you " ſincerely repent of your paſt perfidy, and that " we could depend on your good behaviour for " the future, you might yet hope for mercy and " peace——If I find that you faithfully execute " the following preliminary conditions, I will " not treat you with the ſeverity you deſerve.

" I GIVE you twelve days from this date to " deliver into my hands at Wakatamake all the " priſoners in your poſſeſſion, without any ex- " ception; Engliſhmen, Frenchmen, women

" and

" and children; whether adopted in your tribe, " married, or living amongſt you under any de- " nomination and pretence whatſoever, together " with all negroes. And you are to furniſh the " ſaid priſoners with cloathing, proviſions, and " horſes, to carry them to Fort Pitt.

" When you have fully complied with theſe " conditions, you ſhall then know on what terms " you may obtain the peace you ſue for."—

This ſpeech made an impreſſion on the minds of the ſavages, which, it is hoped, will not ſoon be eradicated. The firm and determined ſpirit with which the Colonel delivered himſelf, their conſciouſneſs of the aggravated injuries they had done us, and the view of the ſame commander and army that had ſo ſeverely chaſtiſed them at Buſhy-Run the preceding year, now advanced into the very heart of their remote ſettlements, after penetrating through wilderneſſes which they had deemed impaſſable by regular troops——all theſe things contributed to bend the haughty temper of the ſavages to the loweſt degree of abaſement; ſo that even their ſpeeches ſeem to exhibit but few ſpecimens of that ſtrong and ferocious eloquence, which their inflexible ſpirit of independency has on former occaſions inſpired. And though it is not to be doubted, if an opportunity had offered, but they would have fallen upon our army with their uſual fierceneſs, yet when they ſaw the vigilance and ſpirit of our troops were ſuch, that they could neither be attacked nor ſurprized with any proſpect of ſucceſs, their ſpirits ſeemed to revolt from the one extreme of inſolent boldneſs, to the other of abject timidity. And happy will it be for them and for us, if the inſtances of our humanity and mercy, which they experienced in that critical ſituation, ſhall

ſhall make as laſting impreſſions on their ſavage diſpoſitions, as it is believed the inſtances of our bravery and power have done; ſo that they may come to unite, with their fear of the latter, a love of the former; and have their minds gradually opened, by ſuch examples, to the mild dictates of peace and civility.

THE reader, it is to be hoped, will readily excuſe this digreſſion, if it ſhould be thought one. I now reſume our narrative. The two Delaware chiefs, at the cloſe of their ſpeech on the 17th, delivered eighteen white priſoners, and eighty-three ſmall ſticks, expreſſing the number of other priſoners which they had in their poſſeſſion, and promiſed to bring in as ſoon as poſſible. None of the Shawaneſe Kings appeared at the congreſs, and Keiſſinautchtha their deputy declined ſpeaking until the Colonel had anſwered the Delawares, and then with a dejected ſullenneſs he promiſed, in behalf of his nation, that they would ſubmit to the terms preſcribed to the other tribes.

THE Colonel, however, determined to march farther into their country, knowing that the preſence of his army would be the beſt ſecurity for the performance of their promiſes; and required ſome of each nation to attend him in his march.

KIYASHUTA addreſſed the ſeveral nations, before their departure, "deſiring them to be "ſtrong in complying with their engagements, "that they might wipe away the reproach of "their former breach of faith, and convince "their brothers the Engliſh that they could "ſpeak the truth; adding that he would con-"duct the army to the place appointed for re-"ceiving the priſoners."

MONDAY October 22d. The army attended by the Indian deputies, marched nine miles to camp

camp No. 14. crossing Margaret's creek about fifty feet wide——The day following, they proceeded sixteen miles one quarter and seventy seven perches farther to camp No. 15. and halted there one day.

THURSDAY 25th. They marched six miles, one half and sixteen perches to camp No. 16. situated within a mile of the Forks of Muskingam; and this place was fixed upon instead of Wakautamike, as the most central and convenient place to receive the prisoners; for the principal Indian towns now lay round them, distant from seven to twenty miles; excepting only the lower Shawanese town situated on Scioto river, which was about eighty miles; so that from this place the army had it in their power to awe all the enemy's settlements and destroy their towns, if they should not punctually fulfil the engagements they had entered into.——Four redoubts were built here opposite to the four angles of the camp; the ground in the front was cleared, a store-house for the provisions erected, and likewise a house to receive, and treat of peace with, the Indians, when they should return. Three houses with separate apartments were also raised for the reception of the captives of the respective provinces, and proper officers appointed to take charge of them, with a matron to attend the women and children; so that with the officers mess houses, ovens, &c. this camp had the appearance of a little town in which the greatest order and regularity were observed.

ON Saturday 27th. A messenger arrived from king Custaloga, informing that he was on his way with his prisoners, and also a messenger from the lower Shawanese towns of the like import. The Colonel however, having no reason to suspect the

the latter nation of backwardneſs, ſent one of their own people, deſiring them—" to be punc-" tual as to the time fixed; to provide a ſufficient " quantity of proviſions to ſubſiſt the priſoners; " to bring the letters wrote to him laſt winter by " the French commandant at Fort Charters, " which ſome of their people had ſtopped ever " ſince;" adding that, " as their nation had ex-" preſſed ſome uneaſineſs at our not ſhaking " hands with them, they were to know that " the Engliſh never took their enemies by the " hand, before peace was finally concluded."

THE day following, the Shawaneſe meſſenger returned, ſaying that when he had proceeded as far as Wakautamike, the chief of that town undertook to proceed with the meſſage himſelf, and deſired the other to return and acquaint the Engliſh that all his priſoners were ready, and he was going to the lower towns to haſten theirs.

OCTOBER 28th. Peter the Caughnawaga chief, and twenty Indians of that nation arrived from Sanduſki, with a letter from Colonel Bradſtreet, in anſwer to one which Colonel Bouquet had ſent to him from Fort-Pitt, by two of the Indians who firſt ſpoke to him in favour of the Shawaneſe, as hath been already mentioned. The ſubſtance of Colonel Bradſtreet's letter was " that he had ſet-" tled nothing with the Shawaneſe and Dela-" wares, nor received any priſoners from them. " —That he had acquainted all the Indian nati-" ons, as far as the Ilinois, the bay, &c. with " the inſtructions he had received from General " Gage, reſpecting the peace he had lately made; " that he had been in Sanduſki-lake and up the " river, as far as navigable for Indian canoes, " for near a month; but that he found it im-" poſſible to ſtay longer in theſe parts; abſolute

" neceſſity

"necessity obliging him to turn off the other "way," &c.

COLONEL BRADSTREET, without doubt, did all which circumstances would permit, in his department; but his not being able to remain at Sanduski agreeable to the original plan, till matters were finally settled with the Ohio Indians, would have been an unfavourable incident, if Colonel Bouquet had not now had the chiefs of sundry tribes with him, and was so far advanced into the Indian country, that they thought it adviseable to submit to the conditions imposed upon them.

THE Caughnawagas reported that the Indians on the lakes had delivered but few of their prisoners; that the Ottawas had killed a great part of theirs, and the other nations had either done the same, or else kept them.

FROM this time to November 9th, was chiefly spent in sending and receiving messages to and from the Indian towns, relative to the prisoners, who were now coming into the camp one day after another in small parties, as the different nations arrived in whose possession they had been. The Colonel kept so stedfastly to this article of having every prisoner delivered, that when the Delaware kings, Beaver and Custaloga, had brought in all theirs except twelve, which they promised to bring in a few days, he refused to shake hands or have the least talk with them, while a single captive remained among them.

By

By the 9th of November, most of the prisoners were arrived that could be expected this season, amounting to 206 * in the whole; besides about 100 more in possession of the Shawanese, which they promised to deliver the following spring. Mr. Smallman, formerly a major in the Pennsylvania troops, who had been taken last summer near Detroit by the Wyandots, and delivered to the Shawanese, was among the number of those whom they now brought in, and informed the Colonel that the reason of their not bringing the remainder of their prisoners, was that many of their principal men, to whom they belonged, were gone to trade with the French, and would not return for six weeks; but that every one of their nation who were at home, had either brought or sent theirs. He further said that, on the army's first coming into the country, it had been reported among the Shawanese that our intention was to destroy them all, on which they had resolved to kill their prisoners and fight us; that a French trader who was with them, and had many barrels of powder and ball, made them a present of the whole, as soon as they had come to this resolution; but that, happily for the poor captives, just as the Shawanese were preparing to execute this tragedy, they received the Colonel's message, informing them that his intentions were only to receive the prisoners and to make peace with them on the same terms he should give to the Delawares.

* Virginians	Males,	32
	Females and Children,	58
Pennsylvanians,	Males,	49
	Females and Children,	67
	In all	206

On

On this intelligence they suspended their cruel purpose, and began to collect as many of the prisoners as they had power to deliver; but hearing immediately afterwards that one of our soldiers had been killed near the camp at Muskingham, and that some of their nation were suspected as guilty of the murder, they again imagined they would fall under our resentment, and therefore determined once more to stand out against us. For which purpose, after having brought their prisoners as far as Wakautamike, where they heard this news, they collected them all into a field, and were going to kill them, when a second express providentially arrived from Colonel Bouquet, who assured them that their nation was not even suspected of having any concern in the aforesaid murder; upon which they proceeded to the camp to deliver up the captives, who had thus twice so narrowly escaped becoming the victims of their barbarity.

On Friday, November 9th, the Colonel, attended by most of the principal officers, went to the conference-house. The Senecas and Delawares were first treated with. Kiyashuta and ten warriors represented the former. Custaloga and twenty warriors the latter.

Kiyashuta spoke—"With this string of "wampum, we wipe the tears from your eyes "—we deliver you these three prisoners, which "are the last of your flesh and blood that remained among the Senecas and Custaloga's tribe of "Delawares, we gather together and bury with "this belt † all the bones of the people that have "been killed during this unhappy war, which

† A belt or string is always delivered when thus mentioned.

"the

" the Evil Spirit occaſioned among us. We co-" ver the bones that have been buried, that they " may be never more remembered— We again " cover their place with leaves that it may be no " more ſeen.—As we have been long aſtray, and " the path between you and us ſtopped, we ex-" tend this belt that it may be again cleared, and " we may travel in peace to ſee our brethren as " our anceſtors formerly did. While you hold " it faſt by one end, and we by the other, we " ſhall always be able to diſcover any thing that " may diſturb our friendſhip."—

THE Colonel anſwered that " he had heard " them with pleaſure; that he received theſe " three laſt priſoners they had to deliver, and " joined in burying the bones of thoſe who had " fallen in the war, ſo that their place might be " no more known. The peace you aſk for, you " ſhall now have. The king, my maſter and " your father, has appointed me only to make " war; but he has other ſervants who are em-" ployed in the work of peace. Sir William " Johnſon is empowered for that purpoſe. To " him you are to apply; but before I give you " leave to go, two things are to be ſettled.

1 " As peace cannot be finally concluded here, " you will deliver me two hoſtages for the Sene-" cas, and two for Cuſtaloga's tribe, to remain " in our hands at Fort Pitt, as a ſecurity, that " you ſhall commit no further hoſtilities or vio-" lence againſt any of his majeſty's ſubjects; and " when the peace is concluded theſe hoſtages " ſhall be delivered ſafe back to you.

2. " THE deputies you are to ſend to Sir " William Johnſon, muſt be fully empowered " to treat for your tribes, and you ſhall engage " to abide by whatever they ſtipulate. In that

" treaty

" treaty, every thing concerning trade and other
" matters will be ſettled by Sir William, to ren-
" der the peace everlaſting; and the deputies
" you are to ſend to him, as well as the hoſtages
" to be delivered to me, are to be named and
" preſented to me for my approbation."——

THE Colonel, after promiſing to deliver back two of their people, Capt. Pipe, and Capt. John, whom he had detained at Fort Pitt, took the chiefs by the hand for the firſt time, which gave them great joy.

THE next conference was on November 10th, with the Turkey and Turtle tribes of Delawares, King Beaver their chief and thirty warriors repreſenting the former; and Kelappama brother to their chief * with twenty-five warriors the latter. The Senecas and Cuſtaloga's tribe of Delawares were alſo preſent. Their ſpeech and the anſwer given, were much the ſame as above; excepting that the Colonel inſiſted on their delivering up an Engliſhman, who had murdered one of our people on the frontiers and brought the ſcalp to them; and they ſhould appoint the ſame number of deputies and deliver the ſame number of hoſtages, for each of their tribes, as had been ſtipulated for Cuſtaloga's tribe.

NOVEMBER 11. King Beaver preſented ſix hoſtages to remain with Col. Bouquet, and five deputies to treat with Sir William Johnſon, who were approved of. This day he acquainted the chiefs preſent that as he had great reaſon to be diſſatisfied with the conduct of Nettowhatways, the chief of the Turtle tribe who had not appeared, he therefore depoſed him; and that tribe were to

* The Chief of the Turtle tribe, for ſome reaſon, choſe to abſent himſelf.

chuſe

chuſe and preſent another for his approbation. This they did a few days afterwards—Smile not, reader, at this tranſaction; for though it may not be attended with ſo many ſplendid and flattering circumſtances to a commander, as the depoſing an Eaſt Indian Nabob or chief; yet to penetrate into the wilderneſſes where thoſe ſtern Weſt Indian Chieftains hold their ſway, and to frown them from their throne, though but compoſed of the unhewn log, will be found to require both reſolution and firmneſs; and their ſubmitting to it clearly ſhews to what degree of humiliation they were reduced.

BUT to proceed. The Shawaneſe ſtill remained to be treated with, and though this nation ſaw themſelves under the neceſſity of yielding to the ſame conditions with the other tribes, yet there had appeared a dilatorineſs and ſullen haughtineſs in all their conduct, which rendered it very ſuſpicious.

THE 12th of November was appointed for the conference with them; which was managed on their part by Keiſſinautchtha and Nimwha their chiefs, with the Red Hawke, Laviſſimo, Benſivaſica, Eweecunwee, Keigleighque, and forty warriors; the Caughnawaga, Seneca and Delaware chiefs, with about ſixty warriors, being alſo preſent.

THE Red Hawke was their ſpeaker, and as he delivered himſelf with a ſtrange mixture of fierce pride, and humble ſubmiſſion, I ſhall add a paſſage or two from his ſpeech.

"BROTHER,

"YOU will liſten to us your younger bro-
"thers; and as we diſcover ſomething in your
"eyes that looks diſſatisfaction with us, we now

 "wipe

" wipe away every thing bad between us that
" you may clearly ſee—You have heard many
" bad ſtories of us—We clean your ears that you
" may hear—We remove every thing bad from
" your heart, that it may be like the heart of
" your anceſtors, when they thought of nothing
" but good." [Here he gave a ſtring.]

" BROTHER; when we ſaw you coming this
" road, you advanced towards us with a toma-
" hawk in your hand; but we your younger bro-
" thers take it out of your hands and throw it up
" to God † to diſpoſe of as he pleaſes; by which
" means we hope never to ſee it more. And
" now, brother, we beg leave that you who are
" a warrior, will take hold of this chain (giving
" a ſtring) of friendſhip, and receive it from us,
" who are alſo warriors, and let us think no
" more of war, in pity to our old men, wo-
" men and children."—Intimating, by this laſt expreſſion, that it was mere compaſſion to them, and not inability to fight, that made their nation deſire peace.

HE then produced a treaty held with the government of Pennſylvania 1701, and three meſſages or letters from that government of different dates; and concluded thus—

" Now, Brother, I beg WE who are war-
" riors may forget our diſputes, and renew the
" friendſhip which appears by theſe papers to

† Their uſual figure for making peace is burying the hatchet; but as ſuch hatchets may be dug up again, perhaps he thought this new expreſſion of " ſending it up to God, or the Good Spirit," a much ſtronger emblem of the permanency and ſtedfaſtneſs of the peace now to be made.

" have

"have ſubſiſted between our fathers."—He promiſed, in behalf of the reſt of their nation, who were gone to a great diſtance to hunt, and could not have notice to attend the treaty, that they ſhould certainly come to Fort-Pitt in the ſpring, and bring the remainder of the priſoners with them.

As the ſeaſon was far advanced, and the Colonel could not ſtay long in theſe remote parts, he was obliged to reſt ſatisfied with the priſoners the Shawaneſe had brought; taking hoſtages, and laying them under the ſtrongeſt obligations, for the delivery of the reſt; knowing that no other effectual method could at preſent be purſued.

He expoſtulated with them on account of their paſt conduct, and told them—"that the ſpeech "they had delivered would have been agreeable "to him, if their actions had correſponded with "their words. You have ſpoken, ſaid he, much "of peace, but have neglected to comply with "the only condition, upon which you can ob-"tain it. Keiſſinautchtha, one of your chiefs, "met me a month ago at Tuſcarawas, and ac-"cepted the ſame terms of peace for your nation, "that were preſcribed to the Senecas and Dela-"wares; promiſing in ten days from that time "to meet me here with all your priſoners—After "waiting for you till now, you are come at laſt, "only with a part of them, and propoſe putting "off the delivery of the reſt till the ſpring.—"What right have you to expect different terms "from thoſe granted to the Delawares, &c. "who have given me entire ſatisfaction by their "ready ſubmiſſion to every thing required of "them?——But I will cut this matter ſhort "with you; and before I explain myſelf further,

 "I inſiſt

" I insist on your immediate answer to the fol-
" lowing questions—

1st. " Will you forthwith collect and deliver " up all the prisoners yet in your possession, and " the French living among you, with all the " Negroes you have taken from us in this or any " other war; and that without any exception or " evasion whatsoever?"

2d. " WILL you deliver six hostages into my " hands as a security for your punctual perfor- " mance of the above article, and that your nati- " ons shall commit no farther hostilities against " the persons or property of his majesty's sub- " jects?"

BENEVISSICO replied that " they agreed to " give the hostages required, and said that he " himself would immediately return to their " lower towns and collect all our flesh and blood " that remained among them, and that we should " see them at Fort-Pitt † as soon as possible.— " That, as to the French, they had no power " over them. They were subjects to the king " of England. We might do with them what " we pleased; though he believed they were " all returned before this time to their own coun- " try."—

THEY then delivered their hostages, and the Colonel told them " that though he had brought " a Tomahawk in his hand, yet as they had now " submitted, he would not let it fall on their " heads, but let it drop to the ground, no more " to be seen. He exhorted them to exercise " kindness to the captives, and look upon them

† It will appear, by the postscript to this account, that the Shawanese have fulfilled this engagement.

" now

"now as brothers and no longer prisoners; adding, that he intended to send some of their relations along with the Indians, to see their friends collected and brought to Fort-Pitt. He promised to give them letters to Sir William Johnson, to facilitate a final peace, and desired them to be strong in performing every thing stipulated."

The Caughnawagas, the Delawares and Senecas, severally addressed the Shawanese, as grandchildren and nephews, "to perform their promises, and to be strong in doing good, that this peace might be everlasting."—

And here I am to enter on a scene, reserved on purpose for this place, that the thread of the foregoing narrative might not be interrupted—— a scene, which language indeed can but weakly describe; and to which the Poet or Painter might have repaired to enrich their highest colours of the variety of human passions; the Philosopher to find ample subject for his most serious reflections; and the Man to exercise all the tender and sympathetic feelings of the soul.

The scene I mean, was the arrival of the prisoners in the camp; where were to be seen fathers and mothers recognizing and clasping their once-lost babes; husbands hanging round the necks of their newly-recovered wives; sisters and brothers unexpectedly meeting together after long separation, scarce able to speak the same language, or, for some time, to be sure that they were children of the same parents! In all these interviews, joy and rapture inexpressible were seen, while feelings of a very different nature were painted in the looks of others;—flying from place to place in eager enquiries after relatives not found!

found! trembling to receive an anſwer to their queſtions! diſtracted with doubts, hopes and fears, on obtaining no account of thoſe they ſought for! or ſtiffened into living monuments of horror and woe, on learning their unhappy fate!

THE Indians too, as if wholly forgetting their uſual ſavageneſs, bore a capital part in heightening this moſt affecting ſcene. They delivered up their beloved captives with the utmoſt reluctance; ſhed torrents of tears over them, recommending them to the care and protection of the commanding officer. Their regard to them continued all the time they remained in camp. They viſited them from day to day; and brought them what corn, ſkins, horſes and other matters, they had beſtowed on them, while in their families; accompanied with other preſents, and all the marks of the moſt ſincere and tender affection. Nay, they did not ſtop here, but, when the army marched, ſome of the Indians ſolicited and obtained leave to accompany their former captives all the way to Fort-Pitt, and employed themſelves in hunting and bringing proviſions for them on the road. A young Mingo carried this ſtill further, and gave an inſtance of love which would make a figure even in romance. A young woman of Virginia was among the captives, to whom he had formed ſo ſtrong an attachment, as to call her his wife. Againſt all remonſtrances of the imminent danger to which he expoſed himſelf by approaching to the frontiers, he perſiſted in following her, at the riſk of being killed by the ſurviving relations of many unfortunate perſons, who had been captivated or ſcalped by thoſe of his nation.

THOSE

THOSE qualities in ſavages challenge our juſt eſteem. They ſhould make us charitably conſider their barbarities as the effects of wrong education, and falſe notions of bravery and heroiſm; while we ſhould look on their virtues as ſure marks that nature has made them fit ſubjects of cultivation as well as us; and that we are called by our ſuperior advantages to yield them all the helps we can in this way. Cruel and unmerciful as they are, by habit and long example, in war, yet whenever they come to give way to the native dictates of humanity, they exerciſe virtues which Chriſtians need not bluſh to imitate. When they once determine to give life, they give every thing with it, which, in their apprehenſion, belongs to it. From every enquiry that has been made, it appears—that no woman thus ſaved is preſerved from baſe motives, or need fear the violation of her honour. No child is otherwiſe treated by the perſons adopting it than the children of their own body. The perpetual ſlavery of thoſe captivated in war, is a notion which even their barbarity has not yet ſuggeſted to them. Every captive whom their affection, their caprice, or whatever elſe, leads them to ſave, is ſoon incorporated with them, and fares alike with themſelves.

THESE inſtances of Indian tenderneſs and humanity were thought worthy of particular notice. The like inſtances among our own people will not ſeem ſtrange; and therefore I ſhall only mention one, out of a multitude that might be given on this occaſion.

AMONG the captives, a woman was brought into the camp at Muſkingam, with a babe about three months old at her breaſt. One of the Virginia-volunteers soon knew her to be his wife, who had been taken by the Indians about six months before. She was immediately delivered to her over-joyed husband. He flew with her to his tent, and cloathed her and his child in proper apparel. But their joy, after the first transports, was soon damped by the reflection that another dear child of about two years old, captivated with the mother, and separated from her, was still missing, altho' many children had been brought in.

A FEW days afterwards, a number of other prisoners were brought to the camp, among whom were several more children. The woman was sent for, and one, supposed to be hers, was produced to her. At first sight she was uncertain, but viewing the child with great earnestness, she soon recollected its features; and was so overcome with joy, that literally forgetting her sucking child she dropt it from her arms, and catching up the new found child in an extasy, pressed it to her breast, and bursting into tears carried it off, unable to speak for joy. The father seizing up the babe she had let fall, followed her in no less transport and affection.

AMONG the children who had been carried off young, and had long lived with the Indians, it is not to be expected that any marks of joy would appear on being restored to their parents or relatives. Having been accustomed to look upon the Indians as the only connexions they had, having been tenderly treated by them, and speaking their language, it is no wonder that they considered their new state in the light of a captivity, and parted from the savages with tears.

BUT

BUT it muſt not be denied that there were even ſome grown perſons who ſhewed an unwillingneſs to return. The Shawaneſe were obliged to bind ſeveral of their priſoners and force them along to the camp; and ſome women, who had been delivered up, afterwards found means to eſcape and run back to the Indian towns. Some, who could not make their eſcape, clung to their ſavage acquaintance at parting, and continued many days in bitter lamentations, even refuſing ſuſtenance.

FOR the honour of humanity, we would ſuppoſe thoſe perſons to have been of the loweſt rank, either bred up in ignorance and diſtreſſing penury, or who had lived ſo long with the Indians as to forget all their former connections. For, eaſy and unconſtrained as the ſavage life is, certainly it could never be put in competition with the bleſſings of improved life and the light of religion, by any perſons who have had the happineſs of enjoying, and the capacity of diſcerning, them.

EVERY thing being now ſettled with the Indians, the army decamped on Sunday 18th November, and marched for Fort Pitt, where it arrived on the 28th. The regular troops were immediately ſent to garriſon the different poſts on the communication, and the provincial troops, with the captives, to their ſeveral provinces. Here ended this expedition, in which it is remarkable that, notwithſtanding the many difficulties attending it, the troops were never in want of any neceſſaries; continuing perfectly healthy during the whole campaign; in which no life was loſt, except the man mentioned to have been killed at Muſkingam.

IN the beginning of January 1765, Colonel Bouquet arrived at Philadelphia, receiving where-ever he came, every poſſible mark of gratitude and eſteem from the people in general; and particularly from the overjoyed relations of the captives, whom he had ſo happily, and without bloodſhed, reſtored to ther country and friends. Nor was the legiſlative part of the provinces leſs ſenſible of his important ſervices. The aſſembly of Pennſylvania, at their firſt ſitting, unanimouſly voted him the following addreſs.

In ASSEMBLY, January 15, 1765, A. M.

To the Honourable HENRY BOUQUET, Eſq;

Commander in Chief of His MAJESTY's Forces in the Southern Department of AMERICA,

The Addreſs of the Repreſentatives of the Freemen of the Province of Pennſylvania, in General Aſſembly met.

SIR,

'THE repreſentatives of the freemen of the 'province of Pennſylvania, in general aſ'ſembly met, being informed that you intend 'ſhortly to embark for England, and moved with 'a due ſenſe of the important ſervices you have 'rendered to his majeſty, his northern colonies 'in general, and to this province in particular, 'during our late wars with the French and bar'barous Indians, in the remarkable victory over 'the ſavage enemy, united to oppoſe you, near 'Buſhy-Run, in Auguſt 1763, when on your 'march for the relief of Pittſburgh, owing, un'der God, to your intrepidity and ſuperior ſkill 'in command, together with the bravery of your

'officers

'officers and little army; as alſo in your late 'march to the country of the ſavage nations, 'with the troops under your direction; thereby 'ſtriking terror through the numerous Indian 'tribes around you; laying a foundation for a 'laſting as well as honourable peace with them; 'and reſcuing, from ſavage captivity, upwards 'of two hundred of our chriſtian brethren, pri-'ſoners among them: theſe eminent ſervices, 'and your conſtant attention to the civil rights 'of his majeſty's ſubjects in this province, de-'mand, Sir, the grateful tribute of thanks from 'all good men; and therefore we, the repreſen-'tatives of the freemen of Pennſylvania, unani-'mouſly for ourſelves, and in behalf of all the 'people of this province, do return you our moſt 'ſincere and hearty thanks for theſe your great 'ſervices, wiſhing you a ſafe and pleaſant voy-'age to England, with a kind and gracious re-'ception from his majeſty.

'Signed, by order of the Houſe,

'JOSEPH FOX, SPEAKER.

The

The Colonel's Anſwer was as follows, viz.

To the honourable the REPRESENTATIVES of the FREEMEN of the province of Pennſylvania, in General Aſſembly met.

'GENTLEMEN,

'WITH a heart impreſſed with the moſt 'lively ſenſe of gratitude, I return you 'my humble and ſincere thanks, for the honour 'you have done me in your polite addreſs of the '15th of January, tranſmitted me to New-York 'by your ſpeaker.

'NEXT to the approbation of His Sacred Ma-'jeſty, and my ſuperiour officers, nothing could 'afford me higher pleaſure than your favourable 'opinion of my conduct, in the diſcharge of thoſe 'military commands with which I have been in-'truſted.

'GRATITUDE as well as juſtice demand of 'me to acknowledge, that the aids granted by 'the legiſlature of this province, and the con-'ſtant aſſiſtance and ſupport afforded me by the 'honourable the Governor and Commiſſioners in 'the late expedition, have enabled me to recover 'ſo many of his Majeſty's ſubjects from a cruel 'captivity, and be the happy inſtrument of re-'ſtoring them to freedom and liberty: To you 'therefore, gentlemen, is the greater ſhare of that 'merit due, which you are generouſly pleaſed 'on this occaſion to impute to my ſervices.

'YOUR

'Your kind testimony of my constant attention to the civil rights of his majesty's subjects in this Province, does me singular honour, and calls for the return of my warmest acknowledgments.

'Permit me to take this public opportunity of doing justice to the officers of the regular and provincial troops, and the volunteers, who have served with me, by declaring that, under Divine Providence, the repeated successes of his Majesty's arms against a savage enemy, are principally to be ascribed to their courage and resolution, and to their perseverance under the severest hardships and fatigue.

'I sincerely wish prosperity and happiness to the province, and have the honour to be, with the greatest respect, Gentlemen,

'Your most obedient, and most humble servant,

'HENRY BOUQUET.'

February 4, 1765.

Soon afterwards the Colonel received a very polite and affectionate letter from Governor Fauquier, dated 25th of December, inclosing resolves of the honourable members of his Majesty's Council, and of the house of Burgesses, for the colony and dominion of Virginia.

Those

THOSE reſpectable bodies unanimouſly returned their thanks to him for the activity, ſpirit and zeal, with which he had reduced the Indians to terms of peace, and compelled thoſe ſavages to deliver up ſo many of his Majeſty's ſubjects whom they had in captivity. They further requeſted the Governor to recommend him to his Majeſty's miniſters, as an officer of diſtinguiſhed merit, in this and every former ſervice in which he had been engaged.

THE Colonel, in his anſwer, acknowledged the ready aſſiſtance and countenance which he had always received from the Governor and colony of Virginia in carrying on the King's ſervice; and mentioned his particular obligations to Col. LEWIS, for his zeal and good conduct during the campaign.

THE honours thus beſtowed on him, his own modeſty made him deſirous of transferring to the officers and army under his command; and indeed the mutual confidence and harmony ſubſiſting between him and them, highly redound to the reputation of both. He has taken every occaſion of doing juſtice to the particular merit of Colonel REID who was ſecond in command; and alſo to all the officers who ſerved in the expedition, regulars as well as provincials †.

THE reader will obſerve that the public bodies who preſented theſe addreſſes to the Colonel, not only wiſhed to expreſs their own gratitude, but likewiſe to be inſtrumental in recommending him to the advancement his ſervices merited. And

† The Pennſylvania troops were commanded by Lieutenant Colonel Francis, and Lientenant Colonel Clayton.

ſurely

ſurely it is a happy circumſtance to obtain promotion, not only unenvied, but even with the general approbation and good wiſhes of the public. It ought, however, to be mentioned, that on the firſt account his Majeſty received of this expedition, and long before thoſe teſtimonies could reach England, he was graciouſly pleaſed of his own royal goodneſs and as a reward of the Colonel's merit, to promote him to the rank of BRIGADIER GENERAL, and to the command of the ſouthern diſtrict of America. And as he is rendered as dear, by his private virtues, to thoſe who have the honour of his more intimate acquaintance, as he is by his military ſervices to the public, it is hoped he may long continue among us; where his experienced abilities will enable him, and his love of the Engliſh conſtitution entitle him, to fill any future truſt to which his Majeſty may be pleaſed to call him.——

POST-

POSTSCRIPT.

IT was mentioned in the 31st page of this account, that the Shawanese brought only a part of their prisoners with them to Col. Bouquet at Muskingam, in November last; and that, as the season was far advanced, he was obliged to rest satisfied with taking hostages for the delivery of the remainder at Fort-Pitt, in the ensuing spring.

THE escape of those hostages soon afterwards, as well as the former equivocal conduct of their nation, had given reason to doubt the sincerity of their intentions with respect to the performance of their promises. But we have the satisfaction to find that they punctually have fulfilled them. Ten of their chiefs, and about fifty of their warriors, attended with many of their women and children, met GEORGE CROGHAN, Esq; deputy agent to Sir WILLIAM JOHNSON, at Fort-Pitt, the 9th of last May; together with a large body of Delawares, Senecas, Sandusky and Munsy Indians; where they delivered the remainder of their prisoners, brightened the chain of friendship, and gave every assurance of their firm intentions to preserve the peace inviolable for ever.

THERE

There is ſomething remarkable in the appellation they gave to the Engliſh on this occaſion; calling them Fathers inſtead of Brethren.

Lawaughqua, the Shawaneſe ſpeaker, delivered himſelf in the following terms.——

" Fathers, for ſo we will call you hence-
" forward; liſten to what we are going to ſay
" to you.

" It gave us great pleaſure yeſterday to be
" called the children of the great King of Eng-
" land; and convinces us your intentions to-
" wards us are upright, as we know a Father
" will be tender of his children, and they are
" more ready to obey him than a Brother. There-
" fore we hope our Father will now take better
" care of his children, than has heretofore been
" done.——

" You put us in mind of our promiſe to Col.
" Bouquet; which was to bring your fleſh and
" blood to be delivered at this place. Father,
" you have not ſpoke in vain—you ſee we have
" brought them with us, — except a few that
" were out with our hunting parties, which will
" be brought here as ſoon as they return.

" They have been all united to us by adop-
" tion; and altho' we now deliver them up to
" you, we will always look upon them as our
" relations, whenever the Great Spirit is pleaſed
" that we may viſit them.

" Father, We have taken as much care of
" them, as if they were our own fleſh and blood.
" They are now become unacquainted with your
" cuſtoms and manners; and therefore, we re-
" queſt you will uſe them tenderly and kindly,
" which will induce them to live contentedly
" with you.

" Here

"HERE is a belt with the figure of our Father the King of Great-Britain at one end, and the Chief of our nation at the other. It represents them holding the chain of friendſhip; and we hope neither ſide will ſlip their hands from it, ſo long as the Sun and Moon give light."

THE reader will further remember that one of the engagements which the different Indian Tribes entered into with Colonel Bouquet, was to ſend deputies to conclude a peace with Sir WILLIAM JOHNSON. This has alſo been punctually fulfilled; and we are aſſured that Sir WILLIAM "has finiſhed his congreſs greatly to his ſatisfaction, and even beyond his expectations." Thus every good conſequence has enſued from this important expedition, which our fondeſt wiſhes could have induced us to expect from the known valour and ſpirit of the able commander who had the conduct of it; and we now have the pleaſure once more to behold the temple of JANUS ſhut, in this weſtern world!

REFLECTIONS

ON THE

WAR WITH THE SAVAGES

OF

NORTH-AMERICA.

THE long continued ravages of the Indians on the frontiers of the British colonies in America, and the fatal overthrows which they have sometimes given our best disciplined troops, especially in the beginning of the late war, have rendered them an object of our consideration, even in their military capacity. And as but few officers, who may be employed against them, can have opportunities to observe the true causes of their advantages over European troops in the woods, it is with the utmost pleasure that I now proceed

proceed to lay before the public the following valuable papers, which I mentioned † to have been communicated to me by an officer of great abilities and long experience, in our wars with the Indians.

As ſcarce any thing has yet been publiſhed on a ſubject now become of the higheſt importance § to our colonies, theſe papers will undoubtedly be an acceptable preſent to the reader, and the remarks contained in them may be more and more improved by the future care and attention of able men, till perhaps a compleat ſyſtem is at length formed for the conduct of this particular ſpecies of war.

SECTION I.

OF THE TEMPER AND GENIUS OF THE INDIANS.

THE love of liberty is innate in the ſavage; and ſeems the ruling paſſion of the ſtate of nature. His deſires and wants, being few, are eaſily gratified, and leave him much time to ſpare, which he would ſpend in idleneſs, if hunger did not force him to hunt. That exerciſe makes him ſtrong, active and bold, raiſes his courage, and fits him for war, in which he uſes the ſame ſtratagems and cruelty as againſt the wild beaſts; making

† See the introduction.

§ It will appear by the account of Indian tribes and towns annexed to theſe papers, that the enemies we have to deal with are neither contemptible in numbers or ſtrength.

no

no scruple to employ treachery and perfidy to vanquish his enemy.

JEALOUS of his independency and of his property, he will not suffer the least encroachment on either; and upon the slightest suspicion, fired with resentment, he becomes an implacable enemy, and flies to arms to vindicate his right, or revenge an injury.

THE advantages of these savages over civilized nations are both natural and acquired. They are tall and well limbed, remarkable for their activity, and have a piercing eye and quick ear, which are of great service to them in the woods.

LIKE beasts of prey, they are patient, and deceitful, and rendered by habit almost insensible to the common feelings of humanity. Their barbarous custom of scalping their enemies, in the heat of action; the exquisite torments often inflicted by them on those reserved for a more deliberate fate; their general ferocity of manners, and the successes wherewith they have often been flushed, have conspired to render their name terrible, and some times to strike a pannic even into our bravest and best disciplined troops.

THEIR acquired advantages are, that they have been inured to bear the extremes of heat and cold; and from their infancy, in winter and summer, to plunge themselves in cold streams, and to go almost naked, exposed to the scorching sun or nipping frosts, till they arrive to the state of manhood. Some of them destroy the sensation of the skin by scratching it with the short and sharp teeth of some animal, disposed in the form of a curry-comb, which makes them regardless of briars and thorns in running thro' thickets. Rivers are no obstacles to them in their wild excursions.

ſions. They either ſwim over, or croſs them on rafts or canoes, of an eaſy and ready conſtruction.

In their expeditions they live chiefly by hunting, or on wild fruits and roots with which the woods ſupply them almoſt every where.

They can bear hunger and thirſt for ſeveral days, without ſlackening, on that account, their perſeverance in any propoſed enterprize.

By conſtant practice in hunting, they learn to ſhoot with great ſkill, either with bows, or fire-arms; and to ſteal unperceived upon their prey, purſuing the tracts of men and beaſts, which would be imperceptible to an European. They can run for a whole day without halting, when flying from an enemy, or when ſent on a meſſage. They ſteer, as if by inſtinct, thro' trackleſs woods, and with aſtoniſhing patience can lie whole days motionleſs in ambuſh to ſurprize an enemy, eſteeming no labour or perſeverance too painful to obtain their ends.

They beſmear their bodies with bear's greaſe, which defends them againſt rains and damps, as well as againſt the ſtings of Muſkitoes and Gnats. It likewiſe ſupples their limbs, and makes them ſlippery as the ancient gladiators, who could not be held faſt when ſeized in fight.

Plain food, conſtant exerciſe, and living in the open air, preſerve them healthy and vigorous.

They are powerfully excited to war by the cuſtom eſtabliſhed among them, of paying diſtinguiſhed honours to warriors.

They fight only when they think to have the advantage, but cannot be forced to it, being ſure by their ſpeed to elude the moſt eager purſuit.

Their

THEIR drefs confifts of the fkins of fome wild beaft, or a blanket, a fhirt either of linen, or of dreffed fkins, a breech clout, leggins, reaching half way up the thigh, and faftened to a belt, with mokawfons on their feet. They ufe no ligatures that might obftruct the circulation of their blood, or agility of their limbs. They fhave their head, referving only a fmall tuft of hair on the top; and flit the outer part of the ears, to which, by weights, they give a circular form, extending it down to their fhoulders.

THEY adorn themfelves with ear and nofe rings, bracelets of filver and wampum, and paint their faces with various colours. When they prepare for an engagement they paint themfelves black, and fight naked.

THEIR arms are a fufil, or rifle, a powder horn, a fhot pouch, a tomahawk, and a fcalping knife hanging to their neck.

WHEN they are in want of fire-arms, they fupply them by a bow, a fpear, or a death hammer, which is a fhort club made of hard wood.

THEIR ufual utenfils are a kettle, a fpoon, a looking glafs, an awl, a fteel to ftrike fire, fome paint, a pipe and tobacco-pouch. For want of tobacco, they fmoke fome particular leaves, or the bark of a willow; which is almoft their continual occupation.

THUS lightly equipped do the favages lie in wait to attack, at fome difficult pafs, the European foldiers, heavily accoutred, harraffed by a tedious march, and encumbered with an unwieldy convoy.

EXPERI-

Experience has convinced us that it is not our intereſt to be at war with them; but if, after having tried all means to avoid it, they force us to it, (which in all probabilty will often happen) we ſhould endeavour to fight them upon more equal terms, and regulate our manœuvres upon thoſe of the enemy we are to engage, and the nature of the country we are to act in.

It does not appear from our accounts of Indian wars, that the ſavages were as brave formerly as we have found them of late; which muſt be imputed to their unexpected ſucceſſes againſt our troops on ſome occaſions, particularly in 1755; and from the little reſiſtance they have ſince met with from defenceleſs inhabitants.

It is certain that even at this day, they ſeldom expoſe their perſons to danger, and depend entirely upon their dexterity in concealing themſelves during an engagement, never appearing openly, unleſs they have ſtruck their enemies with terror, and have thereby rendered them incapable of defence——From whence it may be inferred that, if they were beat two or three times, they would loſe that confidence inſpired by ſucceſs, and be leſs inclined to engage in wars which might end fatally for them. But this cannot reaſonably be expected, till we have troops trained to fight them in their own way, with the additional advantage of European courage and diſcipline.

Any deviation from our eſtabliſhed military ſyſtem would be needleſs, if valour, zeal, order and good conduct, were ſufficient to ſubdue this light-footed enemy. Theſe qualities are conſpicuous in our troops; but they are too heavy, and indeed too valuable, to be employed alone in a deſtructive ſervice for which they were never intended.

ed. They require the aſſiſtance of lighter corps, whoſe dreſs, arms and exerciſes, ſhould be adapted to this new kind of war.

THIS opinion is ſupported by the example of many warlike nations, of which I beg leave to mention the following.

THE learned Jeſuit † who has obliged the world with a treatiſe on the military affairs of the ancient Romans, tells us, from Salluſt §, that this wiſe nation, our maſters in the art of war, were never hindered even by the pride of empire, from imitating any foreign maxim or inſtitution, provided it was good; and that they carefully adopted into their own practice whatever they found uſeful in that of their allies or enemies; ſo that by receiving ſome thing from one, and ſome from another, they greatly improved a ſyſtem even originally excellent.

THE defeat of Antony and Craſſus by the Parthians, of Curio by the Numidians, and many other inſtances, convinced the Romans that their legions, who had conquered ſo many nations, were not fit to engage light-troops, which, harraſſing them continually, evaded all their endeavours to bring them to a cloſe engagement; and it is probable that if Julius Cæſar had not been aſſaſſinated, when he was preparing to march a-

† Vid Joannis Antonii Valtrini Lib. de re milit. Vet. Rom.

§ Neque enim Romanis ſuperbia unquam obſtitit, quo minus aliena inſtituta, ſi modo proba fuiſſent, imitarentur; et quod ubique apud ſocios vel hoſtes idoneum viſum eſſet, cum ſtudio domi exſequerentur. —Aliaque ab aliis accepta, ipſi longe facere meliora quæ quidem digna ſtatuiſſent.

gainſt the ſame Parthians, to wipe off the reproach of the former defeats, he would have added to his legions a greater number of light troops, formed upon the principles and method of that nation, and have left us uſeful leſſons for the conduct of a war againſt our ſavages.

THAT he did not think the attack of irregular troops contemptible, appears clearly in ſeveral parts of his commentaries, and particularly in the African war. The various embarraſſments he met with from the enemy he had then to deal with, neceſſarily call to our mind many ſimilar circumſtances in the courſe of our wars with the Indians; and the pains he took to inſtruct his ſoldiers to ſtand and repel the ſkirmiſhes of the nimble Africans, may furniſh inſtruction to us in our military operations againſt the ſavage Americans.

WE are told that while Cæſar was on his march "to Scipio's * quarters, the enemy's "horſe

* Labienus, Afraniuſque cum omni equitatu, levique armatura, ex inſidiis adorti agmini Cæſaris extremo ſe offerunt, atque ex collibus primis exſiſtunt.—Primo impetu legionum equitatus, levis armatura hoſtium nullo negotio loco pulſa et dejecta eſt de colle. Quum jam Cæſar exiſtimaſſet hoſtes pulſos deterritoſque finem laceſſendi facturos, et iter cœptum pergere cœpiſſet; iterum celeriter ex proximis collibus erumpunt; atque in Cæſaris legionarios impetum faciunt Numidæ, leviſque armaturæ, mirabili velocitate præditi; qui inter equites pugnabant, et una pariterque cum equitibus accurrere et refugere conſueverant. Hoc ſæpius facerent, &c—Cæſaris autem non amplius tres, aut quatuor milites veterani, ſi ſe convertiſſent, ei pila viribus contorta in Numidas infeſtos conjeciſſent, amplius duorum millium numero ad unum terga vertebant; ac rurſus ad aciem paſſim, converſis

" horſe and light-armed infantry, riſing all at " once from an ambuſcade, appeared upon the " hills, and attacked his rear. His legions form-" ing themſelves, ſoon beat the enemy from the " higher ground. And now thinking all ſafe, he " begins to purſue his march. But immediately " the enemy break forth from the neighbouring " hills; and the Numidians, with their light-" armed foot, who are wonderfully nimble, al-" ways mixing and keeping equal pace with the " cavalry in charging or retiring, fall afreſh on " the Roman foot. Thus they frequently re-" newed the charge, and ſtill retired when he " endeavoured to bring them to cloſe engage-" ment. If but two or three of his veterans " faced about and caſt their piles with vigour, " two thouſand of the enemy would fly, then re-" turning rally again, making it their buſineſs to " harraſs his march, and to preſs upon his rear, " following at ſome diſtance, and throwing their " darts at the legions.

converſis equis, ſe colligebant, atque in ſpatio conſe-quebantur, et jacula in Legionarios conjiciebant.

CÆSAR contra ejuſmodi hoſtium genera copias ſuas, non ut imperator exercitum veteranum, victo-remque maximis rebus geſtis, ſed ut laniſta tirones gladiatores condocefacere: quo pede ſeſe reciperent ab hoſte, &c.—Mirifice enim hoſtium levis armatura anxium exercitum ejus atque ſollicitum habebat: quia et equites deterrebat prœlium inire, propter equorum interitum; quod eos jaculis interficiebat; et legionarium militem defatigabat, propter velocita-tem. Gravis enim armatura miles ſimul atque ab his inſectatus conſtiterat, in eoſque impetum fecerat, illi veloci curſu facile periculum vitabant.

"CÆSAR, having so subtil an enemy to deal "with, instructed his soldiers, not like a genera "who had been victorious in the most arduous "exploits, but as a fencing-master † would in-"struct his scholars; teaching them with what "pace to retreat from the enemy, and how to "return to the charge; how far to advance, and "how far to retire; and likewise in what place "and manner to cast their piles. For their "light armed infantry gave him the greatest un-"easiness, deterring his troopers from meeting "them, by killing their horses with their jave-"lins, and wearying his legions by their swift-"ness. For whenever his heavy-armed foot "faced about, and endeavoured to return their "charge, they quickly avoided the danger by "flight."

BUT without going back to the ancients, we have seen this maxim adopted in our days. Marshal de Saxe finding the French army harrassed by the Hussars and other Austrian light troops, formed also several corps of them of different kinds; and the king of Prussia in his first war introduced them into his army, and has augmented and employed them ever since with success. We have ourselves made use of them in the two last wars in Europe: But the light troops wanted in America must be trained upon different principles. The enemies we have to deal with, are infinitely more active and dangerous than the Hussars and Pandours; or even the Africans above-mentioned. For the American savages, after their rapid incursions, retreat to their towns, at a great dis-

† Lanista, in Latin, is an instructor of gladiators, 'which in English can only be translated a Fencing-'master.'

tance

tance from our ſettlements, through thickety woods almoſt impenetrable to our heavy and unwieldy corps, compoſed of ſoldiers loaded with cloaths, baggage and proviſions, who, when fatigued by a long march, muſt be a very unequal match to engage the nimble ſavage in woods, which are his native element.

ANOTHER unavoidable incumbrance, in our expeditions, ariſes from the proviſions and baggage of the army, for which a road muſt be opened, and bridges thrown over rivers and ſwamps. This creates great labour, retards and weakens the line of march, and keeps the troops tied to a convoy which they cannot loſe ſight of, without expoſing it to become a prey to a vigilant enemy, continually hovering about to ſeize every advantage.

AN European, to be a proper judge of this kind of war, muſt have lived ſome time in the vaſt foreſts of America; otherwiſe he will hardly be able to conceive a continuity of woods without end. In ſpite of his endeavours, his imagination will betray him into an expectation of open and clear grounds, and he will be apt to calculate his manœuvres accordingly, too much upon the principles of war in Europe.

LET us ſuppoſe a perſon, who is entirely unacquainted with the nature of this ſervice, to be put at the head of an expedition in America. We will further ſuppoſe that he has made the diſpoſitions uſual in Europe for a march, or to receive an enemy; and that he is then attacked by the ſavages. He cannot diſcover them, tho' from every tree, log or buſh, he receives an inceſſant fire, and obſerves that few of their ſhot are loſt. He will not heſitate to charge thoſe inviſible enemies, but he will charge in vain. For they are as cautious to avoid a cloſe engagement, as indefatigable in harraſſing his troops; and notwithſtanding all his endeavours, he will ſtill find himſelf ſurrounded by a circle of fire, which, like an artificial horizon, follows him every where.

UNABLE to rid himſelf of an enemy who never ſtands his attacks, and flies when preſſed, only to return upon him again with equal agility and vigour; he will ſee the courage of his heavy troops droop, and their ſtrength at laſt fail them by repeated and ineffectual efforts.

HE muſt therefore think of a retreat, unleſs he can force his way thro' the enemy. But how is this to be effected? his baggage and proviſions are unloaded and ſcattered, part of his horſes and drivers killed, others diſperſed by fear, and his wounded to be carried by ſoldiers already fainting under the fatigue of a long action. The enemy, encouraged by his diſtreſs, will not fail to encreaſe the diſorder, by preſſing upon him on every ſide, with redoubled fury and ſavage howlings.

HE will probably form a circle or a ſquare, to keep off ſo daring an enemy, ready at the leaſt opening to fall upon him with the deſtructive tomahawk: but theſe diſpoſitions, tho' a tolerable ſhift for defence, are neither proper for an attack, nor a march thro' the woods.——

THIS is not an imaginary ſuppoſition, but the true ſtate of an engagement with the Indians, experienced by the troops who have fought againſt them. Neither is there any thing new or extraordinary in this way of fighting, which ſeems to have been common to moſt Barbarians †.

† Vid. Cæſ. Comm. lib. V. de bello Gallico, et lib. II. de bello civili.

WHAT

WHAT is then to be done to extricate our little army from impending destruction?

THIS is a problem which I do not pretend to resolve. But as every man would, in similar circumstances, determine himself some way or other, I will propose my own sentiments, founded upon some observations which I believe invariable in all engagements with savages.

THE first, that their general maxim is to surround their enemy.

THE second, that they fight scattered, and never in a compact body.

THE third, that they never stand their ground when attacked, but immediately give way, to return to the charge.

THESE principles being admitted, it follows—

1st. THAT the troops destined to engage Indians, must be lightly cloathed, armed, and accoutred.

2d. THAT having no resistance to encounter in the attack or defence, they are not to be drawn up in close order, which would only expose them without necessity to a greater loss.

AND, lastly, that all their evolutions must be performed with great rapidity; and the men enabled by exercise to pursue the enemy closely, when put to flight, and not give them time to rally.

THESE remarks will explain the reasons of the alterations proposed in the formation of a corps of troops, for the service of the woods. It is not, however, to be expected that this method will remove all obstacles, or that those light troops can equal the savages in patience, and activity; but, with discipline and practice, they may in a great

 measure

meaſure ſupply the want of theſe advantages, and by keeping the enemy at a diſtance afford great relief and ſecurity to the main body.

SECTION II.

GENERAL IDEA OF AN ESTABLISHMENT OF LIGHT TROOPS, FOR THE SERVICE OF THE WOODS.

I SHALL only venture a few notions ſuggeſted by experience upon this ſubject, chiefly with a view to recommend it to the conſideration of perſons capable of propoſing a proper method of forming ſuch an eſtabliſhment: and, in order to be better underſtood, I will ſuppoſe a corps of 500 men to be raiſed and diſciplined for the woods, beſides two troops of light horſe, to which a company of artificers might be added. The fitteſt men for that ſervice would be the natives of America bred upon the frontiers, and inliſted between the age of 15 and 20 years, to be diſcharged between 30 and 35.

CLOATHING.

THE cloathing of a ſoldier for the campaign might conſiſt of a ſhort coat of brown cloth, lappelled, and without plaits; a ſtrong tanned ſhirt, ſhort trowſers, leggins, mokawſons or ſhoe packs, a ſailor's hat, a blanket, a knapſack for proviſions, and an oiled ſurtout † againſt the rain. To this

† The following Watch-coat was contrived by an officer, whoſe name I do not remember. But inſtead of

this might be added, in winter quarters or time of peace, three white ſhirts and ſtocks, with a flannel waiſtcoat.

of the oiled linen to be put under the hat, a cap might perhaps anſwer better. He writes as follows, viz.

" As the Indian war will require frequent incur-" ſions into a wild country, where a man ſick or " wounded, is in ſeveral reſpects more detrimental " to the ſervice than a man killed, every thing that " may contribute to the health of the men is of mo-" ment.

" In this view, I propoſe a ſort of ſurtout, to pre-" ſerve men, in a great meaſure, both from wet and " cold.

" Take a large checked ſhirt, of about half a " crown ſterling per yard, for it ſhould be pretty " fine; cut off the wriſt-bands, and continue the " opening of the breaſt down to the bottom; ſew up " the ſides from the guſſets downwards; rip out the " gathers in the fore parts of the collar as far as the " ſhoulder ſtraps, and reſew it plain to the collar.

" The ſhirt will then become a ſort of watch-" coat like a bed-gown, with very wide ſleeves.

" Take a quantity of linſeed oil, and boil it gently " till one half is diminiſhed, to which put a ſmall " quantity of litharge of gold, and when it is well " incorporated with the oil, lay it on with a bruſh " upon the watch-coat, ſo that it ſhall be every " where equally wet.

" I ſuppoſe the watch-coat, hung in a garret, or " other covered place, and ſo ſuſpended by crooked " pins and packthreads in the extremities of the " ſleeves and edges of the collar, that one part ſhall " not touch another. In a ſhort time, if the wea-" ther is good, it will be dry; when a ſecond mix-" ture of the ſame kind ſhould be laid on with a

ARMS.

THEIR arms, the beſt that could be made, ſhould be ſhort fuſils and ſome rifles, with bayonets in the form of a dirk, to ſerve for a knife; with powder horns and ſhot pouches, ſmall hatchets and leathern bottles for water.

" bruſh as before. When the ſecond coat of painting is dry, the greaſe will not come off, and the ſurtout is an effectual preſervative from rain; it is very light to carry, and being pretty full on the back, will not only keep the man dry, but alſo his pack and ammunition.

" The ſleeves are left long and wide to receive the butt end of a firelock (ſecured) and to cover it below the lock. The coat is double breaſted to be lapped over, according to which ſide the rain drives. A man will be kept dry by one of theſe ſurtouts as far as the knees. If, from the vicinity of the enemy, it is improper to make fires at night, he may place his pack on a ſtone, and, ſitting upon it, change his ſhoes and leggins, and, if he pleaſes, wrap his blanket round his legs and feet, then drawing the watch-coat cloſe to his body, it will keep him warm, as no air can paſs through it, and, leaning againſt the trunk of a tree, he may paſs a tolerable night, both warm and dry.

" It would be of ſervice to have a ſmall piece of the ſame oiled linen to put under the hat or cap to carry the rain down to the watchcoat or ſurtout, otherwiſe whatever wet ſoaks through the hat or cap, will run down the neck, and thereby, in ſome meaſure, defeat the deſign of the watch-coat.

" Perhaps it might be uſeful to mix ſome dark or greeniſh colour with the oil of the ſecond coating, to make the watch-coat leſs remarkable in the woods."

EXER-

EXERCISES.

THE ſoldiers being raiſed, cloathed, and formed into companies under proper officers, muſt, before they are armed, be taught to keep themſelves clean, and to dreſs in a ſoldier-like manner. This will raiſe in them a becoming ſpirit, give them a favourable opinion of their profeſſion, and preſerve their health. The firſt thing they are to learn is to Walk well, afterwards to Run; and, in order to excite emulation, ſmall premiums might from time to time be given to thoſe who diſtinguiſh themſelves. They muſt then run in ranks, with open files, and wheel in that order, at firſt ſlowly, and by degrees increaſe their ſpeed: this evolution is difficult, but of the utmoſt conſequence to fall unexpectedly upon the flank of the enemy. They are to diſperſe and rally at given ſignals; and particular colours ſhould be given to each company, for them to rally by; the men muſt be uſed to leap † over logs and ditches, and to carry burthens proportioned to their ſtrength.

WHAT

† Vegetius gives an account of many ſimilar exerciſes, which the Romans found neceſſary to eſtabliſh among their military. Miles ſylvam cædebat, æſtivis temporibus natabat, ad palum dimicabat, ſaltabat, currebat. Exempla hujus exercitationis crebra ſunt apud Livium. Sic ille de Scipione Africano, 3 decad. lib. VI. "Primo die legiones in armis IV. "millium ſpatio decurrerunt. Secundo die arma "curare et tergere ante tentoria juſſit. Tertio die "ſudibus

WHEN the young soldiers are perfect in these exercises, they may receive their arms, with which they are to perform the former evolutions in all sorts of grounds. They will next be taught to handle their arms with dexterity; and, without losing time upon trifles, to load and fire very quick, standing, kneeling, or lying on the ground. They are to fire at a mark without a rest, and not suffered to be too long in taking aim. Hunting and small premiums will soon make them expert marksmen.

THEY ought to learn to swim, pushing at the same time their cloaths, arms, and ammunition before them, on a small raft; and to make use of snow shoes. They must then be set to work, and be taught to throw up an intrenchment, open a trench, make fascines, clays and gabions; likewise to fall trees, square logs, saw planks, make canoes, carts, ploughs, hand and wheel barrows, shingles and clap-boards, casks, batteaus and bridges, and to build log houses, ovens, &c.

BY example and practice, the most ingenious among them will soon become tolerable good carpenters, joyners, wheelwrights, coopers, armourers, smiths, masons, brickmakers, saddlers, taylors, butchers, bakers, shoemakers, curriers, &c.

" sudibus inter se in modum justæ pugnæ concur-
" rerent, præpilatisque missilibus jaculati sunt.
" Quarto die quies data. Quinto iterum in armis
" decursum est."—Quibus porro modis obviam eatur elephantis. Veget. lib. III. cap. 24.

LIGHT

LIGHT HORSE and DOGS.

I SAID that, to compleat this eſtabliſhment, they ſhould have two troops of light horſe, ſuppoſed of 50 men each, officers included. The men are to perform the ſame exerciſes as the foot, and afterwards be taught to ride, and particularly to be very alert at mounting and diſmounting with their arms in their hands, to gallop through the woods up and down hills, and leap over logs and ditches.

THE horſes ought to be bought up on the frontiers, where they are bred and uſed to feed in the woods, and are ſtrong and hardy. They are to be thoroughly broke, made to ſtand fire, to ſwim over rivers, &c. their ſaddles and accoutrements very ſimple, ſtrong and light. The number of horſes might be reduced to one half, in time of peace, tho' they would be of little expence, as they might be bred and mantained without charge in the military ſettlement. This corps ſhould be equipped as the foot, having only a ſhort rifle in lieu of a fuſil, and a battle ax with a long handle, the only ſort of arms they ſhould make uſe of in the charge.

EVERY light horſe man ought to be provided with a Blood-hound, which would be uſeful to find out the enemies ambuſhes, and to follow their tracts; they would ſeize the naked ſavages, or at leaſt give time to the horſe men to come up with them; they would add to the ſafety of the camp at night by diſcovering any attempt to ſurprize it.

ARTI-

ARTIFICERS.

THE company of artificers should be composed of the most useful tradesmen, and ought to be maintained at all times for the instruction of the soldiers, the use of the settlement, or the service of the army, during the campaign. It will now be time to draw forth this military colony and remove them to the ground laid out for that use in the woods, and at a good distance from the inhabitants. The nature of this settlement will hereafter be more particularly described.

NECESSITY creating industry, our young soldiers will soon provide themselves with the most useful articles, and in a couple of years be able to raise provisions for themselves.

WHILE the greatest part would be employed in clearing the ground, fencing, ploughing, sowing, planting, building and making utensils and houshold furniture, others might hunt with their officers, and remain a fortnight or a month out of the camp, without other provisions than a little flour, and what they could procure by hunting and fishing: then to be relieved, and the whole trained up in that way.

THE military exercises must still be kept up and practised, and great care taken to inculcate and preserve purity of manners, obedience, order and decency among the men, which will be found much easier in the woods than in the neighbourhood of towns.

IN order to make this military establishment more generally useful; I would propose that the soldiers should only receive a very small part of their

their pay; leaving the remainder in the military cheſt.

THEIR accounts ſhould be ſettled every year, and when their ſervices ſhould intitle them to their diſcharge, I could wiſh that each of them had 200 acres of land given him, in a diſtrict appropriated for that purpoſe; and receiving then the whole ballance of pay due to them, they would be enabled to compleat their ſettlement. This inſtitution appears not only practicable, but eaſy, if attended to with patience, aſſiduity and firmneſs. The plan I would propoſe is as follows.

Method of forming ſuch SETTLEMENTS upon the Frontiers, as might ſupport themſelves during an INDIAN WAR.

LET us ſuppoſe a ſettlement to be formed for one hundred families, compoſed of five perſons each, upon an average.

LAY out upon a river, or creek, if it can be found conveniently, a SQUARE of one thouſand ſeven hundred and ſixty yards, or a mile for each ſide.

THAT Square will contain - - 640 acres

Allowing for ſtreets and public uſes	40	640 acres
To half an acre for every houſe -	50	
To one hundred lots at five and half acres - - - - - -	550	

THE four ſides of the ſquare meaſure 7040 yards, which gives to each houſe about 70 yards front to ſtockade, and the ground allowed for building will be 210 feet front, and about 100 feet deep.

AN acre of ground will produce at leaſt 30 buſhels of Indian corn. Therefore, two acres are

ſufficient

ſufficient to ſupply five perſons, at the rate of twelve buſhels each perſon. Two other acres will be a paſture for cows and ſheep, another acre for hay, to be ſown with red clover. The remaining half acre may be laid out for a garden.

ROUND the town are the commons, of three miles ſquare, containing, excluſive of the lots above-mentioned, 5120 acres. On three ſides of the town, five other Squares will be laid out of three ſquare miles, containing 5760 acres each, one of which is reſerved for wood for the uſe of the Settlement; the other four to be divided into 25 out-lots or plantations, of about 230 acres each, ſo that in the four Squares there will be one hundred ſuch plantations, for the 100 families.

ANOTHER townſhip may be laid out joining this, upon the ſame plan, and as many more as you pleaſe upon the ſame line, without loſing any ground.

THUS

THE following is a rough ſketch of the whole.

Townſhip A.		Townſhip B.		Townſhip C.		Townſhip D.	
1	1	2	2	3	3	4	4
5760 acres wood for the Town A	Commons A Commons	Commons B Commons	Wood for the Town B	Wood for the Town C	Commons C Commons	Commons D Commons	Wood for the Town D
25 lots of 230 acres 1	1	2	2	3	3	4	4

THUS the town, A, has its commons, its woodland, and its 4 ſquares marked No. 1. each containing 25 plantations of 230 acres, as propoſed above. In like manner, the other towns, B, C, D, have their appurtenances reſpectively marked.

LET us now ſuppoſe this plan accompliſhed, and ſuch corps as theſe fully ſettled, trained and diſciplined, in the manner above-mentioned; I would aſk whether any officer, entruſted with an expedition againſt the ſavages, would not chuſe to have them in his army? I may ſafely anſwer for all thoſe who have been employed in that ſervice, that they would prefer them to double the number of the beſt European troops. And when they had ſerved the time limited, namely from their 15th to their 35th year, what vaſt ſatisfaction would it be to pay over to them their ſhare of ſavings from the public cheſt; and, as a reward of their faithful toils, to veſt them and their heirs with their ſeveral plantations, which they would now be enabled to cultivate as their own? This proſpect would engage many people to enter their ſons, in ſuch corps; and thoſe veterans, when thus diſcharged, would not only be the means of forming and animating others by their example, but in caſe of a war would ſtill bravely maintain the property they had ſo honourably acquired, and be the greateſt ſecurity of the frontier where they are ſettled.

PRE-

PREPARATIONS FOR AN EXPEDITION IN THE WOODS AGAINST SAVAGES.

It is not practicable to employ large bodies of troops against Indians; the convoys necessary for their support would be too cumbersome, and could neither be moved with ease, nor protected. It would be better to fit out several small expeditions, than one too unwieldy: I will therefore suppose that a corps intended to act offensively shall not exceed the following proportions.

Two regiments of foot - - - - -	900
One battalion of hunters - - - -	500
Two troops of light horse - - -	100
One company of artificers - - -	20
Drivers and necessary followers - -	280
In all	1800

The first article to provide is the provisions, and next the carriages.

The daily ration of a soldier in the woods should consist of one pound and a half of meat (which requires no carriage) and one pound of flour, with a gill of salt per week.

Upon that allowance 1800 men will require for six months or 182 days - -	327,600 lb. Flour.
Allowing one fourth for accident - - - - - - -	81,900
For six months	409,500 lb. Flour.

Meat

MEAT for the ſame time with a fourth part more for accidents, or 2048 beeves at 300 lb. each	614,400 lb. Meat.
Salt for 26 weeks - -	182 Buſhels.

THE above quantity would ſerve the whole campaign, but one half would be ſufficient to penetrate from the laſt depoſite into the heart of the enemy's country: therefore we ſhall compute the carriages for this laſt quantity only.

EVERY horſe carries about 150 lb. neat weight, therefore, to carry flour for three months or 204,750 lb. will require 1365 horſes.

HORSES for flour - - - -	1365
For 91 buſhels of ſalt - - - -	46
Ammunition - - - - - - -	50
Tents - - - - - - - -	50
Tools - - - - - - - -	50
Hoſpital - - - - - - -	20
Officers baggage and ſtaff - - -	150
	1731

TO reduce this exorbitant number of horſes, and the great expence attending it, I would propoſe, for ſuch parts of the country as would admit of it, to make uſe of carts, drawn each by four oxen, and carrying about 1300 lb or ſix barrels of flour. The above quantity of 204,750 lb. will then be carried by 160 carts drawn by 640 oxen

Spare oxen with the army - -	384
The number of oxen wanted -	1024

THIS

THIS method would not be as expeditious as the carriage by horſes, and would require more time and attention in cutting the road, and bridging the ſwampy places, &c. but, on the other hand, what an expence would be ſaved! and by killing the oxen in proportion as the flour is uſed, and abandoning the carts, the convoy is daily reduced, and the graſs near the encampment will not be ſo ſoon conſumed, which is not the caſe with horſes, which muſt equally be fed though unloaded. This is an object of conſequence, particularly near the end of the campaign, when the ſcarcity of fodder obliges to move the camps every day, and to place them in low and diſadvantageous-grounds.

I WOULD therefore incline for the uſe of carts, and they could be made before hand by the hunters and their artificers.

THE oxen ſhould be bought in the provinces where the farmers make uſe of them in their works. One or two ſoldiers would drive the cart and take charge of the four oxen.

THERE are few rivers in North-America deep in ſummer, and which theſe carts with high and broad wheels, could not ford; but if the contrary ſhould happen, the carts, proviſions and baggage, may be rafted over, or a bridge built. In a country full of timber, and with troops accuſtomed to work, no river will ſtop an army for a long time.

BY the above method, 3 or 400 horſes would be ſufficient to carry the baggage, ammunition, tents, tools, &c.

EXPLANA-

EXPLANATION OF THE FOUR PLANS, PLATE II.

Reprefenting the different pofitions of our army in the woods.

ENCAMPMENT.

THE camp (Fig. 1) forms a parallellogram, of one thoufand by fix hundred feet. Eight hundred men of the regular troops (1) encamp on the four fides, which gives twenty-four feet to each tent, containing fix men. The light-horfe (3) encamp within the parallellogram. The referve (7) in the center.

THE provifions, ammunition, tools and ftores (8) and the cattle (9) are placed between the two troops of light horfe and the referve. The hunters (2) encamp on the outfide diagonally at the four angles, being covered by redoubts (5) formed with kegs and bags of flour or fafcines. Befides thefe four redoubts, another is placed to the front, one to the rear, and two before each of the long faces of the camp, making in all ten advanced guards of 22 men each, and 7 centries, covered if poffible by breaft works of fafcines or provifions. Before the army lay down their arms, the ground is to be reconnoitred, and the guards pofted, who will immediately open a communication from one to the other, to relieve the centries, and facilitate the paffage of rounds.

THE centries upon the ammunition, provifions, head quarters, and all others in the infide of

the

the camp are furnished from the reserve. The officers, except the staff and commanders of corps, encamp on the line with their men.

THE fires are made between the guards and camp, and put out in case of an attack in the night.

LINE of MARCH, Plate II. Fig. II.

PART of the hunters (2) in three divisions detaching small parties (5, 6) to their front and to their right and left, to search the woods and discover the enemy.

THE artificers and axe-men (4) to cut a road for the convoy, and two paths on the right and left for the troops.

ONE hundred and fifty of the regular troops (1) in two files, who are to form the front of the square; these march in the center road.

TWO hundred and fifty regulars (1) in one file by the right hand path; and 250 (1) by the left hand path, are to form the long faces.

THESE are followed by 150 regulars (1) in two files, who are to form the rear of the square.

THE reserve (7) composed of 100 regulars in two files.

THE rest of the hunters (2) in two files.

THE light horse (3.)

THE rear guard (5) composed of hunters, follows the convoy at some distance and closes the march. The scouting parties (6) who flank the line of march, are taken from the hunters and light horse, and posted as in plan (Fig. 2) some orderly light horsemen, attend the General and field officers who command the grand divisions,

to

to carry their orders. Two guards of light horſe take charge of the cattle (9)

THE convoy (8) proceeds in the following order.

THE tools and ammunition following the front column.

THE baggage.

THE cattle.

THE proviſions.

THE whole divided into Brigades, and the horſes two a breaſt.

DEFILES.

IN caſe of a defile, the whole halt until the ground is reconnoitred, and the hunters have taken poſſeſſion of the heights. The center column then enters into the defile, followed by the right face; after them the convoy; then the left and rear face, with the reſerve, the light horſe, and the rear guard.

THE whole to form again as ſoon as the ground permits.

DISPOSITION TO RECEIVE THE ENEMY, Fig. ( )

THE whole halt to form the ſquare or parallellogram, which is done thus. The two firſt men of the center column ſtand faſt at two yards diſtance. The two men following them, ſtep forward and poſt themſelves at two yards on the right and left. The others come to the front in the ſame manner, till the two files have formed a rank, which is the front of the ſquare.

THE

THE rear face is formed by the two file-leaders turning to the center road, where having placed themselves at two yards distance, they face outwards, and are followed by their files, each man posting himself on their right or left, and facing towards the enemy the moment he comes to his post.

As soon as the front and rear are extended and formed, the two long faces, who have in the mean time faced outwards, join now the extremities of the two fronts, and close the square †.

TO REDUCE THE SQUARE.

THE right and left of the front, face to the center, where the two center men stand fast. Upon the word "march" these step forward and are replaced by the two next, who follow them, and so on; by which means, that front becomes again a column. The rear goes to the right about, and each of the two center men leads again to the side paths followed by the rest.

WHILE the troops form, the light horse and each division of the convoy take the ground assigned to them within the square, as if they were to encamp; and the horses being unloaded, two parallel lines will be formed, with the bags and kegs of provisions, to cover the wounded and the men unfit for action. The hunters take post on the most advantageous ground on the out side, and skirmish with the enemy, till the square is formed; when, upon receiving their orders, they retire within the square, where they take their post as in Fig. (3)

† These evolutions must be performed with celerity.

THE ſmall parties of rangers (5) who have flanked the line of march, remain on the outſide, to keep off the enemy and obſerve their motions.

WHEN the firing begins the troops will have orders to fall on their knees, to be leſs expoſed till it is thought proper to attack.

THE four faces, formed by the regular troops, are divided into platoons *chequered*. One half, compoſed of the beſt and moſt active ſoldiers, is called the firſt Firing, and the other half the ſecond Firing.

THE eight platoons at the angles are of the ſecond Firing, in order to preſerve the form of the ſquare during the attack.

IT is evident that, by this diſpoſition, the convoy is well covered, and the light troops, deſtined for the charge, remain concealed; and as all unexpected events during an engagement are apt to ſtrike terror, and create confuſion, among the enemy, it is natural to expect that the ſavages will be greatly diſconcerted at the ſudden and unforeſeen eruption, that will ſoon pour upon them from the inſide of the ſquare; and that, being vigorouſly attacked in front and flank at the ſame time, they will neither be able to reſiſt, nor, when once broke, have time to rally, ſo as to make another ſtand. This may be effected in the following manner.

GENERAL ATTACK, Fig. IV.

THE Regulars (1) ſtand faſt.

THE hunters (2) ſally out, in four columns, thro' the intervals of the front and rear of the ſquare, followed by the light horſe (3) with their bloodhounds. The intervals of the two columns

who

who attack in the front, and of thoſe who attack in the rear, will be cloſed by the little parties of rangers (5) poſted at the angles of the ſquare, each attack forming in that manner, three ſides of a parallelogram. In that order they run to the enemy (X) and having forced their way through their circle, fall upon their flanks; by wheeling to their right and left, and charging with impetuoſity. The moment they take the enemy in flank, the Firſt Firing of the regular troops march out briſkly and attack the enemy in front. The platoons detached in that manner from the two ſhort faces, proceed only about one hundred yards to their front, where they halt to cover the ſquare, while the reſt of the troops who have attacked purſue the enemy, till they are totally diſperſed, not giving them time to recover themſelves.

THE ſick and wounded, unable to march or ride, are tranſported in litters made of flour bags, through which two long poles are paſſed, and kept aſunder by two ſticks, tied acroſs beyond the head and feet to ſtretch the bag. Each litter is carried by two horſes——

THESE remarks might have been extended to many other caſes that may occur in the courſe of a campaign or of an engagement, but it is hoped this ſketch will be ſufficient to evince the neceſſity of ſome alteration in our ordinary method of proceeding in an Indian war.

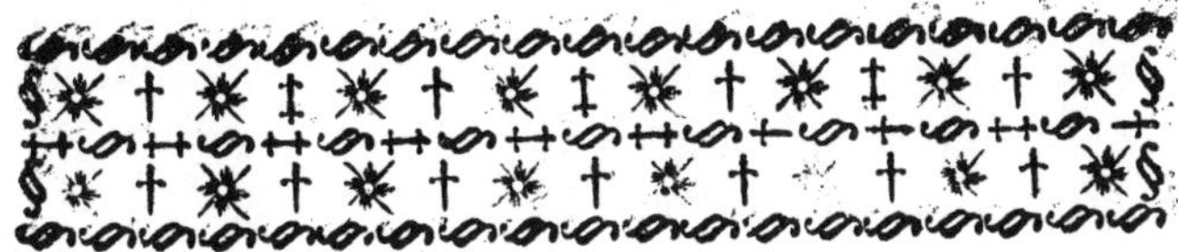

APPENDIX I.

CONSTRUCTION OF FORTS AGAINST INDIANS.

AS we have not to guard here againſt cannon, the ſyſtem of European fortification may be laid aſide, as expenſive, and not anſwering the purpoſe. Forts againſt Indians, being commonly remote from our ſettlements, require a great deal of room to lodge a ſufficient quantity of ſtores and proviſions, and at the ſame time ought to be defenſible with one half of their compleat garriſons, in caſe of detachments or convoys.

 I AM

I AM therefore of opinion that a ſquare or pentagon, with a block-houſe of brick or ſtone * at every angle, joined by a wall flanked by the block-houſes, would be the beſt defence againſt ſuch enemies. A ditch from ſeven to eight feet deep might be added, with loop holes in the cellars of the block-houſes ſix feet from the ground, to defend the ditch.

ALONG the inſide of the curtains the traders might build houſes and ſtores, covered as well as the block-houſes with tiles, or ſlate, to guard againſt fire arrows. There will remain a ſpecious area for free air and uſe, in which as well as in the ditch, gardens might be made and well dug.

THE powder magazines might be placed in the center of the area, keeping only a ſmall quantity of cartridges in each block-houſe for preſent uſe.

THE garriſons of ſuch forts would be free from ſurprizes, even if they had no centries, for nothing can get at them, while the doors are well bolted and barred.

* Experience has demonſtrated that fortifications made of wood decay very ſoon, and are on that account of conſiderable expence.

SOME

SOME REASONS FOR KEEPING POSSESSION OF OUR LARGE FORTS IN THE INDIAN COUNTRY.

As these forts have been one of the causes of the last war and are a great eye-sore to the savages, they have bent their chief efforts against them; and therefore, while thus employed, they have been less able to distress our settlements. Our forts keep the Indian towns at a great distance from us. Fort-Pitt has effectually driven them, beyond the Ohio, and made them remove their settlements at least 60 miles further westward. Was it not for these forts, they would settle close on our borders, and in time of war infest us every day in such numbers as would over-power the thin inhabitants scattered on our extensive frontier. The farmer unable to sow or reap would soon fall back on our chief towns, or quit the country for want of bread. In either case, what would be the fate of the large towns burthened with the whole country, and deprived of subsistance and of the materials of trade and export?

THE destruction of these forts being, in time of war, the chief aim of the savages, they gather above them to distress the garrisons, and to attack the convoy; thereby giving us an opportunity to fight them in a body, and to strike a heavy blow, which otherwise they would never put in our power, as their advantage lies in surprizes, which are best effected by small numbers. Experience has convinced them that it is not in their power to break thoſe ſhackles, and therefore it is not probable that they will continue a check upon them, and ſave the difficulty and expence of taking poſt again in their country. Our forts are likewiſe the proper places for trade, which being cloſely inſpected, it will be eaſy for us to limit their ſupplies, to ſuch commodities as they cannot turn againſt us, and to put a ſpeedy ſtop to all juſt cauſes of complaints, by giving immediate redreſs.

A FEW forts, with ſtrong garriſons, I ſhould judge to be of more ſervice than a greater number weakly guarded. In the laſt war we loſt all our ſmall poſts; but our more conſiderable ones, Detroit and Fort-Pitt, reſiſted all the efforts of the ſavages, by the ſtrength of their garriſons.

APPEN-

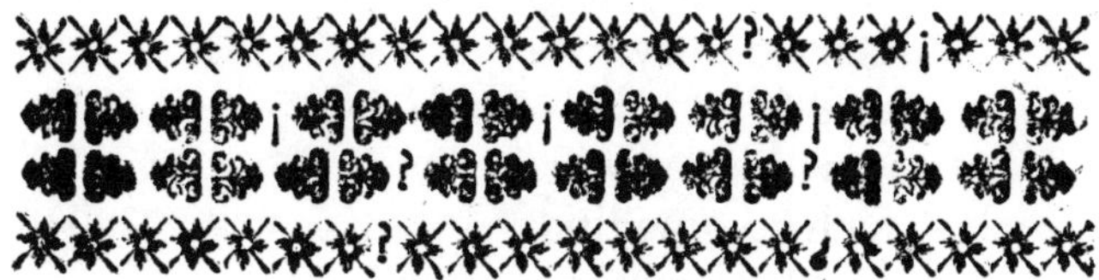

APPENDIX II.

THE following Paper was written by an Officer well acquainted with the places he defcribes; and is thought worthy of a place here, as every thing is material which can encreafe our knowledge of the vaft countries ceded to us, and of the various nations that inhabit them.

ACCOUNT of the FRENCH FORTS ceded to GREAT BRITAIN in LOUISIANA.

THE fettlement of the Illinois being in 40 degrees of latitude, is 500 leagues from New-Orleans by water and 350 by land.

THE moft proper time of the year for going there, is the beginning of February. The waters of the Miffiffippi are then high, and the country being overflowed, there is lefs to fear from the favages, who are hunting in that feafon.

THE encampments should be on the left of the river, as the enemies are on the right, and cannot have a sufficient number of crafts to cross if their party is large.

THEY generally attack at day-break, or at the time of embarking.

THE inhabitants might bring provisions half way, if they were allowed good pay.

THE Delawares and Shawanese lie near Fort Du Quesne, † which is about 500 leagues from the Illinois. The Wiandots and ottawas, (who are at the Detroit) are about 250 leagues from the Illinois by land. And the Miamis about 200 by land.

NEVERTHELESS as intelligence is carried very fast by the Savages, and as all the nations with whom we are at war, can come by the Ohio, ‡ we must be vigilant to prevent a surprize.

† So the French formerly called what is now Fort Pitt.

‡ Part of the navigation of the Ohio, from Fort-Pitt is described as follows, viz.

That the difficult part of the river is from Fort-Pitt about 50 or 60 miles downwards. There are 52 islands between Fort-Pitt and the lower Shawanese town on Scioto; and none of them difficult to pass in the night, but one at the mouth of Muskingham, occasioned by a number of trees lying in the channel. From the lower Shawanese Town to the falls, there are but 8 or 9 islands. At the falls, the river is very broad, with only one passage on the east side, in which there is water enough at all seasons of the year to pass without difficulty. Below the falls, the navigation is every way clear, down to the Missisippi.

THE

THE mouth of the Ohio, in the Miſſiſippi, is 35 leagues from the Illinois.

THIRTEEN leagues from the Miſſiſippi, on the left of the Ohio, is Fort Maſſiac, or Aſſumption, built in 1757, a little below the mouth of the river Cherokee †. It is only a ſtockade, with four baſtions and eight pieces of cannon. It may contain 100 men. In four days one may go by land, from this fort to the Illinois.

IT is of conſequence for the Engliſh to preſerve it, as it ſecures the communication between the Illinois and Fort-Pitt.

FORT Vincennes, which is the laſt poſt belonging to Louiſiana, is upon the river Ouabache ‡, 60 leagues from its conflux with the Ohio. It is a ſmall ſtockade fort, in which there may be about 20 ſoldiers. There are alſo a few inhabitants. The ſoil is extremely fertile, and produces plenty of corn and tobacco.

THE diſtance from this fort to the Illinois, is 155 leagues by water. And it may be travelled by land in ſix days.

THE nation of ſavages living at this poſt is called Pianquicha. It can furniſh 60 warriors.

ALTHO' we do not occupy Fort Vincennes at preſent, yet it would be of the utmoſt conſequence

† River Cherokee falls into the Ohio about 800 miles below Fort-Pitt. This river is in general wide and ſhoal up to the ſouth mountain, paſſable only with bark canoes, after which it grows very ſmall.

‡ Ouabache or Wabaſh empties itſelf into the Ohio about 60 miles above the Cherokee river, on the oppoſite or weſt ſide.

for

for us to settle it, as there is a communication from it with Canada, by going up the Ouabache.

FROM this post to the Ouachtanons is 60 leagues, and from thence to the Miamis (still going up the Ouabache) is 60 leagues further; then there is a portage of six leagues to the river Miamis, and you go down that river 24 leagues to Lake Erie.

MR. DAUBRY went by that rout in 1759 from the Illinois to Venango ||, with above 400 men, and two hundred thousand weight of flour.

|| By the above paper the rout is given up the Missisippi, part of the Ohio, and up the Ouabache to Fort Vincennes, and likewise to the Illinois. Again from Vincennes and the Ouachtanons by water, on the westerly communication to the Miamis portage, then by water down that river by the easterly rout into the Lake Erie, proceeding as far as Presqu' Isle, then by the 15 m. portage into Buffalo or Beef river, lately called French creek, then down the same to Venango on the Ohio. In order therefore, to carry this rout still further, we shall continue it from Venango to the mouth of Juniata in Susquehannah, which brings it within the settled parts of Pennsylvania, viz.

From Venango to Licking creek, 10 miles. To Toby's creek, 13. To a small creek, 1 To the parting of the road, 5. To a large run, 3. To Leycaumeyhoning, 9 To Pine creek, 7. To Chuckcaughting, 8 To Weeling creek, 4. To the crossing of ditto, 4. To a miry swamp, 8. To the head of Susquehanna. 10. To Meytauning creek, 18. To Clear Field creek, 6. To the top of Allegheny, 1. To the other side, ditto, 6. To Beaver dams, 5. To Franks Town, 5. To the Canoe place, 6. To the mouth of Juniatta, 110. Total 239 miles.

THIRTY-

THIRTY-FIVE leagues from the mouth of the Ohio, in going up the Miffifippi, on the right, is the river Kafkafquias. Two leagues up this river, on the left, is the fettlement of the Kafkafquias, which is the moft confiderable of the Illinois.

THERE is a fort built upon the height on the other fide of the river, over againft Kafkafquias; which, as the river is narrow, commands and protects the town.

I DON'T know how many guns there may be, nor how many men it may contain. There may be about 400 inhabitants.

THE Illinois Indians, called Kafkafquias, are fettled half a league from the town; and are able to turn out 100 warriors. They are very lazy and great drunkards.

SIX leagues from Kafkafquias, on the bank of the Miffifippi, is Fort Chartres, built of ftone, and can contain 300 foldiers. There may be 20 cannon at moft, and about 100 inhabitants round Chartres.

THE Illinois Indians at that place, who are called Metchis, can furnifh 40 warriors.

BETWEEN the Kafkafquias, and Fort Chartres, is a fmall village, called *La prairie du Rocher* (the Rock Meadow) containing about 50 white inhabitants; but there is neither fort nor favages.

NEAR Fort Chartres is a little village, in which is about a fcore of inhabitants. Here are neither favages nor fort.

FIFTEEN leagues from Fort Chartres, going up the Miffifippi, is the village of the Cafquiars. There is a fmall ftockade fort; I don't know if there is any cannon. There may be about 100 inhabitants.

THE

THE Illinois Indians living near this village are called Caſquiars, and can turn out 60 warriors.

I COMPUTE there are about 300 Negroes at the Illinois.

THE country of the Illinois is fertile, producing good wheat and corn. All kinds of European fruits ſucceed there ſurprizingly well, and they have wild grapes with which they make tolerable wine. Their beer is pretty good.

THERE are mines of lead, and ſome ſalt. They make ſugar of maple, and there are ſtone quarries.

APPEN-

APPENDIX III.

ROUT from PHILADELPHIA to FORT-PITT.

From PHILADELPHIA	Miles	Qrs.	Per.
to Lancaſter	66	0	38
to Carliſle	55	0	00
to Shippenſburgh	22	0	00
to Fort Loudoun	24	3	00
to Fort Littleton	17	3	00
to the croſſingof the Juniata	18	3	00
to Fort Bedford	14	3	00
to the croſſing of Stoney	29	0	39
creek	20	1	43
to Fort Ligonier	56	0	00
to Fort Pitt	——	----	——
	324	2	40

APPEN-

APPENDIX IV.

NUMBER of INDIAN TOWNS, situated on and near the Ohio River, and its branches, with their distances from Fort-Pitt, and the distances of the principal branches from each other at their conflux with the Ohio.

	FIRST ROUT about N. N. W.	Distance from one another Miles	Distance from Fort-Pitt. Miles
From Fort Pitt	to Kushkuskies Town on Big Beaver-Creek		45
	up the east branch of Beaver Creek to Shanningo	15	60
	up ditto to Pematuning	12	72
	to Mohoning on the West branch of Beaver Creek	32	104
	up the branch to Salt Lick	10	114
	to Cayahoga River	32	146
	to Ottawas town on Cayahoga	10	156

SECOND

SECOND ROUT W.N.W.	Diſtance from one another.	Diſtance from Fort-Pitt.
	Miles	Miles
From Fort Pitt		
to the mouth of Big Beaver-Creek		25
to Tuſcarawas	91	116
to Mohickon John's Town	50	166
to Junundat or Wyandot town	46	212
to Fort Sanduſky	4	216
to Junqueindundeh	24	240

THIRD ROUT about W. S. W.

From Fort Pitt		
to the Forks of the Muſkingam		128
to Bullet's Town on Muſkingam	6	134
to Waukatamike	10	144
to King Beaver's Town on the heads of Hochocking	27	171
to the lower Shawaneſe Town on Sioto river	40	211
to the Salt Lick town on the heads of Sioto	25	236
to the Miamis fort	190	426

FOURTH ROUT down the Ohio; general courſe about S. W.	Diſtance from one another	Diſtance from Fort-Pitt.
	Miles	Miles
By water from Fort Pitt		
to the mouth of Big Beaver Creek		27
to the mouth of Little Beaver Creek	12	39
to the mouth of Yellow Creek	10	49
to the two Creeks	18	67
to Weeling	6	73
to Pipe Hill	12	85
to the long Reach	30	115
to the foot of the Reach	18	133
to the mouth of Muſkingam river	30	163
to the little Canhawa river	12	175
to the mouth of Hockhocking river	13	188
to the mouth of Letort's creek	40	228
to Kiſkeminetas	33	261
to the mouth of big Canhawa or new river	8	269
to the mouth of big Sandy creek	40	309
to the mouth of Sioto river	40	349
to the mouth of big Salt Lick river	30	379
to the Iſland	20	399

to

		Distance from one another	Distance from Fort-Pitt.
By water from FORT PITT	to the mouth of little Mineamie or Miammee † river	Miles 55	Miles 454
	to big Miammee or Rocky river	30	484
	to the Big Bones ‡	20	504
	to Kentucky River	55	559
	to the Falls of the Ohio	50	609
	to the Wabash, or Ouabache	131	740
	to Cherokee River	60	800
	to the Missisippi	40	840

N. B. THE places mentioned in the first three Routs are delineated in the foregoing map, by an officer who has an actual knowledge of most of them, and has long served against the Indians. The fourth Rout down the Ohio was given by an Indian trader, who has often passed from Fort-Pitt to the Falls; and the distances he gives of the mouths of the several rivers that fall into the Ohio may be pretty certainly depended on. Our maps hitherto published are very erroneous in placing some of those rivers.

† These rivers, called Little and Great Mineamie or Miammee, fall into the Ohio between Sioto and the Ouabache, and are different from the Miamis river, which runs into the west end of lake Erie, below the Miamis fort.

‡ So called from Elephant's bones said to be found there.

APPENDIX.

APPENDIX V.

NAMES of different INDIAN NATIONS in NORTH-AMERICA, with the Numbers of their Fighting Men; referred to in the Note, page 48.

THE following liſt was drawn up by a French trader, a perſon of conſiderable note, who has reſided many years among the Indians, and ſtill continues at Detroit, having taken the oaths of allegiance to the King of Great Britain. His account may be depended on, ſo far as matters of this kind can be brought near the truth; a great part of it being delivered from his own perſonal knowledge

		Warriors
Conawaghrunas, near the falls of St. Louis		200
Abenaquis,	St. Lawrence Indians	350
Michmacs,		700
* Amaliſtes,		550
* Chalas,		130
Nipiſſins,	living towards the heads of the Ottawa river	400
Algonquins,		300
Les Tetes de Boule, or Round Heads, near the above	- - - -	2500

Six

Nation	Location	Number
Six Nations, on the frontiers of New-York, &c.		1550
Wiandots, near lake Erie		300
Chipwas,	near the Lakes Superior and Michigan	5000
Ottawas,		900
Messesagues, or River Indians, being wandering tribes, on the lakes Huron and Superior,		2000
Powtewatamis, near S. Joseph's and Detroit		350
Les Puans,	near Puans bay	700
Folle avoine, or Wild-Oat Indians		350
* Mechecouakis,	South of Puans bay	250
Sakis,		400
Mascoutents,		500
Ouisconsins, on a river of that name, falling into Missisippi on the east-side		550
Christinaux,	far north, near the lakes of the same name	3000
Assinaboes, or Assinipouals		1500
Blancs † Barbus, or White Indians with Beards		1500
Sioux, of the meadows	towards the heads of Missisippi	2500
Sioux, of the woods		1800
Missouri, on the river of that name		3000
* Grandes Eaux		1000
Osages,	south of Missouri	600
Canses,		1600
Panis blancs,		2000
Panis piques,		1700
Padoucas,		500
Ajoues, north of the same		1100
Arkanses, on the river that bears their name, falling into Missisippi on the west side		2000

† They live to the north-west, and the French, when they first saw them, took them for Spaniards.

Alibamous,

Alibamous, a tribe of the Creeks -		600
* Ouanakina	Unknown, unleſs the author has put them for tribes of the Creeks	300
* Chiakaneſſou		350
* Machecous		800
* Caoitas		700
* Souikilas		200
Miamis, upon the river of that name, falling into Lake Erie - - -		350
Delawares (les Loups) on the Ohio		600
Shawaneſe on Sioto - - -		500
Kickapoos	on the Ouabache	300
Ouachtenons		400
Peanquichas		250
Kaſkaſquias, or Illinois in general, on the Illinois river - - -		600
* Pianria - - - -		800
Catawbas, on the frontiers of North-Carolina		150
Cherokees, behind South-Carolina -		2500
Chickaſaws	Mobile and Miſſiſippi	750
Natchez		150
Chactaws		4500
		56,500

THE above liſt conſiſts chiefly of ſuch Indians as the French were connected with in Canada and Louiſiana. Wherever we knew the names by which the different nations are diſtinguiſhed, by the Engliſh, we have inſerted them. But the orthography is yet very unſettled, and the ſeveral nations marked with an * aſteriſm are unknown to us, and therefore they are left as they ſtand in the original liſt.

So large a number of fighting men may ſtartle us at firſt ſight; but the account ſeems no where exaggerated, excepting only that the Catawba nation

nation is now almoſt extinct. In ſome nations which we are acquainted with, the account falls even ſhort of their numbers; and ſome others do not appear to be mentioned at all, or at leaſt not by any name known to us.

SUCH, for inſtance, are the Lower Creeks, of whom we have a liſt according to their towns. In this liſt their warriors or gunſmen are 1180, and their inhabitants about 6000. Thus a comparative judgment may be formed of the nations abovementioned; the number of whoſe inhabitants will (in this proportion to their warriors, viz. 5 to 1) be about 283,000.

FINIS.